D1402257

THIS LAND

OF

STRANGERS

The Relationship Crisis That Imperils
Home, Work, Politics, and Faith

ROBERT E. HALL

GREENLEAF
BOOK GROUP PRESS

Published by Greenleaf Book Group Press
Austin, TX
www.gbgpress.com

Distributed by Greenleaf Book Group

For ordering information or special discounts for bulk purchases, please contact Greenleaf Book Group at PO Box 91869, Austin, TX 78709, 512.891.6100.

Design and composition by Greenleaf Book Group LLC
Cover design by Greenleaf Book Group LLC

Publisher's Cataloging-In-Publication Data
(Prepared by The Donohue Group, Inc.)

Hall, Robert E. (Robert Estle), 1948-
   This land of strangers : the relationship crisis that imperils home, work, politics, and faith / Robert E. Hall. -- 1st ed.

   p. ; cm.

   ISBN: 978-1-60832-299-2

   1. Interpersonal relations. I. Title.

HM1111 .H25 2012
302   2012933380

Part of the Tree Neutral® program, which offsets the number of trees consumed in the production and printing of this book by taking proactive steps, such as planting trees in direct proportion to the number of trees used: www.treeneutral.com

TreeNeutral®

Printed in the United States of America on acid-free paper

12 13 14 15 16   10 9 8 7 6 5 4 3 2 1

First Edition

CONTENTS

Introduction: 1

SECTION I: Relationship Lost: Societal Costs of Unrelenting Relationship Decline   9

Chapter 1: Home Alone: The Decline of Family, Friends, and Community   11

Chapter 2: Nobody's Business: Estranged Customers, Employees, Management, and Shareholders   33

Chapter 3: A House Divided Against Itself: A State of Dysfunction   61

Chapter 4: Religious War and (No) Peace: Belief That Divides   85

SECTION II: Relationship: Our Most Valuable Resource   111

Chapter 5: The Value of Relationships   113

Chapter 6: Relationship Math: Looking at the Dollars and Sense   137

SECTION III: Causes of Relationship Decline: Unintended Consequences of Our Advancements   159

Chapter 7: Extreme Consumerism: Me Is Killing Us   161

Chapter 8: Extreme Commercialism: Influence for Sale or Rent   179

Chapter 9: Worshipping at the Altar of High Tech   201

Chapter 10: The Institutionalization of Relationships—Growing
Care-less   221

**SECTION IV: The Age of Relationship: Revaluing And Reclaiming
Relationships   237**

Chapter 11: Revaluing Relationships   239

Chapter 12: Reclaiming Small and Local That Is Bigger and Better   261

Chapter 13: Embracing Relational Leadership: Where Do We Go
from Here?   279

Epilogue: 295

Endnotes: 299

Acknowledgments: 329

Index: 333

Introduction

The year was 1936 and our nation was struggling with economic depression, bank failures, and record summer temperatures. In a small, dusty town in southeastern Oklahoma where the locals were experiencing the worst drought on record, my grandfather, a rancher, was dying of cancer. The cancer was eating away the flesh from the side of his face. The pain was so acute that his neighbors took turns sitting up with him at night. At times, near the end, these men had to physically hold him on the bed.

My grandfather owned one of the largest ranches in the county and was known for his generosity in helping others in need. Years after his death, we found a trunk in the attic of his ranch house filled with IOUs from widows and men without work. My grandfather, Bob Hall, had "loaned" them money or a cow to provide milk for their kids.

But by the time he was ravaged with cancer, he had lost just about everything. My grandmother later recounted the last time he got out of bed. Bankers had come to foreclose on his last few head of livestock.

My grandfather got up, put on his hat, as was his way, and walked outside onto the large front porch and into the yard. As the men on horseback drove the last herd of cattle through the corrals, onto the dusty road, and then westward until they were out of sight, he took off his hat, waved it weakly above his head, and let out a yelp. He then walked back into the house where he died a few weeks later.

My father, 17 years old and a freshman in college at the time, left school to return to the ranch. There were no livestock left, and the family owed substantial taxes on the land. Everyone said, "There's no way those boys will be able to hold on to the ranch." Dad and his two brothers went to every bank in the neighboring town of McAlester looking for a loan, and each time they asked they got the same answer: "We would like to help you boys, but your deal just isn't bankable."

After exhausting all the banks in McAlester, they headed north and west across the South Canadian River to a bank in the little town of Holdenville. They got the same story. But as they were leaving, the banker said, "If you could find someone to cosign the note, I might be able to make a deal work."

As a last gasp, they went to an adjoining neighbor and lifelong family friend by the name of Buzz Newton, who was known to have money but also to be a bit miserly. He used a piece of baling wire for a belt, had toes sticking out of his worn-out shoes, and had holes in his old shirts and pants. One lens in his wire-rim glasses was cracked, and the other one was shattered. Buzz attended church about four times a year. When the offering plate was passed around, he would dig down into his pocket for what seemed like an eternity and then pull out a nickel and put it in the collection plate.

When the three brothers asked Buzz if he would cosign the note, he replied, "I always thought so much of your dad; he was the most generous man I have known. Yes, I'll cosign the note."

On February 9, 1937, the bank note was signed. The boys received $228 to buy livestock, seed for a crop, and implements. They had a good harvest that fall, paid off the note, and made sufficient payment on the taxes to keep the ranch. My father lived on and worked that ranch for the rest of his life. It is where my sisters and

I were born and grew up, it was the site of my younger daughter's wedding, and it remains a family treasure today. That bank note, cosigned by Buzz Newton, is framed and hangs on the living room wall of the old stone ranch house as a reminder of the value of one single, committed relationship.

Most of us have family histories replete with similar stories, and a common thread in many of them is a key relationship that delivered us from difficulty and despair. For all of Grandfather's accumulated assets, skill, and grit, it was a relationship that kept the ranch from being lost. While we often focus on tangible assets like money and possessions as being pivotal to our well-being, it is uncanny how often at crunch time it is the intangible value of our relationships that helps us navigate through individual crises—divorce, illness, financial disaster, loss of a job, loss of faith—as well as collective crises such as the terrorist attacks of September 11, 2001, Hurricane Katrina, or the recent financial meltdown. The truth is, relationships are the most valuable and value-creating resource of any society. They are our lifeline to survive, grow, and thrive.

Today, the unprecedented unraveling of these relationships is destroying us. At home, at work, in politics, and in faith, a cumulating and compounding loss has collectively retarded our growth and development and injured us in ways both known and repressed. It is hard to miss the fact that pieces of our relationship infrastructure—family, friends, community, organizations, politics, churches—are crumbling. But until now, no one has fully connected the broader dots that form the plummeting arc of decline and the rising slope of its cost; nor has anyone pulled together the narrative on its causes and cure. *We cannot build better lives or a stronger society on deteriorating relationships.*

The measurable decline in the strength, number, and duration of genuine relationships has occurred at a time when the array of relational choices and the freedom to exercise them has never been greater. Our democracy, capitalism, freedom of and from religion, technology, and physical and social mobility afford us an incredible array of relational choices regarding whom we select as our leaders, do business with, worship with (or not), and interact with (or not).

Already carrying the baggage of a disposable society, our most harmful waste has become discarded relationships, now piled up and rotting all over our planet. That we have a relationship problem is not news. What is news, however, is just how broad and consequential the relationship demise is across all facets of our lives:

- In homes, growing relationship dysfunction feeds growing economic disparity between "haves" and "have-nots," and the expanding costs of social services threaten government solvency.

- In a tough global economy, businesses strain to compete, while a few profit inordinately on the backs of broken stakeholder relationships (employees, customers, stockholders).

- In the political arena, federal and state government leaders are gridlocked on tough issues like health care, employment, and deficits in an environment of extreme partisan divide.

- In matters of faith and belief, communities whose expressed intention is to heal wounds and to love one another are now characterized by the loud and divisive voices that dominate, throwing fuel on the fire.

This all points to a society exhausted by attempts to function when its core fabric—relationships—is coming apart at the seams.

We have lost our way. Like a native culture invaded by outside forces, suffering the ravages of having lost its beliefs, rites, and customs, we have come to a place where our society seems to be losing its grip on relationships. The loss has come primarily from within.

The collapse of great societies has historically been first and foremost about the collective decay of relationships. While theories on the fall of the Roman Empire abound, a common thread is the change in relationships. British historian Edward Gibbon famously placed the blame on a loss of civic virtue among Roman citizens.[1] He defined civic virtue as cultivation of habits of personal living that kept the relationships of the community healthy, vibrant, committed, growing, and thereby successful. Contrast that to the outsourcing of the Romans' defense to external barbarian mercenaries—relationships for hire. Whether a corporation is outsourcing customer service offshore or an absent father is outsourcing parenting responsibilities to an ex-wife, abandoned relationships create a very heavy load.

In this book we will take a journey through a challenging relational landscape. Brace yourself. Facing this pervasive and consequential relational challenge with all its implications is daunting.

Section I reviews the unrelenting evidence that points to our relational demise at home, at work, in politics, and in faith. We will examine facts and figures to quantify the magnitude of the problem and its costs—economically, socially, physically, and emotionally. We also will share compelling stories that help us get our heads and our hearts around the relationship train wreck we face.

Section II establishes why relationships are the most valuable and value-creating possessions we have. We will examine the central role they have in our growth and development. In doing so, we will weave together social, behavioral, and medical research that places relationships at the center of our health, wealth, and well-being. We'll review examples that will resonate with your own relational life experiences that have helped define who you are.

If relationships are both valuable and value-creating, how and why have we allowed this collapse to happen? Fifty years ago, no one started out with the goal of disassembling relationships. Yet, as you'll see in section III, a series of important societal advancements have had unintended consequences. We will examine four of these that have served us well in many ways but have led us unwittingly to sacrifice our relationships. The result: We have become acclimated to disposing of relationships.

Finally, in section IV, we will look to the hope of the future. Evidence of a movement to revalue and reclaim relationships is popping up in many areas. In fact, as the supply of authentic, trusted relationships declines, there is a growing demand to restore what is a core, organic need. We will examine three key shifts that are central to ushering in a new age—the Age of Relationships. In the process, we will introduce the two important concepts of "relational capacity" and "relational leadership" for moving forward.

Throughout the book the term *relationship* is used as a broad, encompassing concept for examining individually and collectively the set of relational connections we have or might have.

The research and writing for this book has taken more than six years—a much larger undertaking than I initially envisioned. While a little chagrined with how long it has taken, I have felt compelled to stay the course because of a deep conviction that much of the conversation about our most substantive societal problems misses the mark. We all know that our relationships have lost ground in recent decades, but we have failed to see the larger picture and weigh the costs. As founder and corporate CEO of a relationship management consulting and software company for 20-plus years, my life's work has been to build stronger connections with customers, employees, and shareholders in organizations around the world. I am a strong believer in capitalism and in democracy. As a volunteer among the homeless for more than a decade, I am a believer in helping those less fortunate. Yet our broken relationships have a death grip on economic growth, political progress, and social development that capitalism, democracy, and social programs have been unable to break. As a result, we suffer an unfolding relational caste system: Those with strong relationships "have" and those with broken relationships "have-not." *Relationship capital has surpassed financial and political capital as the scarce resource that now dictates society's progress or regress.*

My purpose is to sound the alarm by looking at our society through the lens of relationships. I want to change the conversation regarding our relational challenges and how we move forward. My goal is to make the case for each of us to become a more active force for stronger, longer, and better relationships.

I must warn you about three possibilities. First, I think understanding the facts is crucial for coming to grips with the breadth of what we face. However, if I've quoted more research than you deem necessary for certain topics, you may wish to quickly skim data you already know. Second, section I, about our relational decline, may be overwhelming or depressing. Unfortunately, meaningful change often requires facing the magnitude of our problem, which helps us summon the courage to address it. Third, I have not provided a snappy, simple solution at the end of the book to make our society more relational, because such a solution does not exist. While it is tempting to put the onus on our president and Congress or on corporate, government, and religious leaders to proffer a few, powerful changes—a law, policy, or program—real organic change will come from what each of us does in our respective spheres of influence. The stories at the beginning and end of the last chapter provide examples of how leadership for the Age of Relationship starts with the small, local decisions we make and actions we take.

Our relationships are difficult, time-consuming, unpredictable, exhausting, and sometimes hurtful. Most often they are both our most significant source of pain and our only real source of healing and recovery. In writing this book I draw on my own challenges as a son, brother, husband, father, friend, team member, volunteer, corporate CEO, student of politics, consultant to corporations and governments, and fellow traveler on the journey of faith and belief. To take liberties with a quote by D. T. Niles, I am one beggar telling another beggar about where I found bread.[2]

RELATIONSHIP LOST: SOCIETAL COSTS OF UNRELENTING RELATIONSHIP DECLINE

How serious is our relationship decline?

Everyone knows that relationships in parts of our society are a mess, but few have looked broadly and deeply at the full scope of what we face and the attendant costs. It is its additive effect at home, at work, in politics, and in faith that now roils us into potential crisis.

In this first section of the book, we walk through the relational carnage in those four primary domains of our lives. You will be painfully (maybe numbingly) familiar with some and startled by others, but collectively these four chapters are the story of profound loss. It reminds me of the sign at the entrance to a school for wayward boys: "The truth shall set you free but first it will make you miserable."

Chapter 1

Home Alone: The Decline of Family, Friends, and Community

We lead the world in fatherless families—40% of children fall asleep without a resident father regularly within reach.
—Lionel Tiger, anthropologist, Rutgers University[1]

Several years ago I made a visit to my company's Johannesburg, South Africa, office to meet with a large financial services client. During my stay, our managing director there arranged for me to speak to the management team of a large retail chain. I made the presentation in a large tent out in the bush on a large private game preserve owned by our client's CEO. After a great barbecue cooked over an open fire pit, the owner took a couple of my team members and me on a night tour in his open-top vehicle to observe wild African animals. We saw several white rhinos, two hippopotamuses, giraffes, and hyenas. As we returned to camp, the owner commented that he had previously had some elephants but had to remove them because a couple of younger rogue males in the group had become very disruptive. He went on to explain that they had been raised without their mothers, extended family, and older bulls, and as a result, they became hooligans that really tore the place up.

My South African host's story corroborated that of documentaries on PBS and accounts in newspapers chronicling the ongoing saga of rogue elephants. The abnormal behavior of such elephants, which has included raping and killing rhinos, was the result of a collapse of their culture. Charles Seifert at the *New York Times* described it this way: "Decades of poaching and culling and habitat loss . . . have so disrupted the intricate web of familial and societal relations by which young elephants have traditionally been raised in the wild, and by which established elephant herds are governed, that what we are now witnessing is nothing less than a precipitous relational collapse of elephant culture."[2]

The number of older female caregivers had fallen dramatically—sometimes to zero—as had the number of older bulls, which play a key role in keeping the younger males in line. Calves were being born to and raised by younger and inexperienced mothers. In some cases, where orphans witnessed the death of their parents and elders from poaching and culling, the young elephants exhibited behavior associated with posttraumatic stress and other trauma-related disorders in humans: abnormal startle response, unpredictable asocial behavior, inattentive mothering, and hyperaggressiveness.

The crisis of relationship is nowhere more evident or costly than in the current state of our personal lives. In the elephant culture the disruption to family and herd relationships, decline in relational leadership, and collapse of local community and habitat led to its near demise. It is not unlike our human society where the decline of married, two-parent families has greatly reduced the number of actively involved parents, especially adult males. Mobility has led to a level of separation and transience—a loss of place similar to the elephants' loss of habitat—as well as a decrease in access to extended family members, particularly older matriarchs and female caregivers. There has been a large increase in the number of young females, often with children, left alone to raise a family. We have witnessed an increase of youth-based mayhem and violence over the years, both directly and through cultural platforms such as television, movies, music lyrics, and computer games.

So many of the jarring headlines are really news about relationships:

rising divorce rates, strains on single mothers, homelessness, declining graduation rates, unemployment, child abuse, drug abuse, random shootings, isolation, a growing prison population, and loss of global competiveness. Relationship, society's most elemental and value-creating building block, is falling apart.

Despite our progress in research, technology, social programs, medicine, and living standards, something is profoundly wrong. Our relationship dysfunction is casting growing segments of our society into a perpetual spiral of destruction and poverty.

A speaker I once heard asked his audience what word in the English language had the strongest positive resonance. The answer was "home." Home serves as the base for family, friends, and community. "Home" comes in a variety of venues. It's the bar where everyone knows your name, as portrayed in the 1980s sitcom *Cheers*. It's the coffee bar where everyone gathers to weave the tangled relationship web of the 1990s sitcom *Friends*. It's the loving support and gritty conflicts of the more recent show *Brothers and Sisters*. The ideal of home is the place where family, friends, or community treasures and develops you in spite of fights, faults, and tensions. In today's world, it may even be an electronic place where people connect deeply, albeit virtually, on subjects that impassion them. Home is both the "people" and the "place" where precious relationships reside and we matter.

The concept of home has undergone a seismic shift in the past 50 years. In the language of genetics, our relationship DNA, which contains the formula for how families, friends, and communities function, has been materially altered. If we are to adjust to advance relationships in the good ole new days going forward, we must begin by asking ourselves a critical question: When did we decide that relationships aren't really all that important? To answer that question we must examine our relational decline.

The Decline of the Family

Out-of-wedlock births have risen to almost 70 percent in black America, almost half of Hispanic births and more than a fourth of white births. In 1950, the rates for all three were about 10 percent. Add in the high rates of divorce and other parental break-ups, and you have large numbers of American children growing up in single-parent households. As Roland Warren . . . has said, "Kids have a hole in their soul the shape of their dad."

—*Clarence Page,* Chicago Tribune[3]

The first clue to the plummeting value of family relationships is the significant decrease in the rate of marriage. We have all seen the headlines—single is the new majority. According to information analyzed by the Brookings Institute, married couples represented just 48 percent of American households in 2010.[4] People increasingly are choosing single life over married life, along with shorter, less committed (legally) relationships. The state of our family unions is troubled. A report from the National Marriage Project at Rutgers indicates that close to half of first marriages in the United States end in divorce.[5] Today's divorce rate is still nearly double what it was in 1960,[6] even though it has declined slightly since the early 1980s.[7]

If our buildings or bridges started collapsing or the number of auto accidents doubled in 50 years, as a society at large we would be alarmed. Yet we have become numb to the dramatic shift that affects spouses, children, grandparents, friends, schools, neighborhoods, social circles, and businesses—even church and state. Separation or divorce is a very disruptive, painful, expensive, and time-consuming process for the parties involved. However, it is important to point out that staying in a dysfunctional relationship is not a piece of cake, either, and has its own set of issues. Regardless of the outcome, relationships that do not work have significant consequences.

Similarly, forming marriage relationships has become considerably less attractive. From 1970 through 2004 the number of marriages per 1,000 unmarried women dropped by nearly 50 percent.[8] Pew reports that the rate of new marriages between 2009 and 2010 declined by 5 percent among all groups but most dramatically fell 13 percent among young adults.[9] Similar declines have taken hold in most other postindustrial societies. If marriage were a product, it would have lost market share over the past 50 years at about the same rate as the U.S. automotive industry.

The future does not look promising. For example, recent research from Japan, a country struggling to sustain its current population levels, reports that sexual interest and sexual activity of the young and old alike are in serious decline. A whopping 36.1 percent of teenage boys between the ages of 16 and 19 said they had little to no interest in sex, and in some cases even despised it; that's more than twice the 2008 figure of 17.5 percent. A 2010 survey found that 83.7 percent of Japanese men who turned 20 this year were not dating anyone, while 49.3 percent said they had never had a girlfriend. About 59 percent of girls in the same age group felt the same way, up 12 percent from 2008, while 40.8 percent of married people said they had not had sex in the past month, up from 36.5 percent in the 2008 survey. Kunio Kitamura, head of the Japan Family Planning Association, concluded: "The findings seem to reflect the increasing shallowness of human relations in today's busy society."[10]

Here in the United States, of the percentage of those who do marry, relational satisfaction has declined. The number of women who consider their marriage to be "very happy" has gone down since the 1970s, from 68.6 percent to 60.3 percent.[11] Interestingly, the drop for men is slightly less—from 69.6 percent to 64.6 percent.

The number of children born to unwed mothers continues to reach record highs. From 1960 to 2006, the percentage of births to unwed mothers increased a mind-boggling 726 percent. In 2006 (the latest data available), 38.5 percent of children born in the United States were to unmarried women.[12] By 2012, for women under 30, more than 50 percent of births were outside marriage.[13] In most of these cases, the children grow up in a single-parent family, usually without a father. That means they have only half of the on-site parental relationship resources of a traditional two-parent family.

The percentage of children under 18 living with both biological parents in the United States is 63 percent, the lowest among Western industrialized nations.[14] The second lowest is Sweden, at 73 percent. More than one-third of American children lack one or both biological parents at home.

Finally, according to census information released in 2008, the number of unmarried couples cohabiting has increased from less than a million to 6.4 million over the past 30 years.[15] (Cohabiting refers to couples who are sexual partners, not married to each other but sharing a household.) Unmarried cohabitation is particularly common among the young. About a quarter of unmarried women ages 25 to 39 are currently living with a partner, and an additional quarter have lived with a partner at some time in the past.

Also according to the U.S. Census Bureau, 50 to 60 percent of all first marriages are preceded by the couple living together, as compared to virtually no prior cohabitation 50 years ago.[16] Cohabitation is most common among those of lower educational and income levels. Among women ages 19 to 44, 60 percent of high school dropouts have cohabited, compared to 37 percent of college graduates. Cohabitation is also more common among those who are less religious than their peers and those who have been divorced or have experienced parental divorce, fatherlessness, or high levels of marital discord during childhood.

Since cohabiting relationships are more than twice as likely to dissolve than marriages,[17] and since more than 40 percent of cohabiting-couple households now contain children, growing numbers of children are growing up in families where their parental connections are more transient.

In putting a high value on the presence of both parents in a household, raising their children together, it is easy to fall into the trap of devaluing the relative importance of a single mom or dad. While we may lament the pain of divorce, we cannot ignore the abuse, dysfunction, or destruction that can be present in marriage. Likewise, gay couples or single parents who have chosen to have children absent a mother or father have opened up nontraditional approaches and access to family relationships for groups historically excluded. It has led to "mothering and fathering" roles that don't conform strictly to traditional male/female and mother/father identity. This has led to clashes between those who advocate for traditional relationships versus those who advocate for relational inclusion and access for all. One thing is clear: married, divorced, cohabiting, raising children or not, with or without extended family, straight or gay—relationships come in many forms, and ultimately we need the best relationships we can muster in a changing, challenging, and imperfect world.

In a nutshell, divorce is up, marriage is down; unwed mothers are up, very happy marriages are down; cohabitation is up, and the percentage of children living with both biological parents is down. Indeed, there is a growing recognition and anxiety that our society is playing a form of "relationship roulette" that delivers random and often dire consequences because we lack sufficient intention when it comes to relationships. There are many reasons for all of this, but it is irrefutable that, in terms of up or down, the relative quantity, perceived value, and duration of marital relationships are down.

The Costs of Fewer Family Relationships

If you are a middle-class woman, you have more to fear from divorce than from outsourcing. If you have a daughter, you're right to worry more about her having a child before marriage than about her being a victim of globalization. This country's prosperity is threatened more by homes where no one reads to children than it is by big pharmaceutical companies.

—David Brooks, The New York Times[18]

In our society, family relationships serve many functions. They provide protection, learning, support, love, feedback, and accountability. All of these functions share a common benefit. They are a key source of development for all the parties involved. Children, parents, siblings, and extended family members learn from and are influenced by each other. When these relationships are absent, dysfunctional, or abusive, they inhibit the very development so crucial for a society to thrive and advance.

The cost of divorce, and even for not being married, is considerable. Those who are divorced or stay single accumulate only about half per person what those who marry and stay married do.[19] (We will discuss these financial implications in greater detail in chapter 6, "Relationship Math: Looking at the Dollars and Sense.")

Research from Statistics Canada found that men who divorce are six times more likely to report an episode of depression than are men who remain married.[20] Divorcing women are 3.5 times as likely to experience depression, compared to women who stay married. Certainly depression is not only a result of separation and divorce but also often a cause. Tal Ben-Shahar, the popular professor of happiness at Harvard, reports that depression has increased tenfold since 1960.[21] He calls this increase in depression nothing short of an epidemic and points to our relational decline as its primary cause.

Marital discord has a number of additional costs that cannot be so easily quantified, and these include stress, health issues, loss of productivity and eventually unemployment, and addiction. While I have talked mostly about marriage as a surrogate for relationships (most research regarding romantic partners is organized this way), the reality is that broken relationships between partners of any kind—whether they stay together or part ways—are difficult and expensive economically, socially, and emotionally.

The Costs of—and to—Children

Perhaps the most telling trend regarding the value we place on family relationships in our society is the significant decline in the rate of childbearing. The fertility rate—the number of children a woman is expected to have over her lifetime—went from 7.04 in 1800[22] to 2.12 in 2007.[23] This is consistent worldwide—as incomes rise, fertility rates drop. There are many reasons behind this trend: birth control, changing religious beliefs, family income, less support from the extended family, and the disappearance of the family farm where child labor was an economic advantage.

It is ironic that in general, those who have the fewest economic resources are having the most children. The Hispanic fertility rate (2.99) is nearly 60 percent higher and the African American rate (2.13) is about 26 percent higher than the Caucasian rate (1.87). Yet the influx of women into the workforce has dramatically elevated living standards in recent decades across all groups. In the 1950s, 17 percent of women with children worked outside the home; today, better than 68 percent do. Attempting to meet all of the requirements of work and home—child care, shopping and cooking, cleaning, washing, and the like—has added major demands on time, energy, and relationships among dual-income families, and especially women who work outside the home.

Many Americans report that they enjoy life more as empty nesters than they did while raising their children.[24] This certainly doesn't mean parents regret having children—kids have always been disruptive and require a sacrifice of resources. Nor does it mean that parents love their children any less. In fact, some couples are motivated to have fewer children so they can do more for the ones they have, such as providing them with a better education, which is an increasingly expensive goal when it comes to private schools and colleges.

Fewer children combined with fewer married couples add up to significantly fewer family relationships. If family relationships were a stock, we could easily conclude that something was driving their value down. But it's more complex than that.

For all the costs to spouses or partners in broken relationships, particularly in the short term, the costs to children are greater and more formative (or de-formative) over a longer period of time. Continuing my earlier reference to genetics, broken family relationships have the unique potential to alter the makeup of a child's economic, social, and emotional DNA. The earliest and easiest adverse effect to measure is poverty.

It's a fact: Both divorce and childbearing out of wedlock increase the likelihood that children will be raised in poverty. According to the U.S. Census Bureau, the poverty rate in 2010 for single parents with children was 27.3 percent, compared to a rate of 6.2 percent for married couples with children.[25] Some of this difference is attributed to single parents tending to have less education, but even when married couples are compared to single couples with the same education level, the poverty level for married couples is about 70 percent lower.[26] In fact, being married has the same effect in reducing poverty as adding five to six years to a parent's education level.[27]

It is not easy to sort out cause and effect between relationship problems and poverty. Broken relationships often lead to poverty and poverty often leads to broken relationships. What is straightforward is that the effects of unstable relationships are difficult on the children of those relationships, who have the same needs for love, nurturing, guidance, boundaries, and economic stability as any other children.

Unfortunately, the future does not look promising. Birthrates for all unmarried mothers rose 7 percent and more specifically 3 percent for unmarried teens in 2006, after several years of leveling off, according to the U.S. Department of Health and Human Services (final data for 2006 released in 2009).[28] That increase even extended into the rapidly growing Hispanic population, generally thought of as more family oriented than other groups.

The growth in the number of single moms is compounded by the increase in multiple-father households. Recently, at the transitional housing facility where I volunteer, another volunteer and I were working with a single mother of three sons under the age of eight, each by a different father. Her six-year-old son was acting up at school. She had left work early that day, putting her job in jeopardy, to deal with his issues, and she was at her wit's end. As we discussed her challenge, she shared that the father of her seven-year-old visited his son every week and often brought him a toy truck or took him to McDonald's for a Saturday lunch. By contrast, her six-year-old had never even met his father. The question he repeatedly asked his mother was, "What is wrong with me that my daddy never comes to see me?"

In the previous couple of weeks, the six-year-old had tried to get the attention of her seven-year-old's father. Unfortunately, he just brushed the child off, and the older brother became agitated by his younger brother trying to shoehorn his way into the relationship—a double shot of relational rejection. It tears at this mother to see her one son get so visibly pushed aside by a father figure he so desperately wants. Even among her three boys, none of whom has his father living at home, the difference in relational attention has become a wedge separating the "have-nots" from the "extreme have-nots."

This emerging relational pattern now forms the perfect storm: The birth-rate of unmarried mothers is rising while the rate of multiple fathers per household is increasing. The increase in multiple absent fathers within the same household, producing half-brothers and -sisters, further fragments relationships and adds dramatically to the tension and instability. It is a toxic combination.

Recent research now links the relational stresses of poverty and chaotic households to the neural development that impacts language acquisition and memory of nine- and 10-year-olds. Mark Kishiyama, a cognitive psychologist at the University of California–Berkeley and lead researcher of one such study, stated, "It is a pattern similar to what's seen in patients with strokes that have led to lesions in their prefrontal cortex."[29] Likewise, research shows that the relational environment can impact IQ. For example, when poor children from lower-class families were adopted by upper-middle-class families, their IQs rose by 12 to 18 points, depending on the study. Closely related to poverty and brain development, broken family relationships lead to social problems that span from the teenage years into adult life. Research going back a couple of decades corroborates what we would suspect: Children from single-parent homes (comparing parents of the same race and with similar education) are twice as likely to be arrested for a juvenile crime,[30] treated for emotional and behavioral problems,[31] and suspended or expelled from school,[32] and they are more likely to drop out before completing high school.[32] The grim results do not end there, however.

Broken marriage relationships are also more likely to lead to sexual promiscuity by the couples' offspring. In addition, sexually transmitted diseases currently infect at least one in four girls and young women in America, and the incidence is closer to one in two among high-risk ethnic groups. Those high-risk groups are much more likely to come from broken families.[34]

The Decline of Friends

The same forces that have diminished our family relationships have also eroded the second pillar of our personal lives—friends. Next to family, there is no set of relationships more important to our personal lives than friends and confidants. They play a pivotal role in our development, success, and security.

Right after Hurricane Katrina hit the Gulf Coast, I was part of a team of volunteers in Dallas helping to find temporary housing for displaced evacuees pouring in from New Orleans. The first wave came in cars traveling in caravans. They used their cell phones to be in contact with friends and relatives as they traveled. The second wave arrived several days later. They had been evacuated off of rooftops, rescued by boats, or somehow made their way to the large shelter in the Louisiana Superdome before being bused to Dallas. We met with them to sign them in and address such urgent needs as missing family members, medical prescriptions, and loss of eyeglasses. In meeting with scores of these evacuees in a makeshift shelter filled with row after row of cots in the basement of the Dallas Civic Center, I found that most did not know where key family members, friends, or even their pets were. What was different about this second group who had been left behind for a few days? There were several things, but what really stood out as I talked with them is how many had no friends with cars.

This is very consistent with my experience in mentoring homeless families. One of the most common circumstances preceding homelessness is the lack or breakdown of not only family relationships but also friendships. Such breakdowns can push a distressed family over the edge. Some individuals and families have no people to whom they can turn. Others have imposed on their friends and relatives until those individuals reached a breaking point. When these concerned people can no longer provide a loan, child care, or lodging, families spiral down to homelessness.

All of us are subject to reaching places in our lives where we are socially, emotionally, economically, or even spiritually homeless—places where we are estranged and separated, in need of love, advice, help, and other forms of relational support that help us find our way "home." Our relationships are our lifelines.

Often, close friends take on the role of family and become a source of joy, comfort, and support in good times and bad. When single mothers watch each other's kids, older friends serve as surrogate grandparents, and neighbors provide support during financial strain, friends become extended family. That's why the decline of close friends and confidants is so disturbing.

Recent research published by the American Sociological Review (ASR) finds that the number of people who report they have no one with whom they discuss important matters has nearly tripled over the past 20 years, with the average number of confidants decreasing by about a third (from 2.94 to 2.08).[35] Further evidence of this growing isolation comes from a U.S. Census report published in 2009 that the percentage of people living alone jumped 59 percent—from 17 percent in 1970 to 27 percent in 2007—while the average household size declined from 3.1 to 2.6.[36]

SURROGATE FAMILY MEMBERS

The decline in the number, depth, and tenure of relationships probably explains why there has been such growth in the households with pets (63 percent in 2007 versus 56 percent in 1988). According to Harris Interactive, the number of dog owners who agree their dog "is just like a family member and just as important" has risen from 55 percent in 1995 to 88 percent in 2007.[37] In other words, households where family members are viewed as more important than the family dog decreased from 45 percent to 12 percent. Pets are picking up some of the slack from our loss of human relationships.

If you calculate the loss, it is easy to make a case that well over one-half to three-quarters of our relational resources have disappeared. We have truly become the "help-less" society.

There are two alarming concerns here. First, the loss of about a third of our close-friend relationships is even greater than our loss of kin.[38] Even though we are experiencing demographic shifts such as an aging population, the ASR analysis ruled out these factors as significant causes of this decline. Can you imagine the headlines had there been an adverse shift in life expectancy or ocean temperatures of over 30 percent in 20 years?

Second, and perhaps more troubling, is that according to this research, the mode—the most frequent occurrence—has collapsed from three confidants 20 years ago to zero confidants today. Having no confidants is like being sentenced to relational solitary confinement. The loss translates into poorer decision making, greater loneliness, less support in times of need, and measurably declining mental and physical health.

In addition to becoming sparse, our relationship networks have become narrower. We are exposed to less diversity: Christians hang out with Christians, affluents hang out with other affluents, and so on. Narrowing of relationships has two effects: (1) It may isolate and prejudice us against others who are different; (2) It leads to less informed decisions. In his book *The Wisdom of Crowds*, James Surowiecki identifies diversity of input as a key to effective decision making.[39] Those who have access to more, diverse, and better opinions win. Thus, the decline in and narrowing of the range of friend relationships is painful and costly for us as both individuals and a society.

The Decline of Community

*Community is the place where the person you least want to
live with always lives.*

—Henri Nouwen[40]

Compounding the decline in family and friends is the significant erosion in our community relationships, the third pillar of our personal relationships. Community can be defined as a group that shares a common locale (such as a neighborhood) or a set of interests (such as a volunteer program). Community is both place and persons.

The very qualities that make community great also make it challenging and sometimes painful. We learn from others, but not without pain that is sometimes unbearable. Elizabeth O'Connor captured it when she said, "The pain of belonging is essential to the joy of being."[41]

The United States is a country founded mostly on the idea of escaping an oppressive society. Our roots go back to escaping religious, government, and even family oppression in pursuit of freedom and independence. We have long valued and romanticized the virtues of rugged individualism and independence. It is a central part of the culture of this country. Yet as the pendulum has continued to move us to greater freedom and self-sufficiency, we find ourselves too often alone and without help. Sometimes we are defined by what we have lost.

Robert Putnam, in his bestselling book *Bowling Alone*, reported on the loss of community and resulting decline in "social capital"—the value flowing from the connection of individuals.[42] Putnam's seminal research at Harvard documented diminished local participation in associations, clubs, and numerous other civic and community activities in the 1980s and '90s.

Increased mobility, travel by car, use of electronic garage openers and back-alley garages, the disappearance of porches, the predominance of air-conditioned homes, the prominence of television and computers that keep us inside and glued to our screens, and the demise of local shops are just a few of the developments that have contributed to our local community estrangement. Not only are we bowling alone; we also are living alone in our neighborhoods with less support from others.

Combined, these factors have led to diminished trust in community. In the *Atlantic*, Caitlin Flanagan wrote: "'It takes a village' philosophy is a joke, because the village is now so polluted and desolate of commonly held, child-appropriate moral values that my job as a mother is not to rely on the village but to protect my children from it."[43] Too often the village becomes a jungle. Despite the many new positive options available, like online support groups, negative alternative communities like gangs, youth peer groups, and various forms of online communities such as suicide assistance groups have supplanted neighborhood community. As the presence of working parents at home decreased, the role of peers increased. Boys who need and long for dads are more susceptible to authority figures and structures such as a gang. Community, historically a force for reinforcing established values, has increasingly become a source of alternative values—sometimes functioning more as the enemy inside the gate than as a protector of what we hold dear.

Yet another trend has fed our estrangement. The global economy, technology, and worldwide mobility have exposed us to unprecedented diversity. As a country grounded in diversity, we have seen the benefits of welcoming peoples of all nationalities and races. In fact, research has shown that diversity is a causal factor in innovation. Yet diversity can lead to greater isolation and the absence of relationships.

Robert Putnam's more recent research has produced findings that he and others have been reluctant and very careful about discussing. His study, based on interviews with 30,000 people, found that the more diverse a community is, the less likely people in those communities participate in elections, volunteer, donate to charity, or participate in community projects. The study found that the more diverse the community, the less neighbors trusted each other.[44]

Beyond a point, diversity can have a chilling effect on communities. The increasing proportion of strangers present in today's world seems to be dangerously close to our ability to absorb them, elevating our fear and distrust.

We see growing evidence of people going to their respective corners to be with people like themselves. We need diverse local community, but we are probably running low on relational energy, tolerance, or the will to invest in managing communal differences. When we mostly deal with strangers, we may lose a sense of our own identity. Estrangement wears many hats, all more expensive than we thought.

As a result, two worries emerge: (1) not enough constructive communities, and (2) too much influence from separated or even destructive communities. Supply of community support—even if it is negative—responds to relational demand.

Language is a signaling device that clues us to our loss regarding community. Words like *village, tribe, clan, local,* and *gang* seem to have made a comeback. Why? They are our cry for lost community or an acknowledgment that community has served relationships poorly.

Our society has been on a long journey away from personal relationships toward strangers. The word *stranger* has always carried an onerous reputation with the distrust it elicits. Even today the definition from the *American Heritage Dictionary* reflects an alien tone: "One who is neither a friend nor an acquaintance . . . an outsider."

Strangers do not share community and they typically lack love, positive influence, or investment in us (or we in them). Everywhere we look today, we see trends that make us more reliant on strangers. Our move to more independent, mobile groups of one is reflected in the indoor, solitary activities our children choose to pursue. Having grown up with baseball as a key source of community, I was taken aback to find out that the number of children under the age of 18 skateboarding—an individual sport—has overtaken those playing the team sport of baseball.[45] It is part of a longer-term trend, as participation in baseball declined 27 percent from 1987 to 2003.[46] Overall participation in the top seven team sports declined in 2010 over 2009.[47]

Just as with family and friends, the consequences of absent or false community represent loss of constructive direction, learning, feedback, support, and resources crucial to our development—not just for children or youth but for all of us. Whether you are stranded on a rooftop in the midst of rising water, the target of a home break-in, or a youngster raising money by selling Girl Scout cookies, constructive, caring community is not a "nice to have" but a necessity. Longmont, Colorado, police chief Mike Butler said it very well in Peter Block's book *Community: The Structure of Belonging*: "For 80 percent of the calls we receive, people do not need a uniformed officer, they need a neighbor."[48]

The Real Costs When Personal Relationships Are Lost

Personal relationships are fundamental in creating our emotional, social, and economic wealth—or poverty. While the impact of our society's relational decline in each of three key areas—family, friends, and community—is quite disturbing, it is the cumulative interaction of these factors and their compounding that is even more so. Crumbling infrastructure is what we call deteriorating roads, bridges, and sewer systems. In essence, we now have a crumbling relational infrastructure nationwide.

When discussing how to reduce poverty, William Galston, a former assistant to President Clinton, put the matter simply: Finish high school, marry before having a child, and produce a child after you are 20 years old. Only 8 percent of people who do all three will be poor; of those who fail to do them, 79 percent will be poor.[49]

The difference between 8 percent in poverty versus 79 percent is staggering. How could we be so far off this success formula? Broken and chaotic relationships have infected what happens at home and in the community, particularly at school. The demise of functioning relationships at school has led to unemployment, gangs, and crime. Having sex absent a committed relationship, especially at an early age, sets in motion a series of risks that too often has meant becoming a single parent, dropping out of school, loss of income potential, and limited future opportunities for marriage and a two-parent family. Decline in personal relationships affects virtually every part of society.

The adverse multiplier effect of relationship deprivation—making do with less family, fewer friends, and diminished community—has reached critical mass and spiraled out of control. The divorced, the children of single or unstable parents, those isolated with no friends, and the communally estranged have become mainstream in our culture, with no end in sight. The adverse effects of relational dysfunction are now bolted on and permanently structured into the costs of our school, welfare, law enforcement, judicial, and prison systems. However inadequately, we now budget, staff, train, and equip to serve an ever-increasing "relationship-less" underclass.

The scale of ever-expanding relationship problems and their costs has outstripped the resources and capabilities of the solution. If it takes a village to raise a child, it takes a small city of caregivers, welfare workers, counselors, law enforcement officers, and corrections workers to cope with the relational carnage of a citizenry growing up deprived of functional family, friends, and community relationships. The collapse of personal relational support ultimately shows up in society as larger government budgets, fewer taxpayers and diminished tax receipts, larger deficits, lower productivity—and eventually that society's inability to compete in a global economy.

Yet the consequences of this collapse are not evenly shared. Recent shifts in size and quality of relationship networks (loss of friends and confidants) disproportionately affect the "have-nots." The social networks of those who are less educated, black, male, or elderly are smaller than the social networks of those who are white, female, or younger.[50] These "have-nots" are more likely to live disrupted lives or be single moms, have higher divorce rates, have more abortions, and experience more interpersonal strife than their middle- and upper-class counterparts.[51] For women ages 25 to 34 in the best-educated third, the rate of single parenthood was 5 percent in 1960 and is about that today. For the least-educated third it has nearly tripled, and the trends continue to increase.[52]

As for men, there are obviously exceptions, but in general, they talk less, disclose less, express fewer feelings, and have fewer friends than women have. In a world where relationships are in short supply and, accordingly, social networks are increasing in value, masculine traits such as physical strength and aggressiveness, which are so valuable for combat or certain sports, seem to hold less value. Men accounted for nearly 80 percent of the loss in employment during the 2008–2009 recession, resulting in the widest gap in unemployment rates since World War II: 7.2 percent for women and 10 percent for men.

Unfortunately the loss is circular. Longer-term unemployment extracts further costs in terms of important relationships. According to the Pew Research Center, nearly half (46 percent) of those unemployed six months or more say joblessness has strained family relations, and 43 percent say they lost contact with close friends.[53]

Why the Decline in Relationships Is Killing Us

In the United States, one of the most disturbing measures reflecting relationship dysfunction is the ultimate one, violence. According to a study by the American Medical Association, the U.S. homicide rate for males ages 15 to 24 is 21.9 per 100,000, compared to rates of 1 to 3 per 100,000 for most other developed countries.[54] The news is even more disconcerting when you look at the trends for nonwhites. The homicide rate for black males in that age range is 85.6 per 100,000, or more than seven times the rate for white males.

Tragically, the trend only gets worse. Criminal justice professors at Boston's Northeastern University found murders of African-American teenagers rose 39 percent from 2000–2001 to 2006–2007, compared to an overall rise of homicides of 7.4 percent.[55] The study concluded that black youths are much more likely than are white youths to come from communities where there are high rates of single-parent homes, inadequate adult supervision, inferior schools, and widespread gang activity. In the extreme, relationship dysfunction kills.

The relational devastation not only kills, it imprisons, too. The United States leads the world in the percentage of its population that is behind bars.[56] The impact for Hispanic and African-American men is particularly severe:

- One in 36 adult Hispanic men is behind bars, as is one in 15 black men, including one in nine black men ages 20 to 34.[57]

- Among black dropouts [male] in their late 20s, more are in prison on any given day than are working—34 percent compared to 30 percent.[58]

- On average, states spend almost 7 percent of their budgets on corrections, trailing only health care, education, and transportation.[59]

For any segment of our population to have more of its members living in prison than living independent and productive lives outside is appalling. Historically this rate of incarceration of an ethnic segment of a society occurred only when one group captured or enslaved another tribe or occupied another country. The last time this happened in the United States was before the Civil War. Can you imagine how, in a free, democratic, capitalistic society, we got to this place?

Relationships often are skewed when one of the partners is a convicted felon who has spent time in prison. The convicted are more involved in and influenced by their relationships in a community of criminals and more excluded from mainstream society. If you have worked with the homeless or the poor, you know what a detriment a single criminal conviction is to getting a job and how it decreases income and advancement potential for the rest of one's life. More laws, bigger prisons, and more social programs are no match for the mayhem that accompanies relationship disintegration.

Why are men, especially African-American and Latino men, being imprisoned at such an accelerated rate? Among the many reasons (including poverty and discrimination), one that stands out is education. According to "Cities in Crisis: A Special Analytic Report on High School Graduation," the graduation rate in 17 of the country's 50 largest cities is lower than 50 percent.[60] This has occurred in spite of per-pupil outlays more than doubling in real terms between 1970 and 2004 and the federal portion of that spending nearly tripling.[61] In Detroit, for example, only about 25 percent of students entering the ninth grade graduate four years later. In addition to a decline in high school graduation rates, there is a sizable decline in college enrollment rates for males. Thirty years ago men outnumbered women by about 58 percent to 42 percent in college enrollments; according to the Bureau of Labor Statistics, women outnumbered men by about 8 percent in 2009.[62] Young males have had a dramatic shift in attitude toward school. According to a University of Michigan study, the number of high school boys who said they didn't like school rose 71 percent between 1980 and 2001.[63]

What is this force that is pulling boys—especially poor, ethnic ones—out of school and into prison? Amid much speculation and a fair amount of research, there is no clear-cut single answer to the question. However, many educators and others have observed that the absence of a man in a boy's life can have an extremely detrimental effect.

While relationship decline impacts all of us, those who are some combination of poor, uneducated, ethnic, and male appear to be losing more ground. This inequality of pain and consequence now feeds a growing divide that is disabling the American spirit and will eventually sink us.

In recent years, we have heard about two Americas: one that is wealthy and becoming more rich and powerful, and the other that is poor and sinking deeper into poverty and powerlessness. I maintain that there is an even more compelling reality: One America possesses more, stronger, more enduring, and more functional relationships that lead to wealth, opportunity, and advantage. The other possesses fewer, weaker, shorter-term, and less functional relationships that enslave them in poverty—and resultant illiteracy, violence, and overwhelming disadvantage. The middle is shrinking.

This divergence increasingly represents a relational caste system whose undertow is drowning the have-nots at an unprecedented rate. The demise of personal relationships has been a very difficult issue to tackle because these relationships involve individual freedom and choice and are highly subjective. Each of us is relationally scarred and a victim of our own imperfect families, friends, and communities; any attempt to judge others can be hypocritical and ineffective.

* * * *

It has been easier to see the effects of relational decline than its underlying causes. Perhaps the biggest obstacles to understanding the problem have been the ferocious political and religious disagreements and cultural divides that exist among groups regarding the cause of the problem and therefore the best solution. We are distracted by the terms of the debate. Depending on whether you are liberal, conservative, secular, or religious, the preferred issue to address might include some combination of: family values, taxes and redistributed income, larger government programs, less government inter-vention, better schools, less greedy and more benevolent corporations, less glamorization of Hollywood and celebrity culture, stricter laws and greater accountability, stronger incentives and more breakthrough innovation.

The bottom line is this: We are experiencing a wholesale free fall in the most elemental building block of our society—personal relationships. As a society, we have no graver risk and no greater opportunity in our future than improving the depth, breadth, and duration of these relationships that exert such enormous influence on our health, wealth, and well-being.

Our despair over our personal relationship peril is also our source of hope. In hitting rock bottom, we are forced to rethink our priorities and our ways. To close the loop on those African elephants we discussed at the beginning of this chapter, more recently, when South African park rangers introduced a number of older bull elephants into several destabilized elephant herds, the wayward behavior—including unusually premature hormonal changes among the adolescent elephants—abated.[64] Our human solution may be a little more complicated than that, but relationships *can be reclaimed* even in a changing world, and reclaimed relationships *can yield better outcomes*.

Chapter 2

Nobody's Business: Estranged Customers, Employees, Management, and Shareholders

United States corporations now lose half of their customers in five years, half of their employees in four years, and half of their investors in a matter of months.

—*Philip Kotler*, Kotler on Marketing[1]

I n the summer of 1988 I received a call from a top executive at NCNB (now Bank of America). He was calling on behalf of Hugh McColl, their ex-Marine CEO and a legendary deal maker, to ask if I would help them merge the management teams of their newest acquisition, First RepublicBank Corp. First Republic, the largest bank in Texas and eleventh largest in the country then, was itself the marriage of RepublicBank and Interfirst Bank during the troubled real estate era of the mid-'80s. The *Dallas Morning News* caustically referred to the merging of these two storied Texas banks as two drunks trying to prop each other up.

I agreed to work with them and started interviewing executives, including Ken Lewis, who later succeeded McColl as CEO of Bank of America. The acquisition got off to a rocky start when the new management announced that the name of the new enterprise would be

NCNB of Texas. The once proud Texas bank would now go by the alias of NCNB, North Carolina National Bank—of Texas. This acronym was promptly tagged locally as "No Cash for No Body."

In response, the bank ran folksy television ads with Buddy Kemp, the newly appointed Texas CEO, sitting in a rich, red leather chair talking about how friendly they were and how they had the size and resources to better serve their new Texas customers. The ad invited folks to drop by their local branches, have a cup of coffee, and visit with Buddy. The ad was too good, because people actually did drop by. The bank started getting complaints: "Where's Buddy?" Not only was he not there, but the branch offices weren't set up to serve coffee to customers.

As I talked with the executives from First Republic, it became clear they were blown away by the machinelike precision NCNB's management exhibited in transitioning to the merged entity. McColl had led a bevy of mergers and they had it down to a science. Some bank analysts had even concluded it was their core competency—what they did best. In fact, the First Republic executives were back on their heels awaiting orders from the NCNB management team going forward post-merger. The NCNB executives explained that the detailed plan was just for the first 90 days covering the merger and that they were looking to the First Republic executives for the plan after that. When I met with McColl and his team to preview the findings for the upcoming management retreat, they were shocked that each team was looking to the other for direction in moving forward. They knew precisely how to run the merger. The game plan for growing and increasing the value of the merged bank was not so clear.

By 2008, Bank of America's string of serial acquisitions made it the second-largest bank in the country. However, their purchase of Countrywide in July of that year and the messy rescue of Merrill Lynch in January 2009 led to a slew of bad loans and ultimately a $45 billion TARP bailout. Ken Lewis, then CEO, resigned abruptly in October 2009.

Looking back, this episode would play out repeatedly across the corporate landscape in a number of industries. The norm became companies and management teams that were better at doing deals and making money on Wall Street than running businesses and serving customers on Main Street in a way that produced organic revenue and earnings growth. Renaming efforts and advertising claims and bold promises heightened expectations in the short run but often resulted in disappointment and distrust when actual performance declined. Companies consolidated whole industries, becoming dominant and more efficient in the short term but often repelling customers, shareholders, employees, and jobs over time. It is all part of a common theme of today's organization under economic, social, and political duress: An unrelenting series of actions has undermined stakeholder relationships.

The world of work and business (for our purposes, I include business and nonprofit entities in this category) is at its core a series of relationships among stakeholders: customers, employees, management, and shareholders. Success and productivity are greatly influenced by how these relationships function. Yet the state of relationships in this second domain of our lives is increasingly under siege. The relational damage in the workplace—in our organizations—is not unlike the broken homes, declining friendships, and estranged communities that impact personal relationships. Many of the leading lights of the organizational community are now dimmed or dark: Enron, Tyco, WorldCom, Lehman Brothers, AIG, Merrill Lynch, Countrywide, Bear Stearns, Fannie Mae, and Freddie Mac. Their failures have numerous sources, but none is more elemental than the breakdown in relationships that has produced an increasingly detached, transient, and uncommitted set of stakeholders.

A *McKinsey Quarterly* survey of senior executives around the world found that 85 percent indicated that public trust in business had declined, and 72 percent said commitment to free markets had deteriorated.[2] According to the 2009 Edelman Trust Barometer, those executives are reading the public mind correctly: 62 percent of respondents, across 20 countries, say they "trust corporations less now than they did a year ago."[3] Think about that: In less than a year, more than half of the respondents lost trust in corporations.

Over the last several decades, there has been a steady stream of organizational breakthroughs: automation and new technology, growing efficiencies from economies of scale, downsizing, outsourcing and offshoring, reengineering, Six Sigma, top grading, and even customer relationship management. While mixed in their results, these initiatives share a common characteristic—they have been hard on relationships.

Analysts, mathematicians, engineers, consultants, and business schools have used stopwatches, algorithms, analytics, quantitative process analysis, outsourcing, worker rankings, statistical sampling, balanced scorecards, super-computing, and a bunch of other mechanisms to quantify and eliminate work and workers. Virtually everything they have done has diminished human relationships. Unwittingly, we have spent the past three decades deconstruct-ing the most prolific source of growth and development available to us—the relationship. Most would be hard-pressed to identify a single area of business where trusted relationships have grown more abundant, stronger, or longer.

In the organization with which you are most familiar, how much time and energy are spent dealing with relationship issues and problems, such as the impact of upset or defecting customers on revenues; rebates, pric-ing concessions, or special service programs to assuage customers lacking in loyalty or even those disgruntled; unexpected costs or problems that result from personnel issues such as disagreements or turnover; disputes or poor working relationships between executives and their departments over who should get credit or blame for results; shareholders or other stakeholders who are upset?

If we could take all of the relationship management efforts—customer, employee, management, and shareholder—across all sections of the orga-nization and place those efforts into one department we might call the Relationship Department, it would probably be the largest unit in most organizations. What if this Relationship Department were the single most important contributor to the hard metrics of revenue and market share growth, cost, and bottom-line results, along with stock price and market capitalization? What if, in the nonprofit world, it were key to carrying out the noble missions of feeding the poor, supporting the victims of disaster, helping and healing the sick, inventing cures for dreaded diseases and addic-tions, housing the homeless, and nurturing those broken in spirit?

In this chapter, we will look at the current state of organizational relationships: customers, employees, managers, shareholders—four terms defined by their relational connection—and analyze how and why decline is so prevalent.

Customers and Employees: Looking for Revenue in All the Wrong Places

As mortgages became securitized and Wall Street became involved, they became very transactional and there was no relationship built with the borrower and the lender. And I think that makes it easier for someone to see it as an anonymous party at the other end of the transaction and just walk away from it.

—California real estate agent, on the subprime mortgage crisis[4]

Customers is a relational term: those that providers serve. There has been an incredible focus on customer relationship management (CRM) for the past decade. The amount of time, money, and technology devoted to improving the breadth, depth, and quality of relationships with customers is huge. Yet results have mostly disappointed. According to Forrester Research, only 10 percent of business and IT executives surveyed strongly agreed that business results anticipated from implementing CRM were met or exceeded.[5] Unfortunately, CRM has mostly focused on just about everything—technology, pricing power, sales, cost—except building relationships.

Loads of statistics support the conclusion that revulsion, breakup, and divorce between businesses and their customers are thriving activities. Broken relationships and defections cost companies revenue, customers time, and, eventually, employees their jobs. Let's take a closer look at what's happening.

ERODING CUSTOMER LOYALTY—A LOSS OF TRUST

Why are customer relationships, so crucial to the success of organizations, falling apart so universally? Defection is simply the parting shot from a broken relationship where the commitment has disappeared. Customer loyalty, on the other hand, represents the level of commitment customers have to their providers, and vice versa. And research confirms just how valuable strong, loyal relationships are. Loyal customers

- buy a larger share of their products and services from their loyal provider

DIVORCE, BUSINESS STYLE

A clear indication of broken organizational relationships is customer defections, which are to an organization what divorce is to the family—one side firing the other. Just as in our personal lives, broken relationships can be a destroyer of value. In analyzing the customers of 100-plus clients, for instance, my company consistently found that a 5 percent decrease in customer defection could result in a 30 percent or greater increase in profitability.

Although we don't have 50 years of historical data for comparison as with divorce rates, we do have recent trends. Just as the marital divorce rate has risen, the customer divorce or defection rates across industries continue to climb. According to a Group 1 Software research report, "The total defection rate across all global industries increased from 16.9 percent per year in 2003 to 19.1 percent in 2005. This increase in the average customer defection rate occurred despite the fact that loyalty programs and aggressive discounting seem to proliferate more than ever. However, rather than building relationships based on customer needs, many of these loyalty programs amount to nothing more than bribes for transactions, with little effect on actual customer loyalty."[6]

By 2007, Group 1 Software found customer defections had reached 22 percent—a jump of 30 percent since 2005.[7] This means that, on average, businesses are losing better than 100 percent of their customer base every five years, in spite of research, spending, technology installations, and incentives all directed at retaining these relationships.

The cell phone industry provides a glaring example. In 2003, the Yankee Group reported an incredible statistic: More than one-third of the nation's 139 million cell phone users had switched providers in the previous year.[8] Imagine the sheer magnitude of switching that is represented here. Forget about the lost revenue; consider what it cost in terms of staff time to close approximately 46 million accounts and reopen them elsewhere—with no net new business for the industry. And in spite of considerable efforts to strengthen relationships, the subsequent defection rates only increased, rising from

33.4 percent in 2005 to 38.6 percent in 2007.[9]

General Motors went from 44.5 percent market share in 1980 to 22 percent in 2008.[10] Dysfunction in building customer relationships is one of the top factors that have hurt the entire automotive industry. J. D. Power research reports: "25 percent of the people who walked out of a new-vehicle dealership without buying said they did so mainly because they didn't like the way the salesperson handled their business. With its high costs and high pressures, the current system hardly serves or satisfies anyone."[11]

Booz Allen Hamilton likewise reports that 85 percent of a firm's brand image is determined by the direct interaction between the sales force and target buyers.[12] It is not surprising that across many industries, given the decline in relationships, that loyalty to brands has experienced double-digit declines in the past two years.[13]

For most organizations, the fully loaded cost of sales and marketing focused on getting and keeping customers runs from the high teens to 40-plus percent of total costs. The cost of defecting relationships begins with lost revenue from existing customers and continues with the negative effect that defecting customers have on the attraction of new customers and the brand. Since most research indicates that it costs five to seven times as much to get a dollar of revenue from a new customer as an existing customer, anything that makes this harder both diminishes new customer revenue and adds to cost.

- are willing to pay competitive or even slightly higher prices
- recommend providers to their colleagues and friends
- are open to being cross-sold additional items
- show more patience and forgiveness when mistakes happen
- are willing to hang in longer with problems before they defect

In fact, according to a Bain and Company study, companies defined as loyalty leaders grow revenue twice as fast as their competitors and at a lower cost.[14]

My company was a pioneer in discovering just how valuable key customer relationships are.[15] We got our start while conducting sales training for the Royal Bank of Canada, that nation's largest bank. They had begun to focus on customer profitability and wanted our help in designing a process to identify and apply new insights in targeting and managing customer relationships. As we worked with them, it became clear that about 5 percent of their retail customers were generating more than 60 percent of their profits.

In working with local branches, we discovered that a number of their most profitable customers had no real relationship with branch sales and service staff. We developed a process to proactively engage staff to retain and grow more profitable relationships with these key customers locally, and over the years, the Royal Bank of Canada became a recognized leader in CRM.

Over the next 10 years, my company discovered similar ratios in working with more than 100 banks, insurance firms, retailers, travel businesses, and other companies in the United States, Latin America, the United Kingdom, South Africa, and Australia.

As is true in our personal lives, the connection between customer retention and loyalty takes us to the issue of trust. In a report released in 2006, entitled "Building and Profiting from Consumer Trust," Data Monitor reported that 86 percent of consumers surveyed admitted having become more distrustful of corporations within the previous five years—and 64 percent of the 153 industry leaders surveyed agreed that consumer trust in brands had decreased in the two years prior.[16] It is not surprising that the number of retail shoppers stating that they were long-term loyal customers dropped from 83.3 percent in 2005 to 77.2 percent in 2006.[17] The loss of trust is killing loyalty.

One key attribute of loyalty is to trust the intentions of providers. Richard Evans, a drug industry analyst for Sanford C. Bernstein and Company, put it this way: "A lot of the demand that the industry has created over the years has been through promotion, and for that promotion to be effective, there has to be trust. . . . That trust has been lost."[18]

Notice that Evans did not say the products aren't needed, they are lousy, or they are priced too high; he attributed the decline in profits to a decline in trust. How could an industry that has put billions into product development, marketing to consumers, and education of doctors be worse off than when they started? Kaiser Family Foundation research provides the answer: 70 percent of consumers surveyed believed that drug companies put profits ahead of people. It also found that in 2004, for the first time, most people surveyed said drug companies generally do a "bad job" (48 percent) rather than a "good job" (44 percent) of serving consumers.[19] I have heard it stated this way: People don't care how much you know until they know how much you care.

WHAT'S UP, DOC?

In 2005, a Harvard University survey reported 55 percent of respondents were dissatisfied with their quality of health care, up from 44 percent in 2000, and 40 percent said it had gotten worse in the past five years.[20] "The point is that when they talk about quality of health care, patients mean something entirely different than experts do," said Drew Altman, president of the Kaiser Family Foundation, a cosponsor of the study. "They're not talking about numbers or outcomes but about their own human experience." This occurred during a period of incredible breakthroughs in technologies, drugs, and home health care. When the relationship goes wrong, quality suffers. A solid relationship increases the odds that patients follow doctor's orders regarding meds, exercise, diet, and return visits, leading to better outcomes. Relationships matter.

Lawsuits filed against doctors now represent a significant amount of the cost for medical care. In *Blink*, Malcolm Gladwell summarizes it this way: "Patients don't file lawsuits because they've been harmed by shoddy medical care. Patients file lawsuits because they've been harmed by shoddy medical care and something else happens to them. What is that something else? It's how they were treated, on a personal level, by their doctor. What comes up again and again in malpractice cases is that patients say they were rushed, or ignored or treated poorly."[21]

In a word, it is the relational injury—how doctors mistreat their patients—that drives who gets sued.

Customer relationship decline parallels personal relationship decline. Just as more families have only one parent and little or no extended family support, customers have seen a significant relational decline in the support available to them. While much more information and access are often available (more locations and longer hours, 24/7 call centers, online support), human relationships have been stripped out of the interactions and transactions that go on between organizations and their customers. The hyped advantages of self-service and self-help quickly morphed into "no help." There was no available relationship: no coach or advocate to help navigate to the right answers, especially for nonstandard questions. Or, if there was, it was a one-time episode, with no ongoing relationship to lever for future interactions. The world of business and organizations has not only sacrificed but also even repelled customer relationships.

ERODING EMPLOYEE RELATIONSHIPS—
A LOSS OF TRUST

Just as relationships between customers and providers have declined, the connection and commitment between employers and their employees have also lost ground. The term *employee* is relational: one who is employed by another. Most of us know the pain and dysfunction of being in a bad employer-employee relationship.

Turnover is perhaps the most tangible measure of fractured employee relationships, and it is on the rise. Certainly the recent recession, which erased over 2.6 million jobs in 2008 alone, has greatly impacted turnover.[22] But even prior to the recession, turnover was on the rise. From 2004 to 2007, turnover jumped from 4 percent to 8.8 percent for managers, doubled for salespeople, and more than doubled among skilled manufacturing workers.[23] And, according to the U.S. Department of Labor, in 2006 (the latest year for which data are available) nearly half (45 percent) of all private-sector workers experienced some sort of separation—either voluntary or involuntary departures.[24] Although these numbers are skewed by temporary jobs, summer jobs for youth, people working more than one job, and other factors, they nevertheless present a startling picture.

While separation may be the best available option for one or both parties, each side incurs replacement costs: The employee must expend time and effort finding new work, and the employer does likewise in replacing the worker or redistributing the work.

Evidence shows that the rate of overall separation and specifically the rate of quitting are unlikely to decline. Prior to the economic downturn, a survey conducted by the Society of Human Resource Management found that 75 percent of the nation's employees were looking for a new job; executives led the pack, with 82 percent scouting for jobs.[25] Talk about a resounding "no" vote on their work relationship. Can you imagine those three out of four employees wearing a sign on their foreheads to work each day that said, "I am looking to leave this job"? It just might be a little unnerving for customers, colleagues, and their bosses alike—who, in most cases, are also trying to exit. It is no wonder that so many workers want to leave if their bosses are transient. Instability breeds instability. Similar problems exist in the public sector. Forty-six percent of new teachers, for instance, leave the profession after only five years, with overall attrition up 50 percent in the past 15 years.[26]

In 2010, the Conference Board reported that only 45 percent of Americans were satisfied with their jobs, down from almost 61 percent in 1987 and the lowest they have recorded. Fifty-one percent say they are satisfied with their boss, down from 55 percent in 2008 and around 60 percent two decades ago. Fifty-six percent say they like their coworkers, down from 68 percent in 1987.[27] Other research has shown that among those who felt they worked for an ethical organization, 55 percent were truly loyal. For those who didn't feel they worked for an ethical organization, the loyalty figure was 9 percent.[28] As a consumer or a leader, it is disconcerting to deal with providers in key fields like medicine or financial services who are so indifferent. This lack of commitment affects all stakeholders.

Why are so many dissatisfied with work? Do we have a bunch of disloyal whiners who don't know when they are well off? Or is something going on that is driving a wedge between employee and employer?

Loss of Faith in the Employer

We increasingly see evidence that employees have lost belief or faith in what their organization is about—its purpose.

As organizations jumped through hoops to meet short-term financial targets, they at times directed employees to focus on work considered counterproductive and even unethical. My first evidence of this showed up in a large research project I led in 2001 with the Bank Administration Institute.[29] Our findings were surprising, and they still ring true 10 years later:

- 78 percent of frontline bankers felt pressured to sell beyond customer need.
- 49 percent said their sales goals were unfair.
- 50 percent felt that senior management in large banks was not actively involved in developing a customer-focused bank.

In retrospect, the employees were telling us that the heavy and often heavy-handed approach to selling was violating the relationship they had with their customers, which concerned them greatly. The irony is that employers either have people who are committed to relationships or employees who don't care about customer relationships—an even bigger problem. When workers who value relationships are asked to carry out actions they perceive to be detrimental to relationships, it leads to weakened employee relationships and loss of commitment.

Mixed Messages about Valued Employees

Corporate leaders today swim in an ocean of employee distrust. The steady stream of downsizing and cutbacks has taken a toll. Yet they face a difficult challenge. Wall Street has had an inherent belief in cutting costs by getting rid of people—the preferred disposable asset. All of this has led to a frequent schizophrenia: our annual reports proclaim people as "our most important asset" yet our word to the Street announces we are divesting ourselves of as many of these most precious assets as possible—mostly to the applause of the shareholders.

And clearly, their concerns over job security are further compounded by their concerns over employee compensation. Since the end of 2000, gross domestic product per person expanded 8.4 percent and profits rose from 6 percent to almost 9 percent, but average weekly wages edged down 0.3 percent.[30] According to the *Wall Street Journal*, workers at the 90th percentile (those who earn more than 90 percent of all workers) earned 4.5 times as much as those in the 10th percentile in 2004; 25 years earlier, they were earning 3.5 times as much.[31] Headlines of outrageous executive pay only fueled the fire—a topic we will address later in this chapter. And while lower inflation, greater purchasing power, and the wage pressures of a global economy were all very real, the effect was to further undermine employee relationships.

Employee Peer Networks

Peer connections at work also affect the employee-employer relationship. Among the many changes in recent years that have affected the solidarity of worker-peer relationships are the

- decline of unions
- increase in outsourcing/offshoring
- racial/ethnic/gender divide
- decline in average work tenure
- increase in the use of temporary and part-time workers
- option to work at home
- move to multiple shifts
- mixing of domestic and international workers
- language differences among workers

The perception is that we are less connected to our fellow workers. Thus, we are losing relationships both vertically (with management) and horizontally (with peers).

EMPLOYEE RELATIONSHIP DECLINE: THE COST

The cost of transient, uncommitted employee relationships in both expense and lost revenue is significant. Yet most of the recent focus has been on the cost of having employees, not of losing them. Even our language signals the fatalistic and inevitable mind-set we often appropriate to our human relationships. We talk about them as the soft side even though the costs are very hard. Employees are "just human," which makes it sound as if hard assets, such as wood, steel, plastic, or electronic blips, are somehow more valuable. We talk about employee "emotion" as if it were something to be stamped out like typhoid fever rather than acknowledge that it is the source of innovation, motivation, and commitment.

One of the easiest employee relationship costs to quantify is the cost of turnover. Not all turnover is bad, but all turnover is expensive. When David A. Brandon became CEO at Domino's Pizza, he was appalled to find that annual employee turnover was 158 percent, and that it cost about $2,500 each time an hourly employee left and $20,000 each time a store manager quit.[32] Domino's found that turnover cost actually exceeded profits.

Domino's recruits, hires, and trains approximately 180,000 people a year. The direct cost and the cost in management time are enormous. It raises the question: Is Domino's in the pizza delivery business or in the staffing and training business? Even small improvements in targeting, developing, and retaining relationships would pay a very high dividend. Targeting committed "relationships" is different from filling positions.

Many companies have hit their profit targets by focusing on downsizing. Yet in the considerable effort spent, they have run into issues that negatively impact customers: more errors, faulty handoffs, loss of relationship with key employees or customers. It costs money to form, dissolve, and then re-form relationships. When all is said and done, relationship, revenue, and results are lost.

Corporate America has increasingly embraced a model of employee turnover and relationship instability: interchangeable, disposable, relationshipless. To the accountants and the financial analysts, it looks like an efficient model, but relationship destruction is not sustainable over the long run. Too often estrangement and disengagement are the response of broken relationships that stay together. Disengagement means withholding resources—energy, creativity, skills—from the work and work relationships.

As organizations view employees as an expendable cost, the employee/employer relationship is becoming endangered. Herbert Meyer, former associate editor of *Fortune* magazine, described the change this way: "The restructuring of American business means we are coming to the end of the age of the employer and employee. With all this fracturing of organizations into different and smaller units, employers can't guarantee jobs anymore because they don't know what their companies will look like next year. Everyone is on their way to becoming an independent contractor."[33]

Yet, when employee relationships are strong, customers notice and it helps build strong customer relationships. *Fortune* pointed this out when it chose Wegmans Food Markets as one of their Best Companies to Work For: "You cannot separate their strategy as a retailer from their strategy as an employer . . . its annual turnover rate for full-time employees is just 6 percent, a fraction of the 19 percent figure for grocery chains with a similar number of stores, according to the Food Marketing Institute."[34]

Stable, committed employee relationships not only reduce the cost of turnover but work to build strong customer relationships and revenue streams. A simple truth abides: You can't get committed work and committed customers from uncommitted workers. The very fabric of an organization is its employee relationships.

Management and Shareholders: Looking for Profits in All the Wrong Ways

Management and shareholders join customers and employees in the world of work with their own relationship midlife crisis. They have certainly suffered the organizational version of infidelity, divorce, shotgun weddings, cohabitation, and an almost endless string of merger and acquisition suitors. Management and shareholders have instigated the breakup of units, which has resulted in customer and worker relationships being split up or thrown together in ill-fitting, estranged couplings. Some of these changes succeed and some fail, but they all take a toll on relationships.

Increased global competition has been a powerful force for lower prices and lower cost and has produced many benefits. But stripped-out middle management, reliance on remote workers, technology-based communication that replaces face-to-face interactions, less coaching and mentoring, leaner staffing, self-service, and online purchasing have all weakened relationships in the workplace. It is no surprise that workers often resemble neglected children who suffer the ravages of inattentive parents.

DISCORD, DISTRUST, AND ESTRANGEMENT AT THE TOP

Confidence in all leaders dropped in 2008, but confidence in business leaders fell 13.5 percent, exceeding the decline in all other sectors, including that of politicians.

—National Leadership Index 2008[35]

Perhaps there has never been a time when management relationships, especially executive management, have made so many nasty headlines. We lived through and continue to live through the debacles of the late Ken Lay and Jeffrey Skilling at Enron, Bernie Ebbers at WorldCom, and Dennis Koslowski at Tyco. More recently, the death march claimed Rick Wagoner, CEO of General Motors, Robert Nardelli as CEO of Chrysler, and Ken Lewis, CEO of Bank of America, to name just a few. While the transgressions range from scandal to poor performance, the prominent fall of these CEOs had a singular deleterious effect: In each case, the relationship between leaders and their stakeholders was severely damaged.

This is something I know firsthand. While it is easy to be critical, as CEO of a private company for more than 20 years and as president of the most profitable division of a public company, I know that nothing is more humbling than trying to juggle the responsibilities of good relationship stewardship and sound financial management.

> I vividly remember a call I received late on a Friday evening in the spring of 1989 from my banker, Robin, who got right to the point. "Robert, I am afraid I have some bad news. As you know, our bank has been taken over by the FDIC and they have put your company loan in the 'bad bank,' which means you must pay off your $800,000 bank note. You have some time but you need to find another bank."
>
> I was almost speechless. I tried to protest. "But Robin, we are current on our payments, have not violated any of our loan covenants, and we are profitable."

He responded, "I know, but there is nothing I can do. The FDIC sent in a team and reviewed all of our commercial loans, and they are calling those they don't want to assume. I am truly sorry."

And that was that. Few things focus the mind like having to make payroll. We had to do two things immediately: cut every penny of expense possible and find another bank. The next Wednesday we terminated 10 people (10 percent of our workforce at that time). I met with each one of them to thank them and to apologize for what had happened. What made it especially tough was that, in the months leading up to all of this, we had expanded substantially as we developed and rolled out some new products. When the economy began to falter and the local banks got into trouble, I held a company rally and said that we would stay the course, without layoffs, no matter what. (Our management team had already confidentially begun a three-month hiatus without salaries.) Everyone cheered. The problem wasn't that people didn't believe me. The problem was that they *did* believe me.

As I announced the layoffs, I could see in their eyes the disbelief and the disappointment. I could feel the very painful sensation of my credibility draining out of me. As a young CEO, I learned two very tough lessons. First, I vowed never to make a promise to my employees unless I was absolutely sure I could fulfill it. Second, financial instability in business (just as at home) breeds relational instability, and vice versa. Fortunately we found a local bank that assumed our loan and we were able to pay it off over the next three quarters. Rebuilding the relationships and my credibility took a little longer.

Executive turnover began to reflect a basic change in the relationships between senior management and their corporate owners in the late 1990s. By 2003, exit rates in the executive suite were nothing short of mind-boggling. Booz Allen reported that turnover among CEOs of the world's 2,500 largest corporations in 2003 had risen 170 percent since 1995.[36]

When a basic metric like CEO turnover more than doubles in a period of seven or eight years, you know something is up. Even more significant, it was occurring among the world's largest corporations where order, control, studied decision making, and succession planning are considered not just an art but also a science. Consulting firm Challenger, Gray & Christmas reported in the first quarter of 2008 that 370 CEOs of public and private companies announced departures, a 7 percent increase over the same period in 2007. Of 118 CEO resignations, many were "less than voluntary."[37]

DIVORCE, EXECUTIVE STYLE

Although the churn in CEOs gets more of the attention, executive churn throughout the corporate world has risen. Spencer Stuart reports that the average tenure for a chief marketing officer (CMO) is just 23 months.[38] In 2007, nearly a quarter of the chief financial officer (CFO) positions at Fortune 1000 companies were open during the year.[39] These relationships begin to sound more like dating or cohabiting than marriage, more like lease than purchase.

During the lead-up to the 21st century and beyond, there was a growing trend in the corporate world to replace executives from outside the "family"—that is, strangers from outside the corporation. Martin Conyon reports that in the United States, the number of executives hired from outside an organization increased from 15 percent in the 1970s to 26 percent in the 1990s. According to the *Wall Street Journal*, by 2005, outsiders were replacing 43 percent of departing CEOs in the United States.[40]

Not only had the turnover rate at the top been rising; increasingly, CEO replacements were strangers from another company, industry, or even country, which means they arrived without relationships with customers, employees, management, and shareholders. This makes the transition more uncertain. It doesn't mean that it won't work, but it does mean more effort is required to build relationships, establish new expectations, and instill trust.

The Economist likewise reported that among the CEOs in Europe pushed out in 2003, 70 percent were chief executives who came in as outsiders.[41] The report pointed out that troubled firms were more likely to bring in outsiders, so those individuals may have been facing a tougher challenge to begin with. Furthermore, outside CEOs may be brought in more often specifically to take the kind of actions that will expressly fracture relationships, such as reducing the size of the workforce, getting rid of existing management, severing relationships with certain suppliers, or increasing prices to customers. Whatever the cause, it does appear that outsiders were exiting at a higher rate than were insiders. It certainly makes sense that relational risk increases the odds that CEO hires from outside the family may not work.

If outsider CEOs are likely to have the least tenured relationship with stakeholders and are being canned at a disproportionate rate, what about the opposite end of the continuum? A study by Rüdiger Fahlenbrach (cited by *Fortune* magazine) looked at a sample of 2,300 U.S. companies over a period of 10 years and found that those run by a founder-CEO outperformed the broader stock market by 8 percentage points a year.[42] He draws some very "relationship-oriented" conclusions about why these founder-CEOs seem to be better corporate stewards: "One is that they simply care more. Their companies are their life's work, so they're more likely to embrace long-term strategies . . . founder-run companies have bigger capital budgets and invest considerably more in research and development than non-founder run firms." Fahlenbrach also concluded that founder-CEOs tend to be industry experts, not "managerial mercenaries." In other words, they are likely to have stronger relationships with a broader range of their stakeholders.

While the trend toward hiring executives from outside the organization is beginning to reverse itself,[43] by almost any measure—trust, performance, duration—the strength of executive and management relationships with their stakeholders has declined significantly in recent years. Stakeholders have become increasingly dependent on strangers at the top of their organizations for employment, delivery of goods/services, and return on investments. It is increasingly difficult to expect better outcomes from those weaker relationships.

EXECUTIVE RELATIONSHIP DISCORD:
A RACE TO THE BOTTOM

Clearly, executive relationship discord and instability can retard employee performance; over time, diminished employee performance fuels executive discord. It's a destructive downward spiral.

Several years ago Gallup found in interviewing more than 2 million workers in 700 companies that how long an employee stays at a company and how
productive she is there is determined by her relationship with her immediate
supervisor. "People join companies and leave managers," said Marcus Buck-
ingham, a senior managing consultant at Gallup and the primary analyst for
the study.[44] We have all experienced working for bosses who drove us to leave
or at least to wish we could leave, as well as bosses who played a big role in
our development and success. This boss/subordinate dynamic shows up in
a number of ways: people who bring out the best in each other, people who
bring out the worst; people who can't get along, people who are such good
friends they are blind to the same things; tough people who challenge us in
positive ways, tough people who intimidate; and soft managers who tolerate
and even reward dysfunctional and poor performance.

Toxic leadership can destroy the emotional climate of the workplace. As
pressures have grown to perform, to meet quarterly targets and ever-increasing expectations, a certain style of overachiever has emerged in corporate
America—one who pushes hard for results but at the sacrifice of relationships. Spreier, Fontaine, and Malloy, writing for the *Harvard Business Review*,
describe overachievers who tend to command and coerce, rather than coach
and collaborate, thus stifling subordinates. Further, they take frequent shortcuts and forget to communicate crucial information, and may be oblivious
to the concerns of others. The authors conclude: "Their teams' performance
begins to suffer, and they risk missing the very goals that initially triggered
the achievement-oriented behavior. Too intense a focus on achievement can
demolish trust and undermine morale, measurably reducing workplace productivity and eroding confidence in management, both inside and outside
the corporation."[45]

Dr. James Kroll, a national expert on handling whitetail deer, provides
an example from the animal kingdom of how oppressive leadership builds
up resentment. He often works with bucks that are in pens and must be
drugged to make them safe to move or handle. He says the rule is never to
drug the dominant buck first. "I'm convinced that whitetails hold a grudge
against older deer that have dominated them. Given a chance to get even,
they will never forget past grievances. At the first sign of weakness, every
subordinate buck in the pen will attack the dominant deer."[46] Relational
oppression has a cost across all forms of organizations.

The incredible pressure to meet quarterly revenue and earnings targets of public companies has similarly put a unique strain on ethics and relationships. A survey of financial executives by professors at Duke and the University of Washington found that 76 percent said they would sacrifice economic value (projects and investments that would yield future value) to keep earnings rising smoothly (and avoid missing short-term earnings targets).[47]

This short-term focus can have far-reaching effects. When workers see smart, ethical, high-performance leaders they admire make dumb, questionable, performance-injuring decisions for short-term gain, they not only lose confidence in the company's leaders but also in its mission and future. Even those who have no fear of losing their jobs find it hard to bring the same level of passion and engagement to their work.

Organizations express what they value by how they invest. In recent years, there has been a tremendous investment in new technology, in expanding into global markets, in finding cheaper labor sources in places like China and India, and in stock buybacks. During this period, spending on employee salaries, training, and benefits such as retirement has lost ground. As the economy recovers, few organizations to date have made investing in human resources a substantive priority—with one exception.

The spending on executive compensation, especially for CEOs, has skyrocketed in recent years. It has become a symbol for lack of fairness, poor stewardship, arrogance, dishonesty, paucity of purpose, and an assault on the value of the team, thus eliciting outrage.

The numbers are startling: In the past 25 years, CEO total average compensation has jumped from about $625,000 a year, or 42 times the average worker salary of $14,900, to $5.4 million, or 340 times the average worker's $15,900.[48] There are a number of reasons for the jump, such as competition for CEOs, with private equity firms offering higher pay and freedom from the shareholder and regulatory stresses of public companies. To the workers asked to be good stewards of scarce resources, this dramatic increase is hypocritical, unfair, and divisive. These increases often translate into destabilizing forces that can harm stakeholder relationships: for executives, there is pressure of higher expectations and shorter time horizons for results; for workers, fewer resources, a class division, and even warfare that ultimately can cost them compensation and jobs; for shareholders, poorer results. And when that happens, the unvirtuous circle is completed as the very worker relationships needed to deliver results—especially crucial to the CEO and his performance—become eroded.

THE PRICE WE PAY FOR TRANSIENT SHAREHOLDER RELATIONSHIPS

In 2009, the average stock turnover appears to have exceeded 250 percent (changed hands two and a half times), compared to 78 percent a decade ago, and 21 percent barely 30 years ago.

—John C. Bogle, founder and retired CEO, Vanguard Group[49]

As with the other stakeholders we discussed in this chapter, the duration, depth, and functionality of shareholder relationships has declined. The simplest way to look at the erosion of shareholder relationships is by examining the turnover of stock holdings.

More shareholders are cashing in more frequently. John Bogle, founder and retired CEO of the Vanguard Group, nets it out: "First, the folly of short-term speculation has replaced the wisdom of long-term investing as the star of capitalism. A rent-a-stock system has replaced the earlier own-a-stock system."[50]

Shorter-term stock holding periods have driven significant changes in relationships. Management operates under tremendous pressure to show favorable short-term results measured in months instead of years. A one-cent-per-share miss for a given quarter can literally cut the value of the company by 25 percent, driving investors to the exits. Companies cater to a new breed of transient shareholders. In essence, divorcing one company and then entering a relationship with another—driven by brokers incentivized to make trades—has become big business. The payoff for these brokers, much as for divorce attorneys, thrives on relationship instability.

Likewise, the growth of mutual funds has also added not only to the transiency and thus instability but also relational estrangement by inserting an intermediary (the fund) between the company and the ultimate stock owner. Many funds have had turnover rates of 100-plus percent, which means their average holding period for a stock was less than 12 months. The pressure for money managers to show their returns for individual and institutional investors has often worked in opposition to holding stocks for the after-tax gains their clients needed. Short-term and frequent trading often meant ordinary income rather than the lower capital gains rates for their investors.

Rent-a-stock does not sound like investment. Instead it sounds like a series of one-night stands where none of the parties is committed to a long-term, mutually rewarding relationship. Companies that make short-term decisions in defense of their stock price are often tempted to mortgage their future. Investors sacrifice after-tax gain to make money managers look good. Stock owners are behaving like much of the rest of society, emphasizing freedom over commitment and shorter-term satisfaction over longer-term gains.

About half of all U.S. households own stocks directly or through mutual funds.[51] Although these stocks are held in a number of ways—company pension plans, mutual funds, direct ownership—the advent of the public company provided a way to expand the pool of owners by separating ownership from management. Most shareholders are not involved in the operation of the business. It is a significant statement to say that half our households are heavily invested in the financial success of our public corporations. In fact, it is about the same percentage of adults who voted in the last presidential election. Participating in capitalism by investing is like participation in democracy by voting. These investments house college funds for our kids, money for retirement and dreams for second homes, great vacations, and more. This trend has provided tremendous capital to our publicly owned businesses and has enabled them to invest in product development, expand into new markets, increase production capacity, and acquire new technology.

Yet this expansion also has real implications for the sophistication of this growing class of ownership and their relationships with the companies they own. Capitalism in general, and the stock market in particular, is about assessing and managing opportunity and risk. How can the residents of more than 50 million households, who work in fields that give them little insight into the inner workings of corporations and the markets they serve, be adept at knowing how to invest their money wisely? The answer is they can't. These households are primarily invested in mutual funds managed by institutions. While stock ownership is increasing because of mutual funds, the share of stocks owned by individuals has declined significantly—from 90 percent in 1950 to just 32 percent today.[52]

In recent years, as individual investors were getting more removed from their investments, there was a surge in corporate scandals, exorbitant compensation, backdating of stock options, and illegal and legal (but misleading) financial engineering. Distrust in corporate leaders, boards of directors, investment banks, rating agencies, and auditing firms grew rapidly.

These practices have, and continue to, cost shareholders billions of dollars. It has become clear that while certain shareholders are losing money, those who take companies public, advise and finance major mergers and acquisitions, lead divestitures, and take public companies private have been able to prosper in good times and bad. The turbulent business of forming and disbanding corporate relationships—marriage and divorce *Wall Street* style—has been quite lucrative for investment banks and other handlers, agents, and insiders even if it was quite painful for many of the stakeholders—especially employees and certain investors. As *Fortune* magazine pointed out, "Whether they opt for an acquisition, a private-equity buyout, or a Tyco-style dismemberment, Wall Street gets paid."[53] Even after the meltdown of 2008–2009, workers at 23 top investment banks, hedge funds, asset managers, and stock and commodities exchanges made over $140 billion in total compensation in 2009, up 20 percent over 2008 and topping their peak year 2007 by $10 billion.[54]

Too often these inside groups have leveraged their relationships on the backs of the other stakeholders, leaving a path of economic and relational destruction for employees, customers, and unprivileged shareholders. Increasingly, the shareholder relationship has morphed from owners to traders. The function of providing capital to corporations, considered money for longer-term investments requiring years for return, has come to behave more like short-term expense money for this week's lottery ticket. In many cases, the advisers who are benefactors, if not enablers, of the turbulence in the corporate relationships are paid handsomely even when longer-term shareholders' outcomes are negative. Bogle hits the nail on the head when he laments that while once we were an ownership society, we are now an agency society, but the agents charged with looking out for our interests (mutual fund managers and pension fund trustees) have taken too large a portion while too small a portion is delivered to the last-line investors who put up so much of the capital and assumed so much of the risk.[55]

The more things change (i.e., broader participation in the markets), the more they stay the same, in that power is concentrated in the hands of relatively few institutions, which has a corrupting influence. At best, this relational sea change creates unintended consequences for the investor who puts up the capital, and havoc for those trying to lead and manage the organization. When short-term and detached forces exert too much power over the management of public corporations, it distorts reality and leads to dysfunctional management decisions and actions.

The Challenge of Operating in a "Relationship-less" World

Dysfunctional family relationships retard childhood growth and development (school performance) and lead to kids getting in trouble. In organizations, it really isn't that different.

One of the impacts of this short-term, relationship-less pressure has been the increase in financial engineering to meet or beat quarterly financial targets. There are now more doubts about the accuracy of financial statements and the role of CEOs, CFOs, boards, auditors, rating agencies, and government regulators such as the Securities and Exchange Commission in overseeing financial reporting. Too often the numbers have been engineered to obfuscate the true state of the organization. Corporate management has certainly played a role, but so have the detached owners who focused solely on short-term results. In response, there has been a dramatic rise in the number of outside board members deemed more objective and less beholden to CEOs and therefore less vulnerable to the temptation to mess with the numbers.[56] It's like sending the kids off to boarding school for some tough love. Unfortunately, however, the result can be weakened relationships.

This trend has already impacted the types of relationships that govern corporations. Outside directors have lessened the domain expertise of the board. Perfect objectivity is perfect ignorance. Selecting directors and executives primarily on the basis of their compliance pedigree is not likely to result in the candidates with the highest expertise in revenue growth, innovation, or operations. In a shareholder marketplace where the pressure for growth in revenue and earnings is so intense and the punishment for failing to perform is so high, detached and uninformed executive and shareholder leadership can hurt the potential for growth. Once again, the decline in trusted, committed, and competent relationships is a destructive force.

Finally, as pressure mounts for short-term financial results, a number of executives and their boards have turned to ill-advised mergers and acquisitions. Sometimes these marriages are simply a way of disguising pending revenue and earnings shortfalls.

Mergers and acquisitions are tough on customer and employee relationships. I know this firsthand, based on acquisition work for clients and in my experience in buying and selling three of my own companies. No matter how hard you try, it is impossible to pull off a merger without some broken glass. A Marist survey of better than 1,000 merger versus nonmerger telecom industry workers found that merger employees rated their employers 11 to 13 percent lower than nonmerger employees when it came to issues regarding trust and inclusion.[57] Not surprisingly, Marist research studies show that employees who believe their managers don't care about them are less inclined to care about customers.

All of this raises an important question: How do we target and attract the types of shareholder relationships that make sense? Just like the relationships between marriage partners, customers and providers, and employers and employees, organizations are now beginning to think more intentionally about how to match the direction of the company and the needs and preferences of their shareholders. Warren Buffett is known for saying that public companies get the shareholders they deserve. In other words, if organizations seek only short-term results, they will attract only short-term investors. It's a match made in hell.

Not all relationships need to be or should be long-term. But as a society, we are starved for more committed, predictable, stable relationships. We are relationally undernourished, and it shows.

* * * *

We have spent the past century learning how to separate ownership from management—mostly in public companies. But the relational chasm between owner and management has become so wide and detached that it is now exacting an unacceptable cost. It is part of a larger pattern where the duration, depth, and functionality of work and business relationships continue to plummet. The economic, emotional, and social damage is probably more cumulative and circular than we realize. The decline in the strength and value of customer relationships destroys revenue and profit growth over time. Diminished employee relationships lead to eroded customer relationships, which in turn hurt revenue growth. Estranged management relationships are the single most significant factor undermining employee relationships. Detached shareholders translate into greater management pressures for short-term results, shortsighted decision making, and disposable employees. Poor relationships beget poor results, which beget poor relationships.

And the beat goes on. The loss of personal relationships is now compounded as we experience a similar relational litany at work and in our organizational lives. So many of our organizational advances have changed how we do business, and in the process, our relationships have taken a hit.

It is on us to adjust to this new world. The good news? This demise and its attendant costs force examination and the search for better ways. The hopeful signs of a new relational reality will be our focus in section IV. Meanwhile, circling back to my story about Bank of America, here's one of those signs: Brian Moynihan, now CEO of acquisition-plagued Bank of America, has sworn off any future acquisitions.

Chapter 3

A House Divided Against Itself: A State of Dysfunction

Our leaders, even the president, can no longer utter the word "we" with a straight face. There is no more "we" in American politics at a time when "we" have these huge problems—the deficit, the recession, health care, climate change and wars in Iraq and Afghanistan—that "we" can only manage, let alone fix, if there is a collective "we" at work.

—*Thomas Friedman*, The New York Times[1]

Several years ago our family visited the Civil War site of the Battle of Vicksburg. We made our way along the 6.5-mile circular perimeter dug to protect the Confederate Army and the citizens of Vicksburg, Mississippi, from the oncoming Union army, whose intent was to take the city and command of the Mississippi River. Our guide stopped the vehicle at one point and walked us down to a small open meadow tucked between two small hills. He began by reminding us that both the Union and Confederate armies were mostly organized by state and that Missouri was one of the few states with regiments in both armies. Well, the Missouri Union regiments wound up aligned against the Missouri Confederate units at Vicksburg. They were fighting and killing their own neighbors and relatives in a battle that lasted nearly six weeks.

As his eyes moistened, our guide then told us how the two sides would often call a truce at sundown, and soldiers from each side would stroll down to the meadow to meet their fellow Missourians and mortal battlefield adversaries by day and swap stories from home—about family, neighbors, and loved ones—and even play dominoes until after dark. Then they would return to their respective posts and, come daylight, continue the fighting until the Confederates, under siege and nearly starved, surrendered to the Union Army on July 4, 1863, after almost 20,000 soldiers from the two sides had been killed or injured.

It struck me then, as it does now, just how vulnerable our relationships can be and how blind we can become when consumed with what divides us. Nearly 150 years later we find ourselves once again traveling down a political path where too often we define ourselves by how we disagree, whom we disdain, and how morally bankrupt others are. In affairs of state, it seems we have chosen sides, becoming more like the very opposition that is the object of our contempt: louder, more arrogant, and less able to hear other points of view. When we place a higher priority on beliefs that divide us and less on the relationships that bind us together, we come apart.

Beyond home and work, there is a third life domain where relationships play a key role. These relationships involve our individual and collective political role as citizens. They revolve around our government, a set of beliefs and freedoms, a culture, a common history, and elections. We pay taxes, pledge our allegiance, and in some cases sacrifice our lives in order to live in this country. The state of this state of affairs can be a vast source of great relational wealth.

Yet war seems to be the operative state of politics, not only at home but across the globe. The loss of confidence in and animus toward leaders and governing institutions is now certifiably off the charts. Abroad, the proliferation of terrorism and sectarian violence appears to be never ending and has at times driven a wedge between the United States and our allies. In American politics we have witnessed the contempt of a perpetual red state/blue state brawl. Partisan screaming matches on TV and in town hall meetings, movies dedicated to trashing the political opposition and its leaders, and Internet articles on how to assassinate heads of state have become standard fare. Protesting a war at a soldier's funeral, shooting abortion clinic doctors, shouting insults to grieving parents burying gay children—such flamed political discourse has gone mainstream and commercial, and it is now big business.

POLITICAL CONTEMPT GETS PERSONAL

Some of the writings that followed the 2004 presidential election in which George W. Bush was reelected illustrate just how arrogant, condescending, and relationally brutal that race was.

Ted Rall (CommonDreams.com): "So our guy lost the election. Why shouldn't those of us on the coasts feel superior? We eat better, travel more, dress better, watch cooler movies, earn better salaries, meet more interesting people, listen to better music and know more about what's going on in the world. If you voted for Bush, we accept that we have to share the country with you. We're adjusting to the possibility that there may be more of you than there are of us. But don't demand our respect. You lost it on November 2."

Cal Thomas (Fox News): "In war, the defeated side surrenders to the victor. If the left wants to heal the divide, let them move in the president's direction for a change. And if they are in doubt about that direction, they can consult people who live in what the elites consider flyover country: the good people in those red counties who have had enough of the left and said so on Election Day. The nation isn't growing more divided. It is growing more conservative and republican. And a lot of those people think they're pretty intelligent."[2]

Notice how personal and visceral these descriptions are—a tone very common in the blogosphere. My guess is these responses elicited a response in you.

The term that comes to mind here is *contempt*. John Gottman is

a Washington University marriage and relationship guru who has
been able to predict with better than 90 percent accuracy, based on
a 15-minute observation, whether a couple will be together 15 years
later.[3] The emotion he considers most defining in killing relationships
is contempt—trying to speak from a higher level while attempting
to push another down to a lower plane. He says contempt is closely
related to disgust and completely rejecting and excluding someone
from the community.

Contempt has become a dominant weapon in our political discourse. It is ironic that at the very time we are suffering such a broad
loss of relationship and community, the threat of being figuratively or
actually banished as a community member (by friends, from family,
at work) over our politics is relational destruction in its purest form.

How many times have you cringed as a discussion in a social setting moved
to the topic of politics? When it comes to politics, conversation and dialogue
in private homes or the public square are often similarly contentious. As one
of my friends puts it, "It's a good time to either keep quiet or just mumble."
Somewhere along the way it has become personal when our neighbor or
the guy in the next office has a different opinion about politics, the role of
government, the direction of our culture, military engagement, who should
become citizens, and even the role of religion in affairs of state. It started
as a skirmish and has now evolved into full-scale political and cultural war.
The divide is like a thousand points of darkness: Democrat vs. Republican,
including the Occupy Wall Street movement on the left and the Tea Party
on the right; urban versus rural; pro-choice versus right to life; gay versus
straight; union versus nonunion—you name it.

The news is not that we have differences; our differences have always been
a strength. The news is that these differences, in the great melting pot that
once united us, now divide us. As a nation built on relationships, we once
thrived on lively conversation and spirited debate, but we have devolved into
what Andrew Sullivan calls a war within America. He laments what he calls
the high temperature: "Bill O'Reilly's nightly screeds against anti-Americans
. . . Keith Olbermann's 'Worst Person in the World'; MoveOn.org's 'General
Betray Us' on the one side, Ann Coulter's *Treason* on the other; Michael

Moore's accusation of treason at the core of the Iraq War, Sean Hannity's assertion of treason in the opposition to it." He concludes that most striking in all this is the generally minor nature of policy choices on the table. Thus, something deeper and more powerful than the actual decisions we face is driving the tone of the debate.[4]

Strong and healthy debate can help raise our game, but war as the defining construct for politics devours the very relationships that hold us together.

The Rise of Partisan Politics

Not since the Civil War has there been such a fundamental disagreement over basic assumptions about truth, freedom, and our national identity.

—*James Davison Hunter,* **Culture Wars.**[5]

Surely close elections, disputes, and a turnover of leaders are not new. But the gridlock and animosity associated with today's partisan politics are stronger and more vitriolic than in the recent past. Similar to what we're seeing in the corporate world, distrust, disdain, and dissidence have translated into a level of divide that is a part of the overall landscape of relationship decline.

Some people believe that we have overblown the issue of political divide simply because it applies to a relatively small group on the polar extremes. E. J. Dionne reports that approximately 60 percent of us are middle-of-the-road, with the rest evenly divided between extreme right and extreme left.[6] In addition, many defy stereotypes: right-to-lifers for gay marriage; pro-choicers against assisted suicide; devoutly religious liberals; decidedly agnostic conservatives. Reinforcing that view, Stanford professor Morris Fiorina argued that it is the political leaders and elites—not the general public—that are divided.[7] The concern is that political leaders are inducing a "socialization effect" on the average voter and it is only a matter of time before ordinary voters become more polarized.

Clearly, leadership is a big factor in the success or failure and the unity of any enterprise, including our national government. In the executive branch, the George W. Bush administration was one of the most controversial on record, and after his reelection in 2004, his administration experienced a precipitous decline in approval ratings. Critics contend that his style of governing was the most divisive domestically and relationally damaging internationally of any president in memory. But while Bill Clinton enjoyed high approval ratings when he left office, the issues surrounding pardons, extramarital affairs, and impeachment elicited very strong and polar reactions. Now Barack Obama has taken a hit in the ratings, after enjoying high approval at the start of his administration. Congress, whether controlled by Republicans or Democrats, suffers near-disdain.

Just as marital divorce, parentless children, customer defection, and employee turnover are metrics of relationship declines in families and businesses, a similar set of indicators highlights the divide and dysfunction in affairs of state, primarily politics and government.

THE PRICE OF EXTREME PARTISANSHIP

Our decision to lower the [U.S. credit] rating to AA+ from AAA was really motivated by two things. One is the increasing political polarization which we think is going to impede the ability of policymakers to act proactively to get our public finances in order.

—John Chambers, Standard & Poor's[8]

The consequences of our relational divide are significant: a stressed Social Security system, a huge and growing federal deficit estimated at over $546,000 per household,[9] high unemployment, disagreement regarding climate change, continued dependence on hostile foreign energy sources. Thomas Friedman has aptly described the current de facto energy policy of the nation: "Maximize demand, minimize supply and buy the rest from the people who hate us the most."[10] Every president in recent memory, starting with Jimmy Carter, has pledged to move the country toward energy independence. Yet here we sit importing about half of our oil. *Clearly, partisan divide distorts, distracts, delays, and gridlocks.*

One of the real ironies today is how differently we view our personal lives compared with the overall state of our nation. Results of a number of polls show that well over 60 percent of Americans are happy with their lives, but the majority of those surveyed are not happy with our public institutions. According to a 2010 Pew poll, for example, a mere 19 percent are content with the federal government, and only 22 percent say they can trust the government in Washington "almost always or most of the time"—among the lowest measures in half a century and the lowest average of the last 10 administrations (see the chart below).[11] Opinions about elected officials are particularly poor. Only 25 percent expressed a favorable opinion of Congress, the lowest favorable rating in a quarter century of Pew Research Center surveys. While the level of concern is strongest for the federal government, only 34 percent of survey respondents report confidence in local government, while 32 percent felt public schools were on the right track.[12]

Average Trust in Government Over the Course of Each Administration					
		Percent trusting gov't			R-D
Average during each administration	Total %	Rep %	Dem %	Ind %	diff %
Barack Obama	22	12	33	18	-21
George W. Bush	37	50	26	28	+24
Bill Clinton	29	25	34	24	-9
George H.W. Bush	36	44	29	30	+15
Ronald Reagan	42	53	34	38	+19
Jimmy Carter	29	27	33	27	-6
Nixon/Ford	40	51	41	43	+10
Kennedy/Johnson	68	62	72	65	-10
NET:					
Republican admins	39	50	30	33	+20
Democratic admins	30	27	38	27	-11

Figures show the average percent saying they always or most of the time trust the government in Washington to do what is right across surveys conducted over the course of each administration. The Kennedy/Johnson and Nixon/Ford administrations are combined because relatively few surveys were conducted during those periods.

Pew Survey Reports: Distrust, Discontent, Anger and Partisan Rancor, The People and Their Government, April 18, 2010

The basis for much of the dissatisfaction of Americans with their elected leaders is the level of partisanship. At a time when unemployment, deficits, terrorism, climate change, Social Security, and energy self-sufficiency are looming challenges, extreme partisanship is not only ineffective but also a self-centered endeavor that values grabbing power and defeating opponents over arriving at solutions. The National Leadership Index reported more than nine out of 10 Americans believe that their political leaders spend too much time attacking members of the other party.[13]

U.S. Culture Wars and Relationships

Politics is a thin crust on the surface of culture.

—Leo Tolstoy

Conflict, divide, and even violence are not new to us in this country. As Doris Kearns Goodwin notes in *Team of Rivals: The Political Genius of Abraham Lincoln*, government leaders were known to use a gun duel to settle relational differences in Lincoln's time and a few lost their lives in the process.[14]

One way to think of democracy, with all of its imperfections (including occasional violent flare-ups), is a relational form of governing: one that honors human connection and also conflict. Key decisions are derived from a relationship with those governed, guided by the wishes of the majority while protecting the rights of the minority.

It is instructive to understand how terrorism and relational divide abroad have impacted not only our relationships with our allies but also the political and cultural divide in the United States.

THE ROLE OF TERRORISM AND RELATIONAL DIVIDE ABROAD

From 1974 until 2000, the number of electoral democracies worldwide increased from 39 nations to 120 worldwide, seemingly to promise less authoritarian oppression and more freedom and choice for people in those nations.[15] During that period, we witnessed the fall of the Berlin Wall, the end of apartheid in South Africa, the breakup of the Soviet Union as it moved away from Communism, and a decline in violence in Northern Ireland. Relationships among and between a number of formerly hostile groups seemed to be headed in a positive direction.

Consider, then, how surprised and impacted we all were personally when we witnessed the terrorist attacks in New York and Washington on September 11, 2001. There had been previous warning signs, however.

> When the World Trade Center was bombed in 1993, my company's New York regional office was on the 89th floor. I often stayed at the Vista Hotel at the base of the World Trade Center; the hotel was destroyed as a result of the bomb attack. While none of our staff was injured in that explosion, we were unable to get into our offices for three months. In 1999, I was in Nairobi, Kenya, and had a chance to view firsthand the destruction that had taken place a few months earlier when the U.S. embassy was bombed. Yet, the term *terrorism* had not yet become personal and relational. On the morning of 9/11, I was at the Dallas–Fort Worth airport preparing to board a plane when I first saw the images and heard the news that the United States had been attacked. Only then did the word *terrorism* become operative and personal: The targets were civilians or noncombat military, a definite sign of relationships run amok; the act was designed to scare each of us and alter our thinking and behaviors.

Terrorism provides a uniquely broad and instructive view of political relationship dysfunction in the extreme. Terrorism is a tool directed at the heart of relationships. By historic standards, the few thousand people killed in terrorist incidents to date pales in comparison to World War I and World War II, which saw 29 million soldiers and 46 million civilians killed.[16] Terrorism attacks love, trust, and the security of personal and group relationships for the purpose of forcefully exerting control. It has fundamentally shifted the thinking of many regarding how relationships among different people in the world might work or fail.

As we have become more globally connected, we have become more tribal, more differentiated, and more angry toward groups that do not share our beliefs. The fear of becoming homogenized and losing our identity seems to have pushed some in our society to seek closer links with groups or tribes, to seek more distance from those unlike us, pushing back on the progress of a global economy and community. Unfortunately, hate has become a strong organizing force for building dysfunctional relationships.

I write a column for a monthly magazine, and soon after the Iraq war began, I commented that it seems we entered into this war with some hope to demonstrate to those in other parts of the world how our democracy can create order and civility among disparate groups and factions. Yet as things unfolded, we became more fractious, contentious, and unable to focus on what unites us. Perhaps we need to apply the recommendation of General Peter Pace, who, when he was chairman of the Joint Chiefs of Staff, commented on the sectarian violence in Iraq: "If the Iraqi people as a whole decided today that, in my words now, they love their children more than they hate their neighbor, . . . this could come to a quick conclusion."[17] The same question applies to us: Can we love what unites us more than we hate what divides us? Can relationship trump division?

Not only has terrorism impacted our relationships with our enemies, it has impacted our relationships with our friends. It has highlighted differences of opinion among allies regarding the best way to respond. The bickering among Germany, France, the United Kingdom, and the United States during the time leading up to the invasion of Iraq all served to weaken the relationships. At times the spat got pretty petty: Remember the call to boycott "French fries" in the congressional dining hall?

Difficult problems that lack simple solutions can pull us together, but they very often tear us apart. As a nation, our differences over the Civil War and the Vietnam war still haunt us.

Many felt things would improve significantly with the election of a new U.S. president. Yet President Obama has experienced his own rough spots and friction in relationships with former British Prime Minister Gordon Brown, French President Nicolas Sarkozy, German Chancellor Angela Merkel, and most recently with Israeli Prime Minister Benjamin Netanyahu. The issues have ranged from our response to the global financial crisis in 2009 to our Middle East policy and our recent role in Libya.

ELECTIONS THAT DIVIDE, NOT UNITE

The divide in political and government relationships within countries is clearly visible in the election of—and loss of confidence in—leaders. The United States is not the only country where the elections have been raucous, leaving citizens divided.

Spain elected surprise winner Socialist José Luis Rodríguez Zapatero (who had opposed the country's participation in the Iraq war) in 2004, just three days after a major terrorist bomb attack in Madrid that killed 200 people; he received 42 percent of the vote.

Germany experienced a close election in 2005, and as a result, Chancellor Angela Merkel formed a coalition between her conservative Christian Democratic Union and the center-liberal Social Democratic Party.

Mexico experienced an extremely tight presidential race in 2006 that was decided by less than 1 percent, and it resulted in protests that shut down parts of Mexico City and threatened the ability of the new leaders to govern.

Canada elected Stephen Harper as prime minister in 2006 with a total of 36 percent of the vote in a highly divisive election.

The United Kingdom saw Prime Minister Tony Blair step down in 2007 after pressure from his own Labour Party.

Israel's 2009 Prime Minister election results were so close as to be initially inconclusive, leaving the country in political limbo.[18]

The Netherlands elected no clear governing majority in 2010 because voters were split over issues of immigration and the banning of mosques.[19]

THE ROLE OF RELATIONSHIP DIVIDE AT HOME

There have always been noisy debates and disagreements in this country. Certainly wars, terrorists, and external conflicts abroad only add to the pressure, but something has changed. That something is also taking its toll on relationships. How did we get here and is it as bad as it seems? A place to start is to look at voting and the changing face of Congress. In the 95th Congress (1977–1979), 40 percent were moderates, according to the McCarty/Poole/

Rosenthal scale. In contrast, in the 108th Congress (2003–2005), the moderates comprised just 10 percent,[20] and in the 109th (2005–2007) and 110th (2007–2009), the percentage declined even more (as did the percentage of moderates in the Senate).[21] There has been a significant shift away from moderates toward more polar extremes.

VIEWS FROM ABROAD

It is instructive to understand how others outside this country perceive us—especially those who do not view the world through the prism of Western democracy. James McGregor, who runs a Chinese-focused research, analysis, and investment firm, makes this observation: "When the Chinese look at America, they see a media-driven political system with election campaigns featuring crass manipulation of wedge issues that divide the population, while failing to focus on America's real problems."[22]

To them and perhaps others, democracy is very loud, messy, and amoral—a system that in fact magnifies and manipulates differences to create leverage. Freedom—such a positive word to us—can appear as chaos or even evil to others.

Have we, as the Chinese conclude, moved beyond freedom to the point of exploiting our differences, and thus relationships, for purposes of economic, status, or political gain?

Matthew Dowd of the *Washington Post* observes that the average difference between the approval rating of voters from the president's own party and those from voters of the opposition has more than doubled over the past 50 years. During the terms of presidents Dwight Eisenhower, John Kennedy, Lyndon Johnson, Gerald Ford, Richard Nixon, and Jimmy Carter, the average difference between the approval ratings was about 30 percentage points. Under presidents Reagan and George H. W. Bush, it rose to the 50 percent range and moved up to an average of 58 percent under Bill Clinton. It jumped to as high as a 71 percent partisan difference under George W. Bush.[23]

According to the Pew Research Center, by early 2006, a time of vibrant economic growth, 56 percent of Republicans said the economy was excellent or good, while only 28 percent of independents and 23 percent of Democrats concurred. Michael Barone states: "It's hard to resist the conclusion that when Democrats—and, in 2004–2006, independents—were responding to questions about the condition of the economy, they were actually responding, 'I am a Democrat,' or, more emphatically, 'I hate George W. Bush.'"[24]

The presidential election of 2008 brought with it the hope of less division. One of then-candidate Barack Obama's most popular speech lines was, "There is not a liberal America and a conservative America—there is the United States of America." Yet his first-year ratings were the most polarized for a president in Gallup history, with an average 65-point gap between Republicans and Democrats. Obama's approval ratings became slightly more polarized in the early part of 2010, with an average 69-point gap between Democrats (83 percent) and Republicans (14 percent).[25]

To be fair, Obama came into office as the country was in the middle of a mortgage meltdown, Wall Street was in chaos, unemployment was high and rising, and General Motors was on the edge of bankruptcy. The bailout of Wall Street (started under Bush), along with GM and the stimulus package, were all controversial actions in the midst of challenging times. Yet it was the bruising health care reform battle that seemed to energize a Tea Party movement and that led to a doubling (22 percent in 2010) of the percentage of the electorate since 2000 that said they are angry with government.[26] It just keeps getting more personal.

How can people from the same country have such differences of opinion? Compare this level of disagreement to observers rating a basketball referee over several games, supervisors viewing a worker operating a piece of equipment, or an experienced surgeon overseeing a young surgeon in the operating room. Can you imagine a 70 percent difference in opinion on whether Michael Jordan was a great basketball player? In any other field, that level of divide would almost certainly cause one side to think the other side uninformed, very biased, or possibly crazy. This kind of polarity is dysfunctional and is damaging to relationships.

The trend is unrelenting: We have been mostly headed in opposite directions for about 50 years. Similar to marital divorce rates, the rate of abandoning political parties and the partisan divide in assessing presidential performance have all doubled in the past 50 years. This isn't a one-time spike or even an anomaly. This is a sea change.

POLITICAL DIVIDE WITHIN THE DIVIDE

In the 2008 presidential primary, we saw that we are highly divided not only across political parties but also within. Some conservatives were outspoken in their disdain of Republican candidate John McCain and moderate Republicans trashed Sarah Palin. Hillary Clinton was called Nixon in a pantsuit, a whore, a sociopath, and a horror film that never ends. She was accused of pimping out her daughter, Chelsea, and of fascist associations— all by fellow Democrats on liberal sites like Huffington Post and Daily Kos. In response, Clinton supporters accused Obama supporters of "horrid" sexism and urged a writers' strike by contributors to those sites.[27]

Cate Malek describes how this kind of divide can feed on itself. "Escalation is a psychological process that causes the parties involved in a conflict to use more and more extreme measures to try to 'beat' their opponents."[28] As the conflict escalates, each side stereotypes the other. They cut off communication with the adversaries and associate only with their own, which contributes to increased misunderstanding and distrust of the other side. Meanwhile, within the group or party, members become more homogenous as moderate voices are ousted, leading to more extreme leaders, views, and actions. Leaders fear that if they appear weak or conciliatory they will be replaced and so they refuse to admit any past mistakes. The last stage of escalation is violence. In worst-case scenarios, the parties completely *dehumanize* each other. Escalation is one of the most dangerous forces in the world. Although the issues that sparked the conflict may have been legitimate, escalation distorts thinking. Escalation involves not just intellectual differences; it also engages the emotions striking at the heart of the relationship. Political escalation has gone mainstream.

A Conspiracy of Incumbency

It takes a lot of money to look this cheap.

—Dolly Parton

While turnover among CEOs and other top-level executives in business has nearly tripled in recent years and the divorce rate in marriages has about doubled since the 1960s, the number of political leaders leaving office is at record lows.[29] Competition in congressional elections has been declining for more than 50 years, and the 2002 and 2004 House elections were the least competitive of the postwar era, with only five of the 401 incumbents running for reelection defeated, and two of these losses were a direct result of redistricting. This 99 percent reelection rate for incumbents in 2004 equaled the success rate of incumbents in the 2002 midterm election. A broader gauge of competition, the number of relatively close contests, reveals that the 2004 House elections were even less competitive than the 2002 House elections.[30] In 2006 and 2008 the reelection rate eased to 94 percent. In the Senate, average reelection rates over the past 10 years exceed 85 percent. Even in the 2010 House elections, considered a significant change in direction, 87 percent of incumbents who ran were reelected.[31]

The real two-party system in the United States is not Democrat and Republican but incumbent and nonincumbent, and the incumbent party is trouncing the nonincumbent. This incredible lack of turnover for a Congress that has a breathtakingly low approval rate is puzzling on the surface. How could a group with such low approval ratings be so overwhelmingly reelected?

If you look below the surface it becomes a little clearer. First, redrawing of congressional districts in recent years by Democratic and Republican congresses has been done with the express purpose of protecting incumbents of both parties. This redrawing has generally tended to favor the extremes by artificially drawing the district to provide a majority of either liberal or conservative voters, thus protecting the district for either Democrats or Republicans. In addition, the Voting Rights Act was designed to provide minority representation by drawing districts so that ethnic groups would have a majority representation. This creates districts that are designed to be like-minded groups with like-minded political leaders. The net effect is to increase the number of leaders who come from more partisan districts, ones who are more likely to become extreme in their partisanship and unlikely to risk alienation by constituents if they dared to compromise. We have created an election process that is designed to artificially polarize our political leaders, in comparison to the rest of us.

Unfortunately there is perhaps an even a more sinister cause. The inability of challengers to compete financially with incumbents is an even bigger part of the problem. The cost of President Obama's 2008 presidential campaign was $745 million; for the first time in history, the total expenditures for all the candidates exceeded $1 billion.[32] And many analysts expect Obama alone to raise over a billion dollars for the 2012 presidential election. Average congressional House campaign expenditures rose from $87,000 in 1976 to $1.3 million in 2006, and successful Senate campaign spending went from $609,000 in 1976 to $9.6 million in 2006.[33] In 2008, the average congressional incumbent raised over $1.3 million, compared to the average challenger's $335,000. In the Senate, the average incumbent raised $8.7 million compared to the average challenger's $1.1 million. Financing, especially for a lesser-known challenger, can be very difficult.

The role of money in politics is pervasive and growing like an aggressive cancer. In the middle of the "Great Recession," spending in 2009 on lobbyists approached $3.5 billion, up 5 percent from the previous year, breaking all records and doubling since 2001.[34]

Incumbents have an obvious presence that makes them well known and helps them raise money from constituents who seek favors. Special interests are usually the most crucial source of fund-raising and represent a more narrow set of issues than the population at large. So the need to raise money in districts that are already drawn to make them more polar than the population simply adds fuel to the fire. Many challengers are intimidated by the prospect of running.

BENEFICIARIES OF THE DIVIDE

The notion of a culture war gives life to "useful" fund-raising strategies.

—Morris Fiorina, political scientist[35]

It is useful to look at who benefits from all this. The pejorative term *military-industrial complex* was coined many years ago to describe those entities, such as defense contractors, who benefited from the prospect of war. Is there a corollary for cultural and political war in our society? Are there groups who gain power, money, and status through the escalation of divisive wedge issues? The answer is yes—there is a societal "relational-industrial divisiveness complex" that cultivates and feeds off divide.

In recent elections, in addition to such traditional campaign contributors as large corporations and labor unions, new partisan groups such as conservative Christians, the Tea Party, and Moveon.org, along with Internet contributors, have emerged. They have contributed not only money but also research, think tanks, and get-out-the-vote efforts.

The shriller messages of political campaigns are attempts to raise contributions and other resources from these groups. Often one set of narrow, partisan messages is communicated in order to galvanize support. A different, less controversial message is promoted later, especially in moving from the primary election, where parties pick their candidates, to the general election, where a broader set of voters elects a candidate. Of course, all of this ducking and weaving can be very confusing, even amusing, but it also evokes considerable anger. It certainly makes it much harder to govern afterward. The very term *political*—think "politically correct"—has come to mean giving the answer the inquirer wants to hear.

These groups often favor fighting it out on tough issues rather than compromising and building consensus; in other words, they create conflict and disagreement over how to address conflict and disagreement.

It's not surprising that as the role of money keeps expanding, Congress's approval ratings keep declining. Some of these same trends are apparent in the Senate, but since senators are elected at the state level, gerrymandering of local districts is not an issue. The net is that money as the key source of political power corrupts. To paraphrase Dolly, "it costs a lot of money for politicians to look this bad."

Presidential elections, by contrast, provide the national electorate an avenue to express broader frustrations. Salena Zito contends that frustration is often misunderstood: "Main Street keeps trying to send a message to the political class with their presidential votes, and the political class keeps reading these votes as affirmations rather than negations. People voted against Democrats in 2004 and against Republicans in 2008—not for the other party." She concludes that politicians' inability to read those votes correctly may reflect our narcissistic age, in which everyone thinks everything is about them.[36]

Extreme partisanship, along with incumbent politicians who remain in office in spite of historic low ratings, helps explain why self-proclaimed independents have reached their highest level in 70 years (39 percent), exceeding Democrats and Republicans (23 percent each), while favorability ratings for both parties reached record lows.[37] The percentage of these independents has just about doubled in the past 50 years and jumped from 30 to 39 percent (a 30 percent increase) from December 2008 until April 2009.

How ironic: The flight from marriage—the divorce rate—and the flight from political parties have both doubled in the past 50 years. "None of the above" (single and unattached) becomes our dominant marital and political status. Rather than being defined by what we are, we are defined by what we are not; the relationship and community we don't have. Yet another brick in our relational infrastructure falls.

Dysfunctional partisanship is a relationship problem. We will now examine what is driving this divide.

What's Driving the Divide?

The fracturing of political relationships is something that sociologists and political scientists have been tracking for a couple of decades, even though they don't always agree on the causes. James Davison Hunter, referenced earlier, characterized it as a fierce battle, with Christian fundamentalists, Orthodox Jews, and conservative Catholics against their progressive counterparts—secularists, reform Jews, liberal Catholics, and Protestants—with each side struggling to gain control over such fields of conflict as family, art, education, law, and politics. It has become less a process of mutual understanding and negotiation than an exercise of power politics—imposing one agenda to the exclusion of another.[38]

The question is how much of this growing divide comes from our political differences and how much from the aggressive power-wielding tactics? During the 1960s, the counterculture that evolved around issues like sex, drugs, and opposition to war brought to the forefront a very different mindset compared to the conservative thinking of earlier decades. Boomers, who were either opposed to the war in Vietnam or supported it, continue to influence politics even today. Many opponents continued to move to the left, while many supporters moved to the right.

Political parties, the Supreme Court, the media, academia, organized religion, and Hollywood are all institutions of influence regarding issues such as abortion, drug use, birth control, premarital sex, and sexual content of movies and television. The more parochial groups began to feel that the political and cultural tide has moved too far and differences devolved into strong disagreements and conflict that continually pressure relationships.

During the 2008 presidential election, as Andrew Sullivan points out, between John McCain's "No Surrender" banner and the Democrats' "End the War Now" campaign, the real substantive differences were comically overstated.[39] Despite all the focus on change, at the end of 2009 there were still more than 130,000 troops in Iraq, even more troops in Afghanistan, and enemy-combatants at Guantánamo. Most people agreed we needed health care reform but couldn't agree on what that reform should look like.

In fact, in their book, *Disconnect: The Breakdown of Representation in American Politics*, Fiorina and Abrams find the partisan divide between Democrats and Republicans to average a mere 14 percentage points. Citing a 40-item survey conducted consistently by Pew for 20 years, this difference has increased only four points since 1987.[40] Conversely, Alan Abramowitz in *The Disappearing Center* finds that the number of self-reported voters between 1972 and 2008 who identified themselves in the ideological extremes grew from 29 to 49 percent. Further, a rise in education levels only adds to the partisan polarization.[41] It's no wonder that political scholars cannot agree on the disagreement, which actually points to the heart of the issue. Fiorina's research asked about a broader set of issues including specific opinions (like *when does life begin* vs. simply *your stance on abortion*), while Abramowitz focused on more ideological self-identification and narrow hot-button issues.

The apparent contradiction helps explain why 60 percent disagree on the performance of Bush then and Obama now, when there is only a 14 percent difference on key cultural and political issues. The chasm in our relationships and our self-identity greatly exceeds the gap in the specific content of our views. Politics have become personal. Power politics are used to impose one side's will over the opposition, and once-neutral groups are now themselves special interests.[42]

Conservatives have had a strong sense that the universities, mainstream media, and courts that legislate from the bench were partisans for liberal causes. Liberals have lamented the rise of talk radio, a changing Supreme Court, and conservative churches as strong partisans for conservative causes. In both cases, institutions that have the potential to serve as sources for thoughtful analysis, deliberation, and even reconciliation have instead become sources of partisanship, division, and ultimately polarization. Democracy works because it allows for differences, debate, and ultimately resolution. Relationships are fostered and protected when the process allows for all to have a voice.

Perhaps that was what was so powerful about President George W. Bush addressing rescue workers after 9/11, as he stood on a pile of rubble that five days earlier was the World Trade Center. With one arm draped around New York firefighter Bob Beckwith and the other holding a bullhorn, he responded to the workers' plea that they could not hear him: "I can hear you. The rest of the world hears you!" Ever so briefly we were one. To have a voice and have it heard is a profoundly simple but powerful force of relationship.

The concerns about Congress primarily focus not on a broken system but on the members themselves. When presented with a series of criticisms of elected officials in Washington—that they care only about their careers, are influenced by special interests, are unwilling to compromise, are profligate and out-of-touch—large majorities (no fewer than 76 percent) agree with each of the statements.[43] The criticism is described in very personal, relational terms: selfish, obstinate, wasteful, and inattentive. This lack of trust translates into a lack of hope: Another 2010 poll finds that 57 percent of American voters think life for the next generation will be worse, not better.[44]

While confidence in corporate and political leaders has been in free fall, for military leaders it continues to rise. According to Harvard's National Leadership Index, 70 percent view the military leaders as working for the greater good, compared to 37 percent for the executive branch of government and 10 percent for business leaders.[45] The concern is that many of these government and business leaders have become self-absorbed. David Brooks describes a breed of reckless political and corporate leaders who want to leave a mark by hitting grandiose home runs.[46] Clinton tried to transform health care. Bush tried to transform the Middle East. Obama has tried to transform health care, energy, and much more. In swinging for the fences, we have swung from one extreme to the other. Like highly opinionated parents who constantly fight, no matter how noble their beliefs, they create a toxic environment for the kids.

Many Americans, less than enamored with the egoism and heroism of their leaders, are now worn out by the drama. Many believe more moderate approaches in the deficit, Iraq, health care, energy, climate change, and immigration would have been supported by a majority of citizens, had our leaders not overreached. These leaders—public servants—resemble absentee fathers and certain corporate CEOs when they put their egos ahead of those they serve. Healthy relationships cannot exist when leaders are a driving source of division for those they serve—whether children, customers, employees or citizens.

Looking for Insight in All the Wrong Places

As our divide grows wider and more vicious, we become a society not only more polarized but more wounded. After all, it is hard to fully grasp the damage that opposing sides are able to inflict on each other in the form of criticism and ridicule. As citizens of a culture that has suffered loss in personal and work relationships, we are more vulnerable to the relational wounds of political attack. All of this escalation of political divide and its attendant wounds drives a bigger wedge between oppositional groups.

How does this influence our relationships? The greater our humiliation, the more likely we are to seek the solace of the like-minded who will share our views and blind spots. We move from seeking objective sources to biased ones. Moderating influences are replaced by ones that polarize.

Research supports the notion that the more like-minded a deliberating group is on cultural or political issues, the more extreme it is likely to become. An important piece of research on this topic was performed by J.A.F. Stoner at MIT years ago. He expected to find that a group of like-minded people who deliberated on topics would move or moderate to the center, but the opposite occurred.[47] In fact, James Surowiecki validated these findings by coming at the topic from the opposite position, positing that diverse individuals operating independently very often made wiser choices.[48]

Diversity not only has a moderating effect, it makes us smarter. This need for differences of opinion and perspective is pervasive. We have seen repeatedly where organizations or administrations have made stunningly poor judgments because management was engaged in groupthink. Uniformity of thinking may simplify the decision making, but it often hampers the quality of decisions made.

One of the beauties of democracy is the way diverse and independent opinions are aggregated in the voting process. Unfortunately, in recent years people have clustered together for like-minded support. The irony is that as we have grown apart, in many ways we have become more homogenous. In his book *The Big Sort*, Bill Bishop quantifies this shift: "In 1976, less than a quarter of Americans lived in places where the presidential election was a landslide [counties where the spread between the two major presidential candidates was 20 percent or more]. By 2004, nearly half of all voters lived in landslide counties. Minority opinion holders in heavily majority counties not only vote less, but also tend to withdraw from all forms of public life, including volunteering."[49]

Not only have we become physically sorted and separated; technology has made it easier to become more isolated and prejudiced by filtering the information we receive. Just as living in a certain physical space and in a certain way influences the information we receive, so do the books we read, the websites we visit, the bloggers we read, and the music we listen to. As technology has given us more control and the ability to filter out information we don't want, we have become more segregated and relationally hostile—for example, liberals tend to read only liberal books, while conservatives read only conservative books. We gravitate toward the commentators, blog sites, cable news, and opinion we like and that conform to our prejudices.[50] We can virtually dial up the news we want to fulfill our viewing pleasure.

The power of choice also has made news content and channels of delivery more of a consumer product as customers exert pressure to make news more entertaining. Diana Mutz of the University of Pennsylvania pointed out that we are predisposed as humans to avoid boredom by seeking certain kinds of conflict and partisanship—that is, we are drawn to arguments rather than civil discussions.[51]

Accordingly, talk radio and cable television emerged as a political form of professional wrestling. It has elevated the likes of Rush Limbaugh, Bill Maher, Sean Hannity, Chris Matthews, Bill O'Reilly, Keith Olbermann, Glenn Beck, and Jon Stewart to cult hero status. For them, hyperbole, often divisive for the country, is good for ratings.

Not surprisingly, there is a price to pay for all of this drama and fragmentation. Professional wrestling may be entertaining to some, but it is not very trusted, and neither is the media. In 2009, Harvard's Center for Public Leadership found 66 percent do not trust (39 percent not much; 27 percent not at all) what leaders of the media say,[52] and 79 percent thought they primarily represented themselves or special interests. Media has not only joined the parade; it is leading it. Drama sells. Escalation of cultural and political differences is good for the news business, but it tends to polarize democracy's citizens.

Our defense mechanisms—like avoiding personal conflict while seeking to be entertained by observing it in others—often protect us from one evil while creating another. As information bigots, we have created a form of blindness that prevents certain insights and surprises, precludes us from certain relationships, and narrows us, taking away some of what we desperately need for our own development. It precludes and insulates us from relationships that could make us more civil, tolerant, unified, and wise.

In spite of our reputation as confident and even brash, politically, Americans are quite tepid. When compared to citizens from 12 other countries, Americans were found to be the most reluctant to discuss politics with those who had differing beliefs. Only 23 percent of us reported having regular discussions with people who may not share our opinions. This behavior only worsens as we become more educated and wealthy.[53]

We have segregated ourselves: We are affirmed by our friends and entertained by watching enemies go at it, while isolating ourselves. We make easier but less-informed political decisions, confident of our rightness, ignorant of our blindness, and diminished in our relationships.

* * * *

This commercially driven political culture breeds systemic divide, yet another cog in the machinery of our society-wide relationship decline. Witness the results of a 2011 survey from the World Economic Forum: The

United States has tumbled further down a global ranking of the world's most competitive economies, landing at fifth place because of its huge deficits and declining public faith in government.[54] The process began about 50 years ago and has devolved into a system unwittingly rigged to prevent this nation from addressing broad strategic issues, disabling effective political action.

The relationship among and between those who govern and those governed is precious. Democracy is designed to empower the most prevalent view while respecting and protecting the view of the minority through such mechanisms as constitutional rights. It can be messy and at times raucous in the short run, but it is intended to manage relational differences in a way that keeps everyone engaged and as whole as possible. Broken relationships, on the other hand, produce broken societies. Political opposition groups who spend a disproportionate share of their resources fighting and tearing down the other side underinvest in constructive problem solving and innovation that drives development. It starves productive initiatives.

It is easy to chart the decline in job approval and confidence ratings for our politicians and government entities and the flight from political parties. But it is hard to place a cost on the relationship divide that now afflicts our affairs of state. It is hard to know the longer-term financial and other costs of a paralyzing federal debt, energy dependence, or systemic unemployment. The loud, righteous voices of division and partisanship have drowned out the voices of shared solutions, effective negotiation, and relational consensus that define us.

Our differences will always be with us, and while difficult, they are not our primary problem. In fact, differences are the source of new ideas and can serve to strengthen decisions, actions, and relationships. Differences are part of successful relationships. Yet, stalemate, civic unrest, and even civil war await us if we are smitten by a love of hating our adversaries.

The real opportunity is for us to use our current state of conflict as a springboard to better things. We opened this chapter discussing the very costly Civil War that nevertheless abolished slavery and rebuilt the union that still stands 150 years later. Confronting the dark dysfunction and destruction of rabid conflict galvanizes us to seek the light of more civil, productive, relational discourse.

Chapter 4

Religious War and (No) Peace: Belief That Divides

You can safely assume you've created God in your own image when it turns out that God hates all the same people you do.
—*Anne Lamott*, Bird by Bird

In the spring of 2010, I spent two weeks in Israel as part of a religious study group that had previously traveled to Turkey, Greece, and Italy. As we visited a number of famous sites, one of the recurring themes was the incredible history of conflict. In Jerusalem, we counted 13 different layers of tearing down and rebuilding on the sacred site of the holy city. When our travels took us to the ruins of the magnificent Belvoir castle high above the Jordan River in the Great Rift Valley, we reviewed its history. The land, originally owned by a French nobleman, was sold to Crusader Christians in 1168. They built the fortress, which was overtaken by the Muslims under the commander Saladin in the late 1180s. Our tour leader, biblical historian and archaeologist Jim Fleming, ended his lecture with this statement: "The Jews, Muslims, and Eastern Christians memorized the pages of history torn out by Christians and the West."

The history of faith, belief, and even nonbelief—regardless of the version—is one of relational conflict in which too often we magnify the good of our side while we focus on the other side's bad deeds. We often ignore our own excesses: the terrors during the Crusades are often minimized in the Western telling of history, for example. It is that prideful tendency that makes faith, such a potent force for building relationships, a source of divide when our so-called relational doctrine is antithetical to actual relationships.

The cost and pain of broken, fractured relationships is nowhere more disappointing and confounding today than in the fourth domain—faith and religion. The 9/11 attacks opened our eyes yet again to the life-and-death consequences of radical hatred directed toward people who don't share the same religious or cultural beliefs.

We have witnessed Shia and Sunni Muslims killing each other in Iraq: Mosques have been destroyed, people have been set on fire, and torture killings have occurred routinely. Minority sects are treated brutally in many countries. The war in Lebanon between Israel and Hamas resulted in the loss of many lives as well as property. Incidents such as the cartoon controversy in Denmark, ethnic riots in France, the killing of a movie producer who was an heir of the artist Vincent van Gogh in the Netherlands, and a series of bombings in Indonesia, Lebanon, Kenya, the Philippines, Spain, and the United Kingdom are stark reminders of the fractious nature of relationships among various religious and secular groups. The ongoing conflicts and tensions among Jews, Muslims, Hindus, Christians, secularists, and atheists threaten every corner of the globe.

More recently, the Arab Spring in Tunisia, Egypt, Libya, Syria, and other Middle Eastern nations—with all its hope for greater freedom and tolerance—could also become an Arab winter. In Egypt, long-simmering tensions between Muslims and Coptic Christians have now devolved into violence, and with the growing influence of the Muslim Brotherhood and ultraconservative Islamic groups, there is fear that protections under former military governments will evaporate. Even in Iraq, during the eight-plus years of heavy U.S. military presence, at least 54 Iraqi Christian churches have been bombed and 905 Christians killed in various acts of violence. A report released in November 2011 estimates that 500,000 Christians remain in Iraq, down from 800,000 to 1.4 million in 2003. Archbishop Louis Sako of the Chaldean Catholic Church there laments: "It's a hemorrhage. Iraq could be emptied of Christians."[1]

Closer to home, the 2009 murder of Kansas doctor George Tiller, who performed abortions, reminds us of just how intensely broken and volatile relationships can be between pro-life and pro-choice advocates; there is nothing like killing someone in the name of life to give belief a bad name. The factions surrounding faith are numerous: those who believe in God and those who do not; liberal and conservative Christians; Catholics and Protestants; and various denominations split on issues such as the roles of women and gays.

At their core, faith and beliefs are relational. Yet, rather than operating as a force for bridging and building relationships, faith has once again become a battle to impose one group's will on another—a raw struggle for power that ultimately leaves all sides relationally oppressed and weakened.

Faith: Under Attack and Attacking

Sixty-four percent of the American people believe that religion is "under attack" [according to a poll released by the Anti-Defamation League] . . . nearly half of the American people (45 percent) agree that right wing religious leaders are seeking to impose their religious beliefs on everyone else.

—Anti-Defamation League[2]

Most of us hope for a faith and a set of beliefs that can be a source of healing and relationship building in a world of disagreements, strife, and even violence. We keep expecting greater knowledge, more literacy, and enhanced religious freedom to improve relationships among people of varying beliefs. Unfortunately, the opposite has been true in recent times.

The growing partisan political divide discussed in chapter 3 has a very strong religious component. According to Pew Research released in 1999, Republicans and Democrats scored 78 and 76, respectively, on an index of religious commitment. By 2007, however, this minor two-point gap had ballooned to 17 points (79 for Republicans and 62 for Democrats).[3] As is the case with politics, the growing religious divide is impacting our relation-ships in ways that are at times startling.

All the great religions have significant admonitions for mankind about the importance of relationships with God and other humans. In fact, Put-nam reports that nearly half of all associational memberships are church related, half of all personal philanthropy is religious in character, and half of all volunteering occurs in a religious context.[4] And according to Putnam and Campbell's exhaustive analysis, religious people, especially those affili-ated with a religious community, make better neighbors: They are more likely to volunteer, give to charity, assist a homeless person, donate blood, spend time with someone feeling depressed, offer a seat to a stranger, help someone find a job, and take part in local civic life.[5] While religion deals with sin, punishment, evil, and an afterlife, nothing is more central to faith than the need for stronger, deeper, and more enduring relationships.

Yet, part of the mystery of religion and faith is how something that has such great potential to enhance relationships can also lead to such hatred, war, and carnage. Today the religions of the world carry a heavy burden for their role as instruments of hatred and violence rather than love and peace. Most of us could not have guessed 20 years ago that religious conflict could have become so combustible. Religious scholar Martin Marty laments the church's decline as a force for building relationships: "The hugely successful church growth movement had undermined the church's oldest purpose—that of building community. Churches were once built around a geographic community. . . . Now they are constructed around similar lifestyles."[6]

When it comes to religion and values, we have organized ourselves into tribes, like-minded in many ways, and ready for battle but not ready for diverse community or relationship.

The religious divide appears as conflict and animus in three broad cat-egories: (1) between people of religious faith and nonbelievers, including agnostics, atheists, and secularists (defined as those who are indifferent to or reject religion or religious considerations); (2) among worshippers of different faiths, such as Jews, Muslims, Christians, Hindus, and Bud-dhists; (3) within the great religions themselves, such as Shia and Sunni Muslims, and Catholic and Protestant Christians. The common thread is that instead of strengthening our relationships, too often we allow our beliefs to undermine them.

The Growing Divide between Believers and Nonbelievers

God doesn't exist—the bastard.

—Jean-Paul Sartre

The divide between those who see religion as the solution and those who see it as the problem is expanding. In elections, the courts, the media (especially talk radio and cable TV), and the blogosphere battles rage over prayer in school, gay marriage, ordination of gays into the ministry, abortion, legalization of certain drugs, pornography. Debates over profane and vulgar language, attire, nudity, gambling—the "sin" issues—have created a tug-of-war among those with different views based on their faith.

In this country and around the world, as science, technology, the birth control pill, women's rights, and more liberal views on sex and attire have ushered in the changes of a modern era, there has been a resurgence of more conservative beliefs among those who feel the changes have gone too far and violate the teachings of their faiths. Christian conservatives have been horrified by a noticeable decline in moral and family values, while secular liberals have been horrified by the rise of the Christian Right and their desires to impose their views on society. The chart below outlines the rise in the number of believers in the world's largest religions.

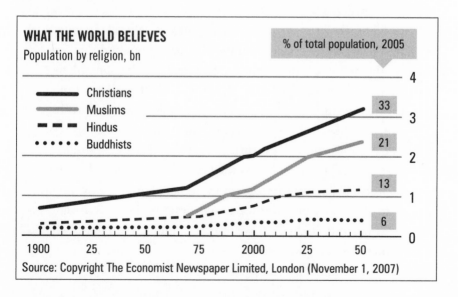

WHAT THE WORLD BELIEVES
Population by religion, bn

% of total population, 2005

- Christians
- Muslims
- Hindus
- Buddhists

Christians 33
Muslims 21
Hindus 13
Buddhists 6

1900   25   50   75   2000   25   50

Source: Copyright The Economist Newspaper Limited, London (November 1, 2007)

Ironically, liberal, conservative, faith-based, and secular populations all seem to feel abandoned in some way by the version of the country and the world they knew and loved, and each has shown a willingness to fight to return to its "proper" place.

Books like Ann Coulter's *Godless: The Church of Liberalism* assert that liberalism has become its own religion—a godless faith that attacks organized religion. Books like Sam Harris's *The End of Faith* and the late Christopher Hitchens's *God Is Not Great* assert that religious belief will likely be the undoing of our society. While the polar extremes get much of the media attention and fit the stereotypes, writers like Jim Wallis (*God's Politics*) and Anne Lamott (*Traveling Mercies*) represent varying views that are less rigid and rules-based, with more focus on forgiveness, peace, the poor, and the environment. It is a reflection of the times that religious belief and the debunking of religious belief are simultaneously so prominent. Debates on evolution, creationism, and intelligent design grace the covers of *Time* and *Newsweek* magazines, are ever present on cable networks, and feed the emergence of books like *The God Delusion* by biologist Richard Dawkins. Francis Collins, head of the project for mapping the genome, laid out his vision of science and belief tied together in *The Language of God*:

> In the twenty-first century, in an increasingly technological society, a battle is raging for the hearts and minds of humanity. Many materialists, noting triumphantly the advances of science in filling the gaps of our understanding of nature, announce that belief in God is an outmoded superstition, and that we would be better off admitting that and moving on. Many believers in God, convinced that the truth they derive from spiritual introspection is of more enduring value than truths from other sources, see the advances in science and technology as dangerous and untrustworthy. Voices are becoming shriller. The God of the Bible is also the God of the genome. He can be worshiped in the cathedral or in the laboratory. His creation is majestic, awesome, intricate, and beautiful—and it cannot be at war with itself. Only we imperfect humans can start such battles. And only we can end them.[7]

The issue of God is very top-of-mind. More than half (53 percent) of Americans believe religion is losing its influence. Conversely, as mentioned earlier, nearly half (45 percent) agree that right-wing religious leaders are seeking to impose their beliefs on everyone else, but 57 percent of conservative Christians disagreed with that assumption.[8]

Atheists, who historically have been relatively passive, have become more vocal. New terms like *missionary secularism* and *secular fundamentalist* reflect the much more proactive, strident role of atheists. Ironically, many of these "nonbelievers" have adopted the very approaches—proselytizing, condemning the other side, elevating conflict—they accuse religious groups of exhibiting.

As nonbelievers have attacked the religious on their lack of scientific evidence, religious believers have extolled research showing they are more than twice as likely as secularists to say they are "very happy" (43 percent versus 21 percent) and a third more likely to be optimistic.[9] This debate looks very much like a political campaign or the rivalry between two competing consumer products such as PCs versus Macs, or Coke versus Pepsi.

In addition, colleges are reporting enrollment increases in classes and majors that focus on religion. Students are seeking out housing where they can integrate faith and spirituality into their daily lives. In a survey of 112,000 freshmen, more than two-thirds reported that they prayed, and close to 80 percent expressed belief in God.[10]

Yet, just as religion has grown in prominence on campus, there has been a growth in each generation in the number of those who consider themselves outsiders to religion, with a heavy skew to the young. Research indicates that this growth is not a passing fad but a sustained trend that is likely to continue. All of this points to two very different groups headed in two very different directions. This does not bode well for relationships.

The Proportion of Those "Outside" Christianity Is Growing with Each Generation

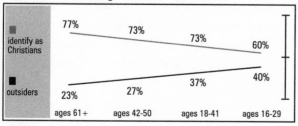

Source: The Barna Group, Ltd. 2007[11]

The Growing Divide Among Worshippers of Different Faiths

The second relationship divide is an almost life-and-death struggle that is going on among religious followers of various faiths. Disagreement and even war among religious groups is as old as history itself. Ironically, many of the most violent struggles go back to a common source—Abraham. Bruce Feiler explains it this way: "The great patriarch of the Hebrew Bible is also the spiritual forefather of the New Testament and the grand holy architect of the Koran. Abraham is the shared ancestor of Judaism, Christianity, and Islam. He is the linchpin of the Arab-Israeli conflict. He is the centerpiece of the battle between the West and Islamic extremists. He is the father—in many cases, the purported biological father—of 12 million Jews, 2 billion Christians, and 1 billion Muslims around the world. He is history's first monotheist."[12] Certainly there are any number of other religious groups such as Hindus, Buddhists, and smaller groups such as the Amish that involve relational conflict, but for purposes here, I have chosen to focus on Judaism, Christianity, and Islam because of the prominence of the conflicts in our Western society.

Historically in the United States, religious discrimination has been primarily directed at Catholics and Jews. In recent years, however, approximately three in four Americans have favorable opinions of Catholics and Jews. Even among white Protestants and secularists, large majorities hold positive views of them. Views toward Muslim-Americans and evangelical Christians, on the other hand, were not as high, and views of atheists ranked the lowest.[13] Groups seen as more extreme on either end of the belief continuum are less highly thought of.

There is another factor in all of this. The extreme groups seem to be more active in attempting to exert change. Whether by proselytizing, supporting political candidates, promoting legislation, influencing the courts, or perpetrating violence, the activist nature of more extreme groups is eliciting a negative response not only from their opposition but also from moderates. Aggressive attempts to inflict unwanted change on others, whether around political issues or issues of belief, create conflict and fracture relationships—and these attempts are increasing.

For decades, the conflict between Muslims and Jews has dominated headlines. The conflict goes back centuries and was exacerbated with the establishment of the state of Israel in 1948. But in recent years, with the violent attacks in countries like Indonesia, Spain, the United Kingdom, and the United States, there has been a growing awareness of the conflict between Western countries and radical Islam. The wars in Afghanistan and Iraq have brought much more attention to this conflict. These events have changed attitudes and ruptured potential relationships within and between countries and religions.

We all face issues regarding how to reconcile ancient religious belief with a modern world, and Islam is no exception. According to Pew, the majority of Muslims who see a struggle between Islamic fundamentalists and those who want a more modern society side with the modernizers.[14] These solid majorities may or may not have solid influence in those countries where the government is under the authority of religious leaders. Interactions on the topic often lead to conflict, strain relationships, and may magnify the perceived conflict between groups. The challenge is not new. If we study religious reformers such as Abraham, Moses, Muhammad, Jesus Christ, Martin Luther, or Gandhi, struggle has been the norm for applying old customs and attitudes to a new world.

We are in an era of conflict and turmoil, but the one thing there appears to be agreement on is that our relationships are suffering. Westerners still view Muslims "as fanatical, violent, and as lacking tolerance," while Muslims see the West as "selfish, immoral and greedy—as well as violent and fanatical."[15] Our views of each other are similar in many aspects.

After 9/11, there was a concerted effort by political and religious leaders imploring citizens not to judge all Muslims based on an isolated attack. Many Muslims went out of their way to say that the violence was not a true reflection of the teachings of Islam. Initially that empathy seemed to translate into higher approval ratings, and Americans felt more positive about Muslims.[16] Over time, however, those approval ratings began to decline as the Muslim radicals seemed to capture more of the public's attention through their words and actions.[17]

As a result, three key trends have emerged: (1) The majority of Americans have a positive impression of Muslims, but only 41 percent have a positive impression of Islam—we are separating individuals from their predominant religious beliefs. (2) In a relatively short period of time, that positive view has declined by 10 percent. (3) Among Americans who hold an unfavorable view of Islam, evangelical Protestants are the group that holds the most negative view. This group is viewed as more extreme and fundamentalist in this country, and it is the one most at odds with Islam.

What's interesting is that the groups who are in many ways most alike—fundamental in their beliefs and aggressive in their actions—oppose each other the most. Conversely, the group most unlike the Islamic radicals—secular or nonreligious U.S. liberals with negative opinions of U.S. fundamental religious groups—view these Islamic believers more positively. For example, Pew found that evangelicals are more likely to see Islam as encouraging violence compared to the rest of the population (50 percent versus 33 percent), while secularists were less so (26 percent).[18] In spite of the decline, it appears that, overall, Americans have a more positive view of Muslims than do people in other countries.[19]

Similarly, it is surprising to find Muslim attitudes regarding Christians to be relatively positive. "While large percentages in nearly every Muslim country attribute several negative traits to Westerners—violence, immorality, selfishness—solid majorities in Indonesia, Jordan, and Nigeria express favorable opinions of Christians."[20]

The Growing Divide within Religious Faiths

American churches today are more culturally and politically segregated than our neighborhoods . . . In the welter of choice provided by our post-materialistic culture, people are choosing the comfort of agreement.

—*Bill Bishop,* The Big Sort

The divide within religious groups such as Islam, Christianity, and Judaism themselves can be just as severe and relationally ruinous as the divide across those groups.

ISLAM

The West has been exposed to the internal battle between the Sunnis and the Shias, the two sects that evolved in the debate over succession after the death of the Prophet Muhammad in the year 632 AD. Worldwide, approximately 85 percent of Muslims are Sunni and about 15 percent are Shia.[21] In Iraq and Iran, however, the majority are Shia. Since a Sunni minority under Saddam Hussein ruled Iraq, there has been bitter conflict regarding a democratic government that would transfer much more power to the Shias. This conflict is not new. According to the Iraq Body Count project, by September 2009, approximately 100,000 civilians died in the Iraqi war.[22] It is safe to say that thousands have died in the conflict between the Shias and the Sunnis. In Pakistan, the BBC reports that in excess of 4,000 people have been killed in Shia versus Sunni violence in the past couple of decades.[23] This kind of religious violence is increasingly the norm in countries around the world.

In 2006, before the surge strategy, Thomas Friedman described the divide between the Shias and Sunnis in Iraq and how hate and differences became increasingly mainstream: "We are failing in Iraq because of what the Shiite and Sunni mainstreams—not the fringes—are tolerating. Democracy fails when centrist forces either won't stand up to extremists or try to use violence for their own purposes."[24] He goes on to share just how rigid the more extreme factions are. Early on, one of the Sunni Arab leaders said to him in private, "Thomas, these Shiites are not real Muslims." While as Americans we may view this as a battle for liberty over oppression, for many there, it has been simply a battle between Shias and Sunnis.

In this battle, moderates often become enablers. It is a dance of dysfunction where one group—blinded by hate and convicted by a narrow view—leads, while the other—with a broader but less passionate view—follows.

Ironically, the very loss of focus on family and community that contributes to our relationship decline in the United States poses the opposite problem in Middle Eastern cultures like Iraq. According to John Tierney, the problem in forming a national identity and government was how localized and tribal that part of the world is. Even though the people of Iraq went to the polls and voted, they voted along sectarian lines. "The shrewdest forecasts I heard came not from foreign policy experts but from anthropologists and sociologists who noted a crucial statistic: Nearly half of Iraqis were married to their first or second cousins."[25]

Clan relationships, at the extreme, have led to relationship dysfunctions that ultimately support a culture of violence and destruction. This is widespread from the clans in Iraq to the gangs in Los Angeles. Whether it is a response to religious differences in the former or the loss of fathers in the family structure in the latter, the common denominator is a decentralized, local team or set of relationships built on, committed to, and organized around hatred and violent acts toward others. So, while stronger family and community ties can be very positive for relationships, they also can be used as a force for relational divide.

CHRISTIANITY

I think we've substituted religion for relationships . . . everything about God is relational.

—William P. Young, author of The Shack, in an interview on Good Morning America

Disagreements and conflict within the Christian religion are legion. The history of various reformations and inquisitions includes the use of raw power for one religious denomination to dominate another. Catholic versus Protestant violence has been a staple of religious conflict for centuries, and only in recent years has it subsided in places like Ireland.

While religious riots and violence in the United States have been constrained compared to the rest of the world, other forms of violence and relationship breakdown have occurred. Recent child molestation charges, convictions, and cover-ups by officials of the Catholic Church have undermined trust and confidence. These events have strained the relationship between the Church and its members, as have such issues as the role of women and birth control.

Likewise, in Protestant churches, an ongoing series of disagreements about symbolic versus literal interpretation of scripture, gay marriage, ordination of gay ministers, and the role of women, among other issues, have led various denominations to splinter. One measure of the differences in the Christian community is the sheer number of denominations that have resulted from these splits: According to the *World Christian Encyclopedia*, there are more than 34,000 separate Christian groups around the world, more than half of them independent and having no intention of joining a big denomination.[26]

At the core, this divide is most often a fight between conservatives and liberals. The following *New York Times* article excerpt provides a microcosm of this phenomenon: "As Presbyterians prepare to gather next month . . . a band of determined conservatives is advancing a plan to split the church along liberal and orthodox lines. Another divorce proposal shook the United Methodist convention earlier this month, while conservative Episcopalians have already broken away to form a dissident network of their own."[27] In each case, the Institute on Religion and Democracy, a small organization based in Washington, helped incubate traditionalist insurrections against the liberal politics of the denomination's leaders. Like the Sunnis and Shias, different Christian faiths are at odds. These disagreements dominate the news about mainstream churches in much the same way that scandals have dominated the news about business.

Other, yet related, differences within Christian groups have to do with organization practice, focus, and worship style. One of the most successful proponents of renewal and growth for Protestant churches is Rick Warren, author of *The Purpose Driven Life*. His earlier book, *The Purpose Driven Church*, provided a model for the incredible success he and his followers have enjoyed in realizing church growth.

As the *Wall Street Journal* explains, however, it is a model that a number of churches have found to be divisive. They object that he has spawned an industry advising churches to become purpose-driven by attracting nonbelievers with lively worship services and invitations to volunteer. Some believe it's inappropriate for churches to use modern management tools such as researching the church "market" and writing mission statements. The *Wall Street Journal* nets out these critics' concerns: "But the purpose-driven movement is dividing the country's more than 50 million evangelicals . . . Anger over the adoption of Mr. Warren's methods has driven off older Christians from their longtime churches. Congregations nationwide have split or expelled members who fought the changes, roiling working-class Baptist congregations and affluent nondenominational churches."[28]

Never have people focused so much on their disagreements and so little on the relationships those beliefs were designed to support.

JUDAISM

Like Christians, Jews seem to be moving in opposite and oppositional directions. Sociologist Barry Kosmin discusses the U.S. perspective: "Just like other Americans, religious Jews seem to be polarizing. Certainly the 'religious' or observant are more 'traditional' today than 30 years ago, and we have all noticed an Orthodox revival. But [also]. . . a strong countervailing trends towards assimilation, which is highlighted by the high rate of intermarriage."[29] In fact, more Jews than other Americans describe their religion as "none" (opting for secular over religious), disagree that God exists, and thus are "unsynagogued." [30]

The diverging trends lead to conflict on a number of fronts. One of the core questions is: What does it mean to be Jewish? The debate over this question plays out on a number of issues here in the United States, in other countries, and certainly in Israel. One particularly divisive aspect regards the path to citizenship in the state of Israel, a challenge heightened by the recent assimilation of thousands of former Russians Jews there.

The question of who is and who is not Jewish is complicated by two historic realities. First, the Jewish people, more than most, have a history of dispersion and only in recent history (1948) re-inhabited what they consider their homeland. This means that where someone is born or raised does not tell you whether are not he or she is Jewish. Second, some people consider Jewishness to be a matter of religion (born or converted to the Jewish religion), while others consider it strictly a matter of race (born to a Jewish mother). It is the issue of exactly who is and who is not in the club that is now creating conflict. For example, someone who is born into or converted to the Jewish religion upon moving to Israel (Jewish Homeland) can become a citizen immediately under the Law of Return. However, if people are not born into or converted to Judaism, they must wait six years to become a naturalized citizen.[31]

A bill was proposed in 2010 to put the Chief Rabbinate (the chief religious authority for Jewish people in Israel, dominated by Orthodox Jews) in charge of determining who may be considered a Jewish citizen. This move triggered deep concern among liberal, non-Orthodox, and secular Jews that narrow, religious standards would be used to exclude less conservative Jews from citizenship. Prime Minister Benjamin Netanyahu expressed his concern that such a bill could "tear apart the Jewish people."[32] So controversial and divisive is the bill that it continued to be negotiated and extended into the middle of 2011.

Time magazine calls the growing Israeli conflict between religious communities a domestic culture war.[33] In 2010, tens of thousands of ultra-Orthodox Ashkenazi (European) Jews paralyzed the streets of Jerusalem and a Tel Aviv suburb in a protest march. The target of their wrath was the imprisonment of 43 ultra-Orthodox couples for refusing to allow their daughters to attend a religious school where they would have to mix with the daughters of Mizrahi Jews. These highly Orthodox parents opposed exposing their more sheltered daughters to unwanted influences from the wider world. Aviad Hacohen, the lawyer who filed the Israeli Supreme Court petition on behalf of a group who battles ethnic discrimination in religious schools, warns that this incident is the tip of an ultra-Orthodox iceberg threatening to sink the rule of law in Israel.

Near the end of 2011 the Israeli Health Ministry awarded a prize to pediatrics professor Dr. Channa Maayan for her book on hereditary diseases common to Jews. At the awards ceremony, because the acting health minister is ultra-Orthodox and other religious people would be in attendance, the author had to sit separate from her husband, as men and women were segregated at the event. Worse, she was instructed that a male colleague would have to accept the award for her because women were not permitted on stage. This is just one of a series of controversies, such as ultra-Orthodox men spitting on an eight-year-old girl whom they deemed immodestly dressed. The *New York Times* stated, "Public discourse in Israel is suddenly dominated by a new, high-toned Hebrew phrase, 'hadarat nashim,' or the exclusion of women." Conflict is likely to increase, as conservative groups are having larger families than they did 30 years ago.[34] At a time when the Jewish people face incredible external pressures in the Middle East and around the world, divisive religious conflict from within is particularly debilitating.

As our society seeks a source for building stronger relationships, the growing divide within the religious community only adds to the fissures of a world of fractured relationships.

Consequences of the Growing Religious Divide

Disagreements are inevitable. But unfortunately, as the level of confidence in and passion about beliefs grow, so do the relational consequences. We will now look at three such results.

WHEN BELIEF BECOMES INTOLERANCE

In the West and other regions of the world, there has been a hopeful view that we can have very different beliefs and still get along. The fact that between one-third and half of today's marriages are interfaith—between groups of different faiths—provides the potential to bridge understanding and tolerance between groups.[35] But there is much evidence that this exposure to diversity has served as a wedge that elevates strife.

In his scathing critique of religion, Sam Harris describes the challenge this way:

> Our situation is this: most of the people in the world believe that the Creator of the universe has written a book. We have the misfortune of having many such books on hand, each making an exclusive claim as to its infallibility. People tend to organize themselves into factions according to which of these incompatible claims they accept—rather than on the basis of language, skin color, location of birth, or any other criterion of tribalism. Each of these texts urges its readers to adopt a variety of beliefs and practices, some of which are benign, many of which are not. All are in perverse agreement on one point of fundamental importance, however: "respect" for other faiths, or for the views of unbelievers, is not an attitude God endorses. . . . Intolerance is thus intrinsic to every creed.[36]

Extremes on one side beget extremes on the other; the extremely religious create a backlash from the extremely secular or those who have opposing religious views, and vice versa. We have certainly seen much violence in religious wars. But we have also seen violence by groups who promote peace, either by what they do or what their appeasement allows. In the 1960s' peace movement, we saw buildings burned and blown up, people killed and wounded in the name of stopping a war. Conversely, the failure to embrace strong belief is no panacea either. World War II saw millions of Jews killed, an atrocity enabled by the passivity of certain groups.

INTOLERANCE OF TOLERANCE

Muslims viewed the uproar in 2009 over controversial Danish cartoons of the Prophet Muhammad very differently than Westerners did. Muslims felt Westerners disrespected their religion while Westerners felt Muslims were being intolerant of freedom of the press. Most Westerners do not think Muslims respect women, while over half of Muslims in Egypt, Indonesia, Jordan, and Pakistan surveyed said the same thing about people in the West![37] Many Americans would agree with Muslims, especially among the more conservative religious, that some of the provocative attire and behavior of cultural icons such as Lady Gaga or the demeaning lyrics of some music is disrespectful of women. Yet it is the differences that stand out, not the points of agreement. This is what happens when relationships get in a dysfunctional state: The differences are highlighted and the similarities are minimized. A 2011 U.S. study of intolerance in Pakistan found just how deeply ingrained is hard-line Islam. The study found that textbooks there foster prejudice and intolerance of Hindus and other religious minorities. It also found that while many Pakistani teachers agreed how important it was to respect the practices of religious minorities, simultaneously 80 percent viewed non-Muslims, in some form or another, as "enemies of Islam."[38]

While the presence of religious differences can be very nasty, we cannot forget that our world has been quite capable of deploying man's inhumanity to man in causes that were primarily secular. Even if we were to rid ourselves of what secularists might call "unproven" religious beliefs, what makes us think that would make the world safer? Few saw Hitler or Mussolini as religious extremists, but they were certainly extremists in their beliefs.

For Americans, it is easy to see the intolerance of countries and religions different from ours. Unfortunately, we have our own issues. The Barna Group conducted a three-year study to understand tolerance between Christians and outsider unaffiliated groups. These are some of their findings:

- Sixteen-to-29-year-olds exhibited a greater degree of criticism toward Christianity than did previous generations when they were at the same stage of life.

- Among young non-Christians, nine out of the top 12 perceptions were negative toward Christians. Common negative perceptions were that present-day Christianity is judgmental (87 percent), hypocritical (85 percent), old-fashioned (78 percent), and too involved in politics (75 percent).

- Half of young churchgoers perceive Christianity to be judgmental, hypocritical, and too political. One-third said it was out of touch with reality.

- Among the nation's evangelicals, 91 percent believe that "Americans are becoming more hostile and negative toward Christianity."[39]

The decline in image experienced by both Christians and non-Christians seems to be tied to relational intolerance—a combination of "too judgmental" and "too hypocritical." At the core, the problems center on how groups relate to each other. Christianity's "brand"—especially conservative ones—involves an emerging new image that has steadily grown in prominence over the last decade. Today, according to Barna, the most common perception is that present-day Christianity is anti-homosexual. Perception drives reality.

As Christianity has taken on a more prominent role in recent years, it has become defined by what it is against, rather than what it supports. Political power exerted on behalf of religion combined with contempt makes for a lethal combination. As one young person I heard about expressed it, "Something is broken in the present-day expression of Christianity." That something is relationship. (In the spirit of full disclosure, my religious background is Southern Baptist, agnostic, and Presbyterian.)

Members of the nonbeliever crowd are now guilty of some of the same overzealous attacks and expressions of contempt. Commentators are beginning to discuss this new development and the data available seems to validate it.

Intended or not, the primary outcome from the elevation and personalization of religious and secular belief has been damaging for relationships. Gandhi admonished us: We must become the change we seek. Unfortunately, the reality has been a little different: We have become the belief we disdain.

THE PROBLEM WITH MODERATION

For many, moderation is an answer to the animus and discord of these emerging extremes. This hope lies in religious or secular belief that accepts differing viewpoints resulting in less conflict and battle. Live and let live.

Yet, moderation as a force for repairing and strengthening of relationships faces two challenges: (1) The more extreme groups are growing at a much faster pace than the moderate ones (more on that later in this chapter), and (2) Moderates have little influence on extremists. Sam Harris concluded that among extreme groups, moderates are viewed as "nothing more than a failed fundamentalist" because they refused to live by the letter of the law when it came to their faith. As a result, they are perceived as weak, wimpy, and with no credibility among the more extreme.[40] As discussed earlier, the process of escalation often roots out moderates as groups become more extreme.

Ironically, by dismissing religious moderation as any part of the solution, Harris's views seem to reflect the very polarization he describes. There is some evidence that the pressures produced by a modern world are exerting pressures for reform. For example, Nicholas Kristof of the *New York Times* writes: "While the thread of fundamentalism is real in Islam, so is the thread of reform. The 21st century may become to Islam what the 16th was to Christianity, for even in hard-line states like Iran you meet Martin Luthers who are pushing for an Islamic Reformation."[41]

Many have hoped education would be a moderating force. Yet Samuel Huntington has pointed out that religious fundamentalism in the developing world has not been led by the poor and uneducated.[42] The privileged education, upbringing, and wealth of Osama bin Laden and other leaders of al-Qaeda are perhaps the most well-known examples. The old assumption was that education would make everyone more postmodern in their view of the world.

The new analysis shows that the more elite, affluent, and educated are more focused on and locked into their own beliefs. Church attendance is a strong predictor of voting behavior among the highly educated and more affluent, not the working class.[43] Larry Bartels says that in contemporary American politics, social issues are the opiate of the elites, whether they be liberal or conservative. Our newfound knowledge has inspired more confidence and even arrogance in the partisan beliefs that now destroy relationships.

Moderation takes its licks for being wishy-washy with no real bedrock of belief, passion, or certitude. Conversely, at the heart of more extreme beliefs is false certitude. As Harris states, "Nothing that a Christian and a Muslim can say to each other will render their beliefs mutually vulnerable to discourse, because the very tenets of their faith have immunized them against the power of conversation."[44] When it comes to religious or secular belief, some are convinced they are right about something that by its very nature cannot be proven—that's why they call it faith. Extreme certitude too often leads to extreme intolerance.

Once we agree that it is not an attack on God, science, or technology to admit that we don't get it all, it opens the possibility that we have something to learn. Often, the more we think we know, the harder it is for us to learn new things. As a result, we become immunized from conversation, the influence of others, and learning. It's a frozen state that is very hard on our relationships.

It is what happens when we put more weight on the details of what we believe than the object of that belief—our relationships with family, friends, community, and our God, however defined.

WHEN INTOLERANCE BECOMES VIOLENCE

Someone once told me that before Christian Crusader soldiers left on the long journey from Europe to the Middle East, they were each baptized. Each man would extend his arm and hold his sword out of the water as he went under. His cleansing, symbolized by baptism, didn't extend to his killing arm and sword. That way, his intent to kill with the sword wouldn't violate his faith.

We do the same thing. We compartmentalize our hatred and contempt for those who are different from what we believe, so as not to contaminate our faith, which compels us to love our neighbors and even our enemies.

Violence is the ultimate form of intolerance and destroyer of relationships. Our hopes for the power of religious tolerance have too often been trumped by religious leaders advocating violent beheadings, forced religious conversion under threat of death, and suicide bombings. In the view of some, violence has become the brand of "organized religion," or at least of certain religious groups. For example, a Pew study found not only an increase in unfavorable views of Islam, but an increase in the number of Americans who think there are more violent extremists within Islam compared with other religions. Accordingly, in 2009, 52 percent of Americans were concerned about the rise in Islamic extremism in the United States, up from 46 percent in 2007.[45]

While the West points to Islamic violence in the beheadings, suicide bombs, and torture associated with terrorism, Muslims see the military actions in Afghanistan and Iraq as acts of violence and violations of their sacred Sharia law. Each side sees the violence of the other but not necessarily its own. Violence in the name of religion has been and continues to be a huge ongoing catalyst in the rupture of relationships between Islam and the West.

Religion and Belief: Growth Trends Undermine Relationships

The trend continues: spouses leaving marriage, customers and employees leaving organizations, citizens leaving political parties, and believers leaving religious affiliation in the United States. According to ABC News, the percentage of Americans who say they have no affiliation (15 percent) has almost doubled in the past 18 years, and the percentage who defined themselves as Christian has dropped from 86 percent in 1990 to 76 percent in 2008.[46] This trend is counter to the overall rise in the number of religious believers around the world presented earlier. It seems to reflect an America that is following in the footsteps of an older, more staid Western European religious culture more than the vibrant and frothy religious cultures of Africa, the Middle East, or Latin America.

Defections from Christianity, the largest domestic religious group, have risen 18 percentage points in 18 years. "Unaffiliated" is now in third place, just behind Catholics (25 percent) and Baptists (16 percent) and exceeding mainline Methodists, Lutheran, Presbyterian, and Episcopalians combined. The percentage of American adults who identify themselves as Protestants dropped below 50 percent around the year 2005.[47] Mainline denominations have been losing membership for decades in the United States, as have Jewish communities (those self-identified as religious—not by ethnicity)—dropped from 3.1 million to 2.6 million from 1990 to 2008.

In spite of the overall decline in affiliation, conservative Pentecostals/charismatics have increased from 5.6 million in 1990 to nearly 8.0 million in 2008.[48] Mormons/Latter Day Saints also have increased, from 2.4 million to 3.1 million for the same period. Nondenominational Christians, including members of Bible churches (independent churches that place a heavy emphasis on biblical teaching) and megachurches, recruiting from denominations, have grown from 194,000 in 1990 to more than 8 million in 2008. Once again, Americans have aggressively joined groups defined by what they are not: not religiously affiliated, not Christian, or not with a mainline denomination. Or, they have joined more conservative, narrow, outspoken groups.

A second factor closely related to fleeing religious affiliation is a rise in the rate of changing affiliations. Pew reports that roughly half of the U.S. adult population has changed religion at some point in their lives,[49] compared to only 15 percent in 1955.[50] This upswing in religious divorce and remarriage is yet another place in our lives where relational volatility reigns.

A third factor to look at is church attendance. According to a *Newsweek* poll, those reporting they attend church weekly remains unchanged over the past 40 years (45 percent),[51] yet independent research reports the number of people actually showing up at a typical Protestant church service has dropped by 13 percent, even though the population of America has increased by 9 percent![52] Catholic church attendance has declined from around 44 percent in 1987 to 33 percent in 2005.[53]

The underlying causes of the decline in organized religion vary by group. For example, two-thirds of former Catholics and half of former Protestants say they left their childhood faith because they no longer believe in God or the teachings of most religions; as discussed, many cite reasons of hypocrisy, judgmental attitudes, and leaders too focused on money and power.[54] Much as in politics, people have lost the faith and given up their relational ties.

As in business and politics, scandal in religion has had an eroding impact on confidence: "From 1973 to the mid-1980s, religious institutions obtained many ratings above 60 percent. Ratings suffered in 1989 due to the televangelist scandals involving embezzlement and sexual improprieties by the likes of Jimmy Swaggart and Jim Bakker . . . by 2002, it had sunk to 45 percent."[55] This represents a 40-year low. The sexual-abuse issues among leaders of the Catholic Church have had an impact. According to Harvard's National Leadership Index, religious leaders rated the lowest in 2009 since the index began, in 2005, ranking just ahead of business: eighth out of 13 sectors.[56]

These findings tell us that when it comes to the eroding relationships with its constituents, religion is often its own worst enemy. While it is tempting to blame the media, Hollywood, and a host of others for the challenges, it suffers most from self-inflicted wounds.

As confidence in institutional religion has declined, a number of churches have followed the corporate practice of attempting to rebrand, including dropping their denominational name, to unload unattractive relational baggage.

Most demographers believe that Christianity is the largest religious group today. Researchers disagree on whether or not that will remain the case going forward. Regardless, Christianity and Islam are both experiencing significant growth worldwide. The reasons behind the growth are varied, but according to Luis Lugo at Pew, it emphasizes a personal sense of relationship with God and community.[57] More revealing than the overall growth are the specific traits of the groups driving the growth and the impact those traits have on relationships.

In the United States, those groups experiencing strongest growth tend to be at the more conservative/fundamental end of the theological spectrum and more aggressive in proselytizing and gaining new members. These two characteristics lead to an interesting paradox. These specific Christian groups are more like Islam in that they are more fundamental, but as discussed earlier, they stand out for their unfavorable view of Islam.

This fits the larger pattern. The groups that are growing market share the fastest—Islam, evangelical/Pentecostal Christian, along with certain conservative (including ultra-Orthodox Jews in Israel) and nondenominational groups, and atheists—are the groups that, according to survey data, have the least tolerance for each other and that foster the greatest conflicts. It validates a rather obvious but ominous point: Strong differences in belief coupled with efforts to grow market share (by conversion or population increase) lead to even greater relationship tension and conflict. You can conclude that because of the passion, proselytizing, and animus among these groups, our relationship discord is likely to get worse.

Conversely, the groups who are most likely to be moderate and tolerant of differences are exerting less influence—just as in politics. While these groups—think mainline churches like Methodist and Presbyterian—appear to be less divisive, many have become highly institutionalized and lacking in passion, which contributes to their shrinking in size. In many respects, they resemble the business and government organizations that have let bureaucracy, size, and distance separate them from purpose, people, compassion, and service. They are often inwardly focused on protecting the status quo, their leaders, and the preferences of incumbents instead of focusing on their changing marketplace. Many are victims of relational atrophy and have lost their connection and their authority to influence others—especially younger segments. So, while more tolerant of differences, they are increasingly impotent to advocate for strong cross-denominational or even cross-religious/cultural relationships.

In democratic countries, the growth of more conflict-oriented groups translates into votes, which translates into power that will likely add to division and erode relationships. These groups, which tend to be very passionate, less institutional, more entrepreneurial, and more autonomous locally—all conducive to stronger relationships within the group—have the potential to initiate changes in law, custom, and culture. The very process of advocating for change will likely elicit more conflict. In theocracies, where government is under the authority of religion, these hard-line groups likely will further limit the practice of beliefs and practices alien to them, further increasing conflict.

The increasing focus on gaining and using political power for religious purposes undermines freedom of belief and tempts the state to use religion as a tool for political gain. Both religious and secular groups run the risk of suffering from overconfidence in their own righteousness. Reinhold Niebuhr nailed it: "The final enigma of history is therefore not how the righteous will gain victory over the unrighteous, but how the evil in every good and the unrighteousness of the righteous is to be overcome."[58]

* * * *

In a time when relationship decline and conflict is so prevalent, it is troubling to see religious organizations lose their influence for harmony and instead be viewed as an instrument of conflict and even violence. The late Peter Gomes, a theologian at Harvard's Divinity School, said, "We have just enough religion to know how to hate, but not enough to know how to love."[59] Likewise, it is disconcerting to see the hypocrisy of those of a secular persuasion who have been so critical of religious dogma, divisiveness, and even violence become what they condemn in religious groups.

In the lexicon of the Greeks, who were careful to define different relational categories of love, *phila* (brotherly love of those in my clan, my group, my denomination) has overwhelmed *agape* love (unconditional love given without consideration to whether others are in my group or are like me). In becoming more divided we have become too confident in our rightness. Again, as Niebuhr observed, "A too confident sense of justice always leads to injustice."

The schizophrenia of our religious and secular state—so rich in intent and yet so laden with divide—is a primary cog in the machinery of relationship destruction. Our beliefs are increasingly applied as offensive weapons, rupturing relationships. Everywhere we turn, relationships are missing in action. Our relational decline has become so ubiquitous that we have become numbed.

Yet the history of religion and belief is also a source of hope. It was in coming to grips with the horrible consequences of religious conflict that helped end the Crusades, reform Christianity, and stem the violence in Northern Ireland. Even today the violence that accompanies radical Islam has resulted in pressures from within that faith to temper some of their more extreme actions.

Just as the disintegration of relationships is our big problem, guess what? Relationships are our shining light and our big solution. Read on.*

---

* You may be asking: What is the state of my relationships—at home and work, in politics and faith? To help answer that question, complete the State of Your Relationships quiz at my website www.robertehall.com. Click on the Book page to see how you score.

SECTION II

RELATIONSHIP:
OUR MOST VALUABLE RESOURCE

What makes our relationships so uniquely valuable? There is no life wisdom more important to understand than the value and hope of relationships. Yet contemporary evidence reflects an American society adrift and struggling to treasure this most vital resource. It is imperative to step back and revisit just how central our relationships are to all we deem precious. Our hope for relational development and advancement hinges on our ability to see anew just how relationships link directly to our health, wealth, and well-being.

In chapter 5, "The Value of Relationships," we make the case that we are built for relationship—emotionally, socially, and economically. Chapter 6, "Relationship Math: Looking at the Dollars and Sense," is for those who need to see hard evidence and proof that these soft relationships are really as valuable as we say.

Chapter 5

The Value of Relationships

For a long time, we measured the health of a country by look-ing at its gross domestic product . . . But our work shows that whether a friend's friend is happy has more influence than a $5,000 raise.

—*James Fowler, coauthor of a major study on social networks and happiness[1]*

I slipped into the local Neiman Marcus store around five o'clock on Christmas Eve. A sales clerk who recognized my not so sub-tle stress appeared from the perimeter of the precious jewelry section and said, "May I help you?"

"Yes," I blurted, "I need to find a Christmas present for my wife, have it gift wrapped, and get to a family gathering in about 15 minutes."

After asking me a couple of questions, she suggested: "How about a pearl necklace?" I nodded. "Let me show you three alternatives," she said as she began my introductory 101 course on the basics of pearls, at the end of which I said, "Let's go with the second set."

"Great! I know you're in a hurry, and there'll be a long line in gift wrapping, so let me see what I can get done here." She disappeared momentarily behind a partition and then reappeared. "Mr. Hall, I have someone here who is going to gift wrap the pearls right now and we'll soon have you on your way." I breathed a sigh of relief.

"By the way, my name is Cynthia. While we have a minute, if I could ask you a couple of additional questions, perhaps I could be a resource for you in the future when you need to buy for your wife." I said sure, and in response proceeded to briefly list the precious jewelry my wife had, along with the dates of my wedding anniversary—January 20—and my wife's birthday—September 14. Cynthia then politely asked for my business address and phone number and warmly wished me a great holiday season as she handed me the nicely wrapped package.

On January 13, I was in my office when the phone rang. "Mr. Hall, this is Cynthia down at Neiman's. I just wanted to check in with you and see how your wife liked the pearl necklace."

"Oh, she really loved it. You can never underestimate the power of really nice pearls."

"Great. You know, you mentioned that you have an anniversary coming up on January 20. I know it is still a week away," she teased, "but I have a couple of ideas. Perhaps if you could come by the store one day this week I could show them to you."

"Yeah, you're right, but I'm headed out of town at the end of the day and will be gone for several days."

"You're in the Oxy Tower, right?" she asked. "I'm going to be out that way this afternoon. What if I come by around 1:30? I promise it will only take five minutes to show you a couple of gift ideas."

Later, as she walked into my office, Cynthia began the conversation by saying, "I know you're busy, so let me make this brief. When you listed your wife's current jewelry, you did not say anything about a nice set of pearl earrings to go with the necklace." She then showed me three options, and I decided, "Let's go with the ones in the middle; that seemed to work well last time."

"Okay. I'll take these back and get them gift wrapped, and when you return from your trip, they will be in your desk drawer."

I wound up buying four gifts from Cynthia over the next two years, and I never physically returned to the store. She provided the single most valuable example of relationship management by a commercial enterprise I have ever experienced. We even had Cynthia as a guest at my company's client conference to talk about customer relationships. She saved me time, made me look good through adroit gift selections, and, most of all, made shopping a pleasure rather than a pain. Obviously, it was also a rewarding relationship for Cynthia and for Neiman's, even though I will never be mistaken for a high roller. The products could have been purchased at a number of places—but the relationship was priceless.

It was the relationship with Cynthia, not the jewels, that was precious. The word *precious* implies both value and scarcity. Economists tell us it is the combination of these attributes that drives up the price of items. Ultimately, water is more crucial to life than diamonds are, but diamonds are scarcer and therefore command a higher price.

Valuable relationships can be deeply emotional and intimate, socially pleasing, economically rewarding, or just a small but pleasant addition to our lives. They come in an infinite array of shapes and sizes: a great spouse or partner, parent, sibling, child, friend, employee, customer, colleague, spiritual confidant, fellow soldier, supplier.

We often treat relationships as if they were optional, but the reality is that we are made for relationships—they are not just something we want; they are something we need.

The Unique Value That Relationships Create

The most important health-care system in the world is a mother.
How do you get things in her hands that she understands and can
afford and can use?

Dr. Richard Klausner, former executive director of global
health, Bill & Melinda Gates Foundation[2]

Relationship, collective and all-encompassing, is the single most valuable possession in the world. How can I make such a bold claim in a society obsessed with money, power, status, technology, and fame? Relationship is the defining source of value creation, whether that value is social, economic, political, or spiritual. Relationship is both valuable, like a diamond, and the source of value creation, like the goose that laid the golden eggs. It is the basic building block for our society and the primary catalyst for growth, development, and advancement. There is nothing more central than—and no equivalent substitute for—a committed, competent relationship.

Notice what Dr. Klausner did not say; he did not say a financial system or an information technology system or a marketing system. Instead, he said that a mother is the most important health care enabler, based on the relationship she has with her child. It begins prior to birth, and it never ends. More valuable than the goose or the golden eggs she lays is the relationship.

Make no mistake about it. Building and sustaining relationships is also difficult, painful and gut-wrenching, unpredictable, sometimes oppressive, and often time-consuming. Healing and recovering from broken relationships takes a long time. It should not be a surprise that many of us have tried to exert control and impose structure to protect ourselves from relationships and the baggage they bring. Yet, relationships are the source of life, feeding us nutrients that we can get nowhere else.

John Gottman, renowned for his insight on marital relationships, looks at the relationship, not each individual, as the crucial unit. It's not either person, it's something that happens when they are together, like a structure they are building by the way they interact.[3] The relationship is the fundamental unit of our society. This premise certainly aligns with what we are learning about the physical world. Richard Rohr points to the power of relationship in the world of physics: "Even the new physics tells us that matter is merely the manifestation of spirit, but spirit, consciousness, relationship itself is the real thing. We used to think all the energy was in the particles of the atom; now it seems that energy is, in fact, in the space between the particles."[4]

In a world where relationships have become scarce, a simple reality has become apparent: Those with strong, growing relationships are prospering emotionally, socially, academically, and economically.

Relationship capital—the wealth or value that flows from productive relationships—is based on compelling research. In 2010, researchers who reviewed 148 studies over several decades reported that people with stronger social relationships had a 50 percent increased likelihood of survival over those with weaker social relationships.[5] Even if you engage in poor habits such as smoking or excessive drinking, if you are engaged in strong relationships, you will probably live longer than people who are fit and healthy but on their own. As John Ortberg said so aptly, "It's better to eat Twinkies with good friends than to eat broccoli alone."[6]

Relationships likewise play an important role in organic growth—that is, the ability to cultivate, develop, and produce. David Brooks postulates that in the world of public policy there are two major types. Type one is the ecologists who believe human beings are formed in a web of relationships. They see behavior as shaped by expectations and motivations that we absorb from the people around us. The second type is engineers who believe all of this soft relationship stuff to be so much "mush." They believe behavior is shaped by incentives: Give people the resources they need, and rational behavior and socially productive outcomes will follow. Brooks concludes,

> "Most politicians are ecologists who turn into engineers once in office. They know how much relationships mattered to their own success. But in government, the major tool they have is a budget appropriation. So suddenly every problem turns into a question of resources. When it comes to helping people flourish, the ecologists are usually right."[7]

Societies that maximize the functional potential of relationships foster development and growth at all levels: personal, business, state, and spiritual. In discussing productive relationships, it is important to include those that can be challenging. Often the words we most need to hear come from someone we don't like or respect. Competitors and, often, the opposition have a way of delivering marketplace truths that we wouldn't have been able to get in any other way. Not only are we incomplete without family, loved ones, and colleagues, we also are incomplete without those who can be tough on us. Difficult relationships can be just as crucial to our development as comfortable ones.

What we have learned from years of throwing strategies, policies, and money at our social problems is just how central functioning relationships are to economic and social gain. This reality helps explain why the social programs to eradicate poverty in the 1960s, massive expenditures on technology to solve human problems, and the focus on improving education have come up short. Only by making relationships the cornerstone of our efforts will we be able to facilitate the kinds of development and growth that give us a shot at resolving our biggest problems.

Looking for Relationship Capital in All the Right Places

A good place to start examining this shift is to look at the demand for more relational jobs. According to findings reported in the *McKinsey Quarterly*, there is a growing demand in the workplace for jobs involving more complex, relational capabilities: "Complex interactions typically require people to deal with ambiguity—there are no rule books to follow—and to exercise high levels of judgment. These men and women (such as managers, salespeople, nurses, lawyers, judges, and mediators) must often draw on deep experience, which economists call 'tacit knowledge.'"[8] Furthermore, about 80 percent of nonagricultural jobs in most developed economies involve these tacit interactions, as compared to 20 percent a century ago. These more complex, tacit interactions—contrasted with the routine transactional ones that are increasingly automated—are rife with relationship subtleties. Yet it is in this growing realm of relationship competence where so much of the opportunity resides. According to the McKinsey researchers, the potential for improving productivity for workers in these tacit interactions greatly outstrips the potential of workers in other areas.

Robert Putnam calls the value produced by social interaction "social capital": "Just as a screwdriver (physical capital) or a college education (human capital) can increase productivity (individual and collective), so too can social contacts affect the productivity of individuals and groups."[9] When we ascribe the term *capital* to something, it implies there is stored energy that has the potential to produce, grow, and multiply in the same way that financial capital is used to start companies or develop new products. When a community of strong positive relationships forms around a big idea, those relationships foster collective commitment, competence, leadership, and resource access that, combined, get things done. I believe social, or relationship, capital—whether the group is small or large in number—is the single most value-creating resource we have. Where two or three are gathered together in a social network with a strong purpose, incredible things are possible.

Investment is used in the business world to describe expenditures that are expected to grow in value over a longer-term time frame. When we look at healthy, functional relationships, that is exactly what we see: growth in value over a longer term. Frederick Reichheld says that loyalty is the willingness of someone—customer, employee, or friend—to make an investment or personal sacrifice in order to strengthen a relationship. For a customer, that could mean sticking with a supplier who gives good value in the long term even if the supplier does not offer the best price in a particular transaction. His bottom line is: "Customer loyalty is about much more than repeat purchases. Indeed, even someone who buys again and again from the same company . . . may be trapped by inertia, indifference, or exit barriers erected by the company or circumstances."[10] As Cynthia from Neiman Marcus demonstrated, loyalty is built on strong relationships where each party invests in the other over time in a way that produces value and growth.

Of course, relationships are not just about business; they are also personal, political, and spiritual. And the relationship capital we need comes from others, but not always the ones we like the most nor under the circumstances we prefer. I recently attended an address by Nobel Peace Prize winner Archbishop Desmond Tutu of South Africa. I first traveled to that country in 1984, and it seemed inevitable that the relational strife over apartheid would lead to a bloody civil war. As I recruited a team to open our office and traveled there frequently over the next few years, I observed leaders like Tutu (then chair of the Truth and Reconciliation Commission, or TRC) use the power of relationship to rescue a wounded nation. Many of our clients shared gripping accounts of local TRC sessions where perpetrators admitted to horrible acts and victims expressed forgiveness. In his address, Bishop Tutu delivered the simple message that we are made for relationships: "I cannot be fully me without you and you cannot be fully you without me." Each of us is missing a part completed only by others.

It is informative to hear people reflect back over their lives. I have been surprised how often professional athletes, who seemed entirely about winning, share that what they miss most is relationships with the other players, the sense of team, and bantering in the locker room. What they most miss is what made them most whole.

My wife has a dear friend who lost her husband not too long ago. Her friend has commented how much she misses the smallest discussions: the ones that seemed so inane at the time—the weather, how well she slept, and what they were going to have for dinner that night.

My younger daughter interviewed a number of people for a college religion class to get their views on faith. She made this interesting observation: The younger people she talked with focused more on the theology—the key tenets of their belief. The older or more mature people talked more about their experiences of, and relationships with, God and with their faith community. The essence of our home, work, politics, and faith is relationships.

Built for Relationships

Social relationships, or the relative lack thereof, constitute a major risk factor for health—rivaling the effect of well established health risk factors such as cigarette smoking, blood pressure, blood lipids, obesity and physical activity.

—House, Landis, and Umberson, Science[11]

Research confirms that the human brain is designed to promote relationships. The parts of the brain that mediate pleasure are linked to the parts that mediate emotional relationships. This ability to get pleasure from relationships creates positive learning in infants and children. (Think about children who want to please their teachers.) We were built for relationships; the physiological evidence can be seen, touched, and proven. In addition, we can testify to the emotional benefits of feeling good, loved, and connected. Let's look at both of these realities.

This line of exploration gets us very close to the question, "Why are we here?" As you may have noticed, not everyone agrees on the answer to that question. Some view the question through the prism of their religion.

For example, if you are a Christian, you might look to the teachings of Jesus. When Christ was asked what commandment was the greatest, His answer in Matthew 23:37–40 gives us his priority: "Love the Lord your God with all your heart and with all your soul and with all your mind . . . Love your neighbor as yourself. All the Law and the Prophets hang on these two commandments."

Love is the central point of this message. It puts relationship at the center of our lives and implies that all laws and prophets exist as subset and support. To me, obedience to the law is a means to a core relationship purpose, which is undermined when we use it as a weapon to exclude, diminish, or destroy relationships.

Alternatively, others would come at this question from a scientific viewpoint. They might say we are built to evolve and survive through natural selection. As it relates to relationship, they may point to sources such as Darwin to understand how relationships play a key role in survival of the fittest. Recent research supports the central role of relationship not only in procreation but also in how social relationships have been crucial to surviving and thriving.

Atheists, too, give importance to relationships. As Sam Harris describes: "We are bound to one another. . . . No tribal fictions need be rehearsed for us to realize, one fine day, that we do, in fact, love our neighbor, that our happiness is inextricably from their own, and that interdependence demands that people everywhere be given the opportunity to flourish."[12]

PHYSIOLOGICALLY HARDWIRED FOR RELATIONSHIPS

Robert Sussman believes that the assumption that our skills as hunters and warriors were key to our evolutionary success is erroneous. He argues, instead, that being hunted brought evolutionary pressure on our ancestors to cooperate and live in cohesive groups. In other words, relationships and social skills have helped us evolve. Findings from genetics and paleoneurology point to a hormone called oxytocin, which promotes trust during interactions with others, leading to relationships that allow us to live together and enjoy common goals.[13]

Stronger bonds and, eventually, relationships fed a breakthrough in our evolution, according to Harvard's Dr. George Valliant. Mammalian evolution has hard-wired the brain for spiritual experience, and specifically joy. He states that developmentally, the child's smile, the kitten's purr, and the puppy's wagging tail emerge at the same time. Thus, these social responses are elicited by, and in turn elicit, positive emotion. He concludes: "They all occur when the infant brain's more primitive limbic system becomes effectively wired to the forebrain. Negative emotions like aggression and fear help us to survive individually; positive emotions help the community to survive. Joy, unlike happiness, is not all about me—joy is connection."[14]

Furthermore, our physical characteristics are designed for ongoing interaction that is cooperative or reciprocal in nature. Michael Tomasello argues that the eyes are not just the windows into the soul; they are also a pointing device that enables close and complex cooperative tasks. He points out that the whites of our eyes are several times larger than those of other primates, which makes it much easier to see where the eyes are pointed. This observation leads to one of the most controversial topics in the study of human evolution: how human cooperation evolved. He argues that one possibility is the cooperative eye hypothesis. It concludes: "Especially visible eyes made it easier to coordinate close-range collaborative activities in which discerning where the other was looking and perhaps what she was planning, benefited both participants."[15]

Just as the human mind and body have evolved to enhance relationships, so, too, have relationships had a concrete impact on human physiology. A dramatic example is the historic discovery that absence of physical touch literally caused infants to die in orphanages in Germany after World War I, and it forever altered the practice of medicine and child care, especially in custodial settings.[16]

More recent research has revealed that girls who grow up in homes without a biological father reach puberty at an earlier age.[17] On average, girls in homes where a stepfather was present reached puberty nine months earlier, and those in divorced homes (absent a father or stepfather) four months earlier, than those in a home with both biological parents present. Researchers provide two possible explanations for this: One is that early puberty may be a response to life in a hostile environment, such as a high rate of conflict and stress associated with divorce and remarriage. The alternate theory is based on the fact that, in many animal species, the presence of a strange male is an environmental cue that induces sexual readiness in young females. Hence, early menarche may be triggered by the presence of a strange male in the household.[18]

Conversely, in humans and animals, the presence of the biological father slows down the maturation process, thus protecting against the risks of early development. All of this reinforces the findings that broken spousal relationships can trigger physical changes that in turn increase the odds of breast cancer,[19] and make it more likely that adolescent girls will become more sexually active and pregnant at earlier ages (pregnancy is five times more likely in the United States vs. three times more likely in New Zealand, after controlling for variables such as race, living standard, etc.)—with dire results.[20]

As for men, just-released research shows that male testosterone drops after a man becomes a parent, and the more he cares for his children, the lower it drops. The lowered testosterone seems to signal a hormonal shift in value for more relational commitment to the mate and children, and parenting behavior further reinforces the physiological change.[21]

FRIENDSHIP AND FAT

Another recent discovery is the way that weight gain is influenced by close relationships. A 2007 study of 12,067 people found that obesity can spread from person to person. If one person is obese, that person's friend is 57 percent more likely to become obese. There was no impact when a neighbor gained (or lost) weight, and, interestingly, family members did not have as much impact as friends did.[22]

This gets to the core of why our relationships are so crucial and valuable—our survival depends on it. Our preoccupation with knowledge, science, logic, and technology has illuminated but also obfuscated by leading us to trivialize the relational, emotional, and spiritual sides of our existence.

EMOTIONALLY ENRICHED BY RELATIONSHIPS

While the emotional impact of relationships is hard to separate from the physical, the emotional aspect affects us in large ways and small. Our relationships, more than anything else, predict our state of happiness. Nobel Prize–winning psychologist and behavioral economist Daniel Kahneman of Princeton listed commuting to work, lack of sleep, watching TV, and even time spent with the kids as low on the mood chart, while having intimate relations and socializing ranked high. The latter resulted in lowered anxiety, less depression at home, and more energy at work.[23]

Intimate relationships are very powerful, but other types of relationships are also proving to be very valuable. A report featured in the *British Medical Journal* explains that relationships are central to happiness and that it spreads readily through social networks of family members, friends, and neighbors: "Knowing someone who is happy makes you 15.3 percent more likely to be happy yourself . . . a happy friend who lives within a half-mile makes you 42 percent more likely to be happy yourself. If that same friend lives two miles away, his impact drops to 22 percent."[24] The research also found that people who were part of large social networks were among the happiest, and that the geographic proximity of a happy person to you could have a significant impact on your own positive outlook.

Social relationships can save lives. When we are in groups of positive social relationships, we are happier, more productive, and able to innovate and create things that simply would not be possible individually. Many major breakthroughs in recent history have come from our ability to work together in much larger groups to invent new medicines, technologies, transportation systems, and more.

Being built for relationships means we are also built to serve and help each other. Professor Daniel Gilbert reinforces this point. He cites research that suggests we are hard-wired with a strong and intuitive moral impulse to help others that is every bit as basic as the selfish urges that get all the press. He provides examples of 18-month-old infants who spontaneously "comfort those who appear distressed and help those who are having difficulty retrieving or balancing objects. Chimpanzees will do the same, though not so reliably, which has led scientists to speculate about the precise point in our evolutionary history at which we became the 'hyper-cooperative' species that out-nices the rest."[25]

Relationships may also be a source for warding off boredom. Sociologist Robert Nisbet reported that boredom is a force that drives us as a species. As we evolved, we encountered boredom and monotony. This boredom pushed us toward war, murder, revolution, suicide, alcohol, narcotics, and pornography.[26] It fits that serial killers are notoriously loners. So while we were built for the positive emotions associated with relationships, we were also built for drama, excitement, and challenge. Being in relationships with others is one of the ways we fulfill our need for that stimulation.

Stress and drama can take their toll if we overdo it, however. How we relate to others triggers our emotions, which in turn directly affect our physiological and biological functions. Dr. Henry Lodge of Columbia Medical School describes what he considers a major revelation of the last decade: "Emotions change our cells through the same molecular pathways as exercise. Anger, stress, and loneliness are signals for 'starvation' and chronic danger. They 'melt' our bodies as surely as sedentary living. Optimism, love and community trigger the process of growth, building our bodies, hearts and minds."[27] A Swedish study that tracked 3,122 men for 10 years found that those with bad bosses suffered 20 to 40 percent more heart attacks (depending on how long they worked for them) than those with good bosses.[28] Men who come home to a family after suffering a heart attack are four times less likely to die from a second heart attack. Women suffering from heart disease or cancer do better in direct proportion to the number of family and friends they have.

In addition to the emotional support, when we interact with others, they influence us on key issues in ways that are valuable. Just as organizations have boards that bring wisdom and influence to decision making and accountability, the friends and family we interact with are able to encourage us to go to the doctor, take our medicine, and exercise in ways that translate into better health and happiness.

The parallel between physical exercise and relationships is interesting. We have spent most of the past century investing in automobiles, work equipment, and home appliances that eliminated much of our physical work. How have we used some of the time saved? To perform unpaid physical work—exercise—because it turns out physical exertion aids our health and well-being.

Likewise, many of the advancements of recent decades—using the ATM, purchasing online, working from home, and pumping self-serve gasoline—have eliminated the need to interact with others. Instead of getting together and having a face-to-face conversation, we text each other (more on that in the next section). I believe the good news is that we are learning that our need for "relational exercise" is just as real as that for physical exercise and that we will apply old ways and invent new ones to be more relationally developed and physically present.

Henrik Ibsen described the richness of relationships in these words: "Money may be the husk of many things but not the kernel. It brings you food, but not appetite; medicine, but not health; acquaintance, but not friends; servants, but not loyalty; days of joy, but not peace or happiness."[29] Relationships are not optional; they are a matter of life and death, emotional but also physiological, and key to our development. We cannot become what we might if we treat them as disposable.

Building Relationship Attachments

Good relationships aren't about clear communication—they're about small moments of attachment and intimacy.

—John Gottman, one of the nation's foremost researchers on relationships[30]

Relationship is a word that means different things to each of us. In its most generic sense, a relationship is the connection between two spheres. Most often when we use the word *relationship*, we are referring to the connection between or among people. That connection or association can be kinship, friendship, romance, business, politics, spirituality, or any number of other possibilities. For some, the use of the word is limited to a strong connection between related parties, such as a married couple. For our purposes, we will use a broad definition of relationship with varying degrees of obligation or commitment.

In a word, what makes relationships uniquely valuable and value-creating is *attachment*. While we have greatly increased the volume of communicating and information exchanged, it has not always translated into stronger, more attached relationships. In the midst of an explosion of electronic communication—e-mail, Facebook, instant messaging, texting, Twitter, cell phones, YouTube, and the Internet—our relationships have suffered. Stronger attachment and intimacy are aided by face-to-face communication and recurring relational contact. Most organizational communication processes are designed for clear communication, efficient exchange of information, and closing of transactions—not for relational attachment or connection.

There are four components that build relational attachment.

1. Ongoing and obligated. The first component of relationship is the ongoing nature of the relating. Relationships are ongoing. They evolve over time. A relationship can be as strong and powerful as marriage or as insignificant as owning a product produced and supported by a company. The link or connection may have long periods of dormancy, but if the link is there, so is the potential for relationship.

According to the entry in *Merrium-Websters*, the word *relate* is derived from the Latin referre, which means to carry, tolerate, or bear. There is some level of responsibility or obligation we are required to tolerate or bear on behalf of those with whom we are connected. When we add the requirement to tolerate or bear with a longer-term view, we quickly tumble to the word *patience*. The word *patient* has its Latin root in the words *pain* and *suffer*.

It is the very act of suffering that is most powerful in growing a connection. Thomas Keating expressed the relationship between love and suffering when he said: "Love alone can change people . . . It offers others space in which to change no matter what they do . . . Although such a practice is extremely demanding, everyone has the capacity to do it because only two things are required—suffering and love. Everyone can suffer and everyone can love."[31] In relationships we experience the pain and the gain of suffering, regardless of our desire to avoid it. In simplest terms, relationships are ongoing and obligated, even those that are dormant from time to time.

2. Enabling give and take. It is ironic how the pain and challenges of relationships are also often salved and held together through the redemptive power of—relationships. The two paradoxical components of relationships that serve to make them functional are lubricant and glue. They can reduce friction so we don't overheat or rupture as we interact with others, and conversely relationships can hold things together when they seem inclined to fly apart. Robert Putnam refers to the lubrication function as "bridging" by including and moving among those who are different. The glue function is "bonding" that holds like-minded groups together while excluding those who are different (think tribes, clubs, political parties).[32]

The paradox, of course, is that these two functions—bridging and bonding— could hardly be more different. We can all think of examples where the power of a relationship helped lubricate interaction between parties with very different views to enable them to cooperate in order to achieve a common goal. Divorced parents who may be very hurt, angry, and at odds can be brought together by the friction-reducing love for their children. A trusted relationship can be instrumental in greasing the skids to get past rough spots. As Nobel Laureate Kenneth Arrow said: "Trust is an important lubricant of a social system. It is extremely efficient; it saves a lot of trouble to have a fair degree of reliance on other people's words."[33]

Trust is one of the most powerful forces for efficiency and productivity. Think of all the steps required to assess the trustworthiness of a service, such as which school our kids attend, which mechanic fixes our car, or which financial planner we invest with, when compared to a strong recommendation from someone you totally trust. The trust that comes from our relationships keeps us from getting stuck and is one of life's great shortcuts. Learning who and how to trust is one of the most crucial skills we develop.

Trusting someone with whom we are aligned and in agreement is relatively easy. What's harder is to trust someone when a relationship has been broken. Yet the ability to reconnect with those in broken relationships presents some of greatest opportunities and upsides. Relationships remain our best hope to both bond us with our like-minded groups and bridge the gap with those who are different. As Putnam said, what the world needs is more relationship WD-40 and Super Glue®.

THE WISDOM OF LINCOLN

Abraham Lincoln's treatment of the rebel armies at the end of the Civil War, as told in *Team of Rivals*, provides a primer in the lubricating power of trust:

> With the war drawing to a close, Sherman inquired of Lincoln: "What was to be done with the rebel armies when defeated? And what should be done with the political leaders, such as Jeff. Davis, etc.?" Lincoln replied that "all he wanted of us was to defeat the opposing armies, and to get the men composing the Confederate armies back to their homes, at work on their farms and in their shops." He wanted no retaliation or retribution. "Let them have their horses to plow with, and, if you like, their guns to shoot crows with. I want no one punished; treat them liberally all around. We want those people to return to their allegiance to the Union and submit to the laws."[34]

3. Serving and being served. In relationships, the need to give and receive is crucial. We often start out serving and caring for others out of a sense of concern and need to help them. Yet we have learned that in helping the other person we are helped as well. Robert Zajonc, who was a psychologist at Stanford, found evidence that tutoring—a natural role for older siblings—benefits the one teaching more than it does the student. "Explaining something to a younger sibling solidifies your knowledge and allows you to grow more extensively," he said. "The younger one is asking questions, and challenging meanings and explanations, and that will contribute to the intellectual maturity of the older one."[35]

The need to be served is one of the innate needs we carry around inside. The experiences of fine dining, first-class air travel, upscale shopping, health spas, stadium suites, and limousine service are testament to our need to be served. Money may not buy you love, but it will buy you service. The root word of *serve* meant to be a *servant*, and at one time it referred to someone who had given up his or her rights. We are served when someone gives up her needs or rights in deference to ours.

It is surprising to me how strong this third element of relationship development is—our need is to serve and to be served by others. My experience with Patricia makes the point. (Note: The names and some related information in this and subsequent stories have been changed to protect anonymity.)

I was at my weekly Tuesday night budget coaching session with Patricia, a resident at the homeless ministry where I volunteer. In the previous week, she had indicated that she had only $105 to get through the week. The money had to buy a week's worth of food for herself and her two young kids, cover the cost of doing laundry, make an installment payment on one of her outstanding traffic tickets, pay for school supplies for her oldest daughter, and cover any miscellaneous things that might arise.

The look in her eyes told me immediately that things had not gone well. "Tell me about it," I asked. A pause. "I ran out of money on Thursday," she replied. Silence. "Well, I got really depressed . . . so a friend and I went to Chili's." I was doing the math in my head as she was telling me her story, thinking that maybe she spent $20. I asked her what the damage was: $32. Thirty-two dollars was nearly a third of her budget for the week.

She read my expression and continued. "We had burgers, fries, desserts, and we left a nice tip." *Nice tip . . . you don't have enough money to buy milk for your children's cereal,* I thought to myself, hoping I had concealed my disappointment. She was deflated and so was I. It was a bad decision made worse by her awareness of exactly how the $105 needed to be stretched to make it through the week.

Her words rang in my head: "I got really depressed." I imagined Patricia and her friend getting various forms of positive attention and respect from a warm and caring server. What Chili's was really selling that night to Patricia was someone who would serve her.

Patricia blew almost a third of her weekly budget for the honor of being served. But it didn't end there. Recall the last part of Patricia's statement: "and we left a nice tip." Not just a tip, but a nice tip. As broke as she was, Patricia reciprocated.

Relationships are about being served and serving, taking care of both sides. The word *integrity* means to keep all the parties "whole." It is a dance with a certain rhythm and flow where each participant gives up rights in order to honor the other. When this dance gets out of balance, a couple of very destructive roles surface—victim and persecutor.

When it works it has an element of reciprocity. Ben Beltzer, the retired founder of the Interfaith Housing Coalition, calls it a ministry of mutuality—where the helper and the helped each has a need and each is served. Robert Putnam contends that this reciprocity is a key part of social capital.[36] The more the focus on giving is mutual, the greater the value and the stronger the relationship. The more the focus on taking is mutual, the more the relationship is at risk.

Reciprocity allows each of us to contribute to the relationship. As Pope John Paul II said, "Nobody is so poor that he or she has nothing to give, and nobody is so rich that he or she has nothing to receive."[37]

Reciprocity—serving and being served—is the polar opposite of captive relationship. This is why retention rates are often poor indicators of loyalty, where customers or employees are held hostage and have few options to leave. Captive relationships are a contradiction in terms. The absence of freedom removes the autonomy to choose and poisons the relationship over time—for customers, employees, spouses, friends, and others.

John Ortberg illustrates the power of serving through attention to small things:

> My great-aunt, for many years a widow, fell in love when she was in her seventies. Obese, balding, her hands and legs misshapen by arthritis, she did not fit the stereotype of a woman romantically loved. But she was—by a man also in his seventies who lived in a nursing home . . . In trying to tell me what this relationship meant to her, my great-aunt told of a conversation. One evening she had had dinner out with friends. When she returned home, her male friend called, and she told him about the dinner.

He listened with interest and asked her: "What did you wear?"
When she told me this, she began to cry: "Do you know how
many years it's been since anyone asked me what I wore?"[38]

John Gottman has found that for a marriage to survive, the ratio of
positive to negative emotions in typical encounters has to be at least five to
one. Call it a spirit of yes, serving, or can-do—it all boils down to leading
with yes instead of no.

A sales or service representative who responds to a request in a begrudging
way, saying "yes" against their will—like waiving the late fee but not the
dirty look—results in the worst of both worlds: taking on whatever risk or
loss is inherent in the yes, while eliciting all of the ill will of no. In essence,
the spirit of yes affirms and serves the person, even when you have to say no
to the person's request.

PAY ATTENTION, PLEASE

When reciprocity drives a relationship, it propels the relationship
forward. It can be as deep as a lifelong love among partners or as
shallow as a business transaction such as serving a fast-food meal
to a customer in 30 seconds or less. In either case, the relationship
means each party is attentive to the other—both in what is spoken
and what remains unsaid. I've heard it expressed this way: Love
is knowing the song in someone else's heart and remembering the
words when they forget.

Paying attention is a powerful form of serving that builds attachment. Research has revealed that one of the most powerful development mechanisms for babies is the amount and type of eye contact
they receive.[39] Starting in infancy with that need for eye contact, we
spend the rest of our lives noticing if others are noticing us—if they
are paying attention. As Jennifer Szetho states, "I believe that most
children at one time or another just want to know that their parents'
eyes light up when they walk into the room."[40]

4. Grace and accountability. The final and perhaps most underrated component of positive relational attachment is the marriage of grace and accountability. Both are needed for the same reason: We struggle to live up to our ideals of relationship. Grace and accountability are support mechanisms to prop us up when we stumble.

Grace may come dressed as recognition, mentoring, advising, trusting, forgiving, any number of other things—the soft stuff that lets us know that we still matter in spite of our performance. Accountability comes in the form of feedback, coaching, criticism, truth telling, standard setting, conflict, and even punishment—the hard stuff that is just as valuable as grace.

For me, grace is best defined as unmerited favor or forbearance provided by someone else. Borrowing from the root of the word *relationship*, it bears or tolerates beyond what is deserved. Because we are all fallible, our relationships cannot thrive without grace—they simply suffocate without it. It is a special form of reinforcement that serves as oxygen when we are losing our relational breath in the midst of challenges and missteps. A recurring phrase I have heard homeless mothers use to describe the feeling of grace when they first walk into their own nicely furnished apartment (provided by the interim housing ministry), with a fully stocked refrigerator and pantry and fresh flowers on the kitchen table, is "I can breathe again."

About a year ago my wife, Linda, was to present to an association of professionals who serve people with HIV. She arrived early and walked into the partially filled room. As she headed to the front, she heard a voice say, "Mrs. Hall, do you remember me?" Toya walked up to her and in a quiet voice said, "I was a resident at your homeless ministry." Linda, not fully recognizing Toya because she had gained several needed pounds and was no longer emaciated, responded vaguely, "Yes, so good to see you."

They moved over to a corner. "Remember, you made me leave." Linda's memory was stirred and she recalled the gut-wrenching decision late on a Friday to put Toya and her nine-year-old daughter out because Toya had gotten back on crack cocaine. It was made more difficult because Toya had used up all of her relationships, which left her with no friends or relatives to rescue her or take her in.

Toya continued. "You know, putting me out was the best thing that has ever happened to me. I was on the streets for a few days, but I finally hit bottom and checked myself into detox and rehab. Nothing short of being back on the street could have gotten me there. I am now working as a drug counselor and I have been sober for two years. Thank you for what I know was a very difficult decision. You tried so hard to help me, but what ended up being most helpful of all was evicting me from the program."

Linda has often shared that story with volunteers and case managers there to remind them that the accountability for abject failure is sometimes a form of "disguised" grace—and what is needed most of all.

Accountability, on the other hand, holds truth up to us like a mirror and makes us responsible for the gaps relative to goals, standards, and boundaries in our relationships. We may go to great lengths to avoid accountability and judgment at times because it can point out areas where change is needed. Sometimes the accountability we need the most comes from those we really dislike, distrust, or fear. We have all rejected advice from those we don't care for—to our own detriment. At other times, it may come to us in much more attractive packaging, but still we are not open to hearing it. As the authors of *Primal Leadership* have stated, "Comfort in relationships brings discomfort in accountability."[41]

Willingness to confront issues honestly in a loving way, for the benefit of the relationship, is one of the most profound forms of accountability. Grace that cultivates and accountability that prunes contribute to strong and healthy relationships.

* * * *

Relationships and the value they create do not exist in a vacuum; they are contained and connected in a web called community. Whether it's a family, workplace, church, school, political party, or club, each community presents the potential for multiplied value and also power—both positive and destructive—depending on how the relationships within it interact.

An old African proverb states a simple but profound truth about community: "If you want to go fast, go alone. If you want to go far, go together." As a society obsessed with going fast, we are now stumbling in our effort to go far. Only through relationship and community—our most valuable possessions—will we be able to attain that goal.

Chapter 6

Relationship Math: Looking at the Dollars and Sense

Fortune magazine's "100 Best Companies to Work for in America" earned more than four times the returns of the broader market over the prior seven years.
—*Stephen M. R. Covey,* The Speed of Trust[1]

T he summer after my senior year in high school I passed up an offer to sign a baseball contract with the New York Yankees for a four-year university athletic scholarship instead. In an intersquad game the following summer, I tore the labrum muscle in my left shoulder, ending my pitching career and launching my three-year janitorial career cleaning the football dressing room to keep my scholarship. Nonetheless, I remained a student of baseball. A statistic that always fascinated me is that the difference between a .250 hitter who struggles to stay in the major leagues and a .300 hitter who has a shot at the Hall of Fame is about one to one and a half hits per week. If you watch every at-bat in the six or seven games played each week, you probably can't discern the difference without keeping records.

Relationships are no different. My earlier personal examples of Buzz Newton's relational support of my family or Neiman saleswoman Cynthia Kelly's relationship management are but isolated examples of the broader value relationships contribute to society.

In my company, we worked with a range of clients (stores, branches, and nonprofit entities) to measurably strengthen their customer relationships. We set goals and tracked the actual impact of enhanced relationships over time. For example, a typical bank branch might have 5,000 customers averaging $100 in annual profit contributions for an annual total value of $500,000. We would ask the bank's staff members what would happen if, among the group, each week they could net one elevated relationship—convert an average customer into a top-tier contributor of $1,100 profit per annum by gaining substantially more business from that customer. Time and again, we found that highly committed teams were able to do that over time, leading to a 10 percent, or $50,000, improvement in annual performance. Repeated over five years, profitability could be lifted by $250,000, or 50 percent! Conversely, the net loss of one key relationship per week destroyed a similar level of value.

At the homeless facility where I volunteer, we don't always make a home run (or even a hit), but around 65 percent of families who arrive broke, homeless, and unemployed have historically left with a job, enough savings for a deposit on an apartment, and a cushion of up to three months of cash reserves. Among the 70 to 80 families the teams serve each year, our aim is to positively influence at least one family a week in getting a job, making better spending decisions, or dealing with a difficult family issue. A recent analysis by a university MBA team quantified the value to society for each family moving from homelessness to independence (meaning government services are no longer required, individuals are able to pay taxes, etc.) to be in the range of $75,000. In my 10 years as a volunteer, more than 500 families have moved to independence. If these numbers are even in the ballpark, that adds up to more than $37.5 million.

To positively touch or enhance one relationship per week—individually or collectively, in our communities of family, friends, or colleagues—is a powerful goal. It won't fix the world, but over time it can make a major-league difference.

We cannot consistently reach financial or social advancement in an economy of broken or neglected relationships. For better outcomes, we must be a part of building better relationships. Relationships are not just nice to have; they are essential for functional and productive outcomes. Until we, as a society, better understand the math and economics of relationships, we will struggle to make the necessary commitments to revalue and restore them.

We live in an economy that runs on relationships. McKinsey estimates that over two-thirds of the U.S. economy is influenced by word of mouth. While only 14 percent of people believe what they see, read, or hear in advertisements, 90 percent believe endorsements from their friends and acquaintances. Word of mouth is valued 50 percent higher today than in the 1970s. [2]

Voting provides a tangible example of relational impact. Research conducted at Yale showed that direct response including mail and phone calls had little effect on voter turnout. However, in-person canvassing raised turnout from 44 percent of registered voters to 53 percent. If the person contacting the voter was someone the voter knew, the response rate was four times higher. [3]

There is an interesting symmetry: Businesses are measured on translating goods and services into money (revenue, profits, market capitalization) and social services are measured on translating money and other resources into good (people helped).

Financial and human (including customer) capital, each of which represents stored and potential value, flows to and is invested where it is welcome and treated well—where relationships work and are productive. Conversely, it flees where it is treated poorly. Treatment is a key variable in relationships. Most of us—in our efforts, our skills, and our money— exercise decisions based on how we are treated. Treatment can mean return on investment to a shareholder, pay or respect to a worker, product or customer service performance to a patron, care to a child, attentiveness to a patient, housing assistance to a homeless person, or trustworthiness to a spouse. Poor or ineffective treatment over time has consequences: divorce, defection, dysfunction, distrust, and loss of loyalty and commitment. Further, economic and social value migrate to healthy, productive relationships while excess costs and destruction accumulate around broken relationships. Consequences matter.

This takes us to the crux of the issue. *Relationship capital has surpassed financial capital as the scarce, crucial resource that now dictates whether societies either advance or regress.* Heretofore, capitalism and our global economy have created unprecedented capacity to fund and produce goods and services. Yet now relationship metrics in just about every segment of society have declined to the extent of constraining us.

For a society focused on measuring results and struggling to assign appropriate value to the softer side of relationships, it is important to look more closely at the financial and social economics and value of relationships. Previously we looked primarily at the cost; we'll now look more broadly, with particular focus on the return.

The *American Heritage Dictionary* defines *economics* as "the social science that deals with the production, distribution, and consumption of goods and services and with the theory and management of economies or economic systems." When we talk about the economics of relationships, we are talking about the role they play in the production, distribution, and consumption of business and social good—or how missing or broken relationships limit business and social gain and contribute to loss. We will begin with the world of business and then examine social services.

The Business Economics of Relationships

Most people think in order to succeed, you just have to have a strong background in finance or marketing. . . . [But] business at the end of the day is about relationships with people.

—*Angel Cabrera, president, Thunderbird School of Global Management*[4]

The business economics of relationships are well documented and compelling.

- Customers with a strong, committed relationship to a company are 49 percent more likely to remain a customer and almost twice as likely to recommend a retailer to friends and family than when the relationship is weak.[5]

- Local business units scoring above the median on both employee and customer engagement metrics are, on average, 3.4 times more effective financially than units that rank in the bottom half on both measures.[6]

- Trust constitutes 60 percent of the criteria used to choose *Fortune* magazine's "100 Best Companies to Work for in America" (cited earlier).

- Engaged employees help create engaged customers who are generally more loyal, and loyal customers are more profitable.

In other words, as a CEO once stated to me, "As a general rule, the value of a franchise is highly correlated with the quality and number of relationships it has."

It's very simple: most and best relationships—in number and quality—win. Figuring out how to get the next sale or solve the next service issue will yield much less than it could if, in the process, relationships are not also developed and advanced.

CUSTOMER RELATIONSHIP ECONOMIES AND DISECONOMIES

If relationships are so valuable, why have business organizations not placed greater emphasis on them? There are many reasons, but at the core, the business world has struggled to recognize and quantify fully the economies of scale that strong relationships create. Over time, nothing is more inefficient than broken or frayed relationships, and nothing is more important than value-creating relationships. In my first book, *Streetcorner Strategy for Winning Local Markets*, I summarized our research regarding the inordinate contribution of certain customer groups and the costs of others:

- 3 to 5 percent of customers generate about half of the profit.

- 50 percent of customers are not profitable.

- 60 percent of cross-sell efforts (sales of additional products) are not profitable; they generate more costs but not greater relationships or revenue.

- 60 to 80 percent of frontline time is consumed by customers generating only 20 percent of the profits.[7]

While these numbers vary across industries and businesses, what is clear is that a small percentage of top relationships contribute a large part of the profits; a large group of lesser relationships contribute little; and a small group of tumultuous relationships absorb a disproportionate amount of costs. In addition, generating new customer relationships can take more than three times as long as getting business from existing ones.[8] It all demonstrates just how much impact the varying types of relationship can have on the bottom line.

Once customer relationships fracture—just as in families, politics, or religion—they are difficult and expensive to salvage. Replacing customers requires significant investment, and developing the relationship typically occurs over a period of time. Maggie Mui, a small-business director at Wells Fargo, describes their approach: "We really don't use cold calling a lot. I don't think that is the best way of getting business; starting with a relationship is usually the best."[9]

THE ECONOMICS OF CUSTOMER EMOTION

Positive customer emotion is at the core of customer value. Yet, because relationships are often messy, expensive in the short run, unpredictable and difficult, business strategies often have been designed to avoid this key human attribute. In removing human judgment, error, and emotion from the equation, organizations have sacrificed customer commitment. When emotion is sucked out, relationship goes on life support and eventually dies.

In recent years as organizations came to better understand customer profitability, they saw just how many of their customers were unprofitable. A certain disdain often emerged regarding these customers, yet often, organizations failed to recognize their own culpability in undermining formerly healthy, profitable relationships.

Research by such firms as Forrester found customers increasingly in need of an advocate.[10] The very need for advocacy implies just how distant, bureaucratic, and rules-based many organizations have become. Relationships between organizations and many of their customers devolved from mutualistic to indifferent to adversarial.

Ironically, the oppressive control so many organizations have exerted over their customers creates a real opportunity to stand out for providers who put their customers first. For example, McKinsey quantified the economic opportunity of putting the customer first in a North American bank by examining the powerful link between customer loyalty and value creation in the differences of its branches. They found a more than 50 percent gap between the best and the worst branches, based on share of wallet and customer retention. The distinguishing feature of its better-performing branches was "the ability to turn moments of truth to advantage by solving problems effectively and a willingness to emphasize the financial needs of customers over the branch's own sales priorities. Growing loyalty toward the bank translated directly into a bigger share of the customer's wallet."

They cite similar research on and analyses of European banks that expose a typical 20 percent gap in share of wallet between customers who have positive experiences and those who have negative or mixed ones. They go on to conclude that the aggressive behavior of some sales teams at leading banks generated negative moments of truth and has conspicuously weakened the reputation of these institutions.[11]

Putting the customer first is not just a strategic or cognitive decision—it is deeper and more meaningful. In a study by Pine and Gilmore, customers reported their greatest sense of sacrifice—getting less than they wanted—for not being rewarded for the size and duration of the relationship.[12]

For the longest time, emotion has been a dirty word in the lexicon of business. Business was rational, quantitative, cold, unbiased, and fact-based. We used phrases like "it's just business" to rationalize decisions and actions that had negative emotional results. Yet the research reveals that emotions play a large role in the revenue and profit-generating relationships central to growth—in addition to good and rational decision making:

- Consumers feel before they think, and "feelings happen fast."

- Emotions are more immediate and act as a gatekeeper.

- Believability "is based on a gut feeling."

- Emotional connections help "jump over the fear of being sold to, which is rampant in today's skeptical marketplace."

- Emotional connections lay the groundwork for loyalty. [13]

So much of what we do in business is based on information, analysis, and rational thinking, yet emotion is the major gatekeeper and decision maker for customers.

If it is not personal, then it is not a relationship. It costs real time and resources to create a relationship. Often we are much clearer on the cost of relationship—time, expense, pain—than on the cost of not having one. A Gallup survey found that shoppers who were emotionally connected to a supermarket spent 46 percent more than satisfied shoppers who lacked an emotional bond with the store."[14] It's one of the reasons Trader Joe's stores, with their mom-and-pop feel, sell an estimated $1,750 in merchandise per square foot annually, more than double the figures of their main competitors.[15] Satisfaction is a positive, but emotional commitment is what really pays.

Starbucks's meteoric rise came from dressing up a highly commoditized product (coffee) and creating an emotional relationship with its customers. CEO Howard Schultz defined the company as not being in the coffee business (serving people) but in the people business serving coffee.[16] Starbucks went to great lengths to create a customer experience that was relationship-centered. J.D. Power reported that in most industries customer experience accounts for more than half of customer commitment—65 percent in wireless providers, 64 percent in restaurants, and 56 percent in retail banks.[17] When Starbucks added drive-through service and began selling packaged products in supermarkets, some customers felt relationally abandoned.

Customers in dire need can turn into lifetime customers if the provider gets it right. If not, they walk away and tell everyone else about their negative experience. Heightened or charged moments elevate emotions, opportunities, and risk. Bureaucratic rules and policies of traditional organizations are usually obstacles to seizing these opportunities and translating them into positive emotions. Organizations committed to strong customer relationships must develop the capacity to see and address these challenging relational episodes and the attendant emotion as opportunity.

THE ECONOMICS OF EMPLOYEE RELATIONSHIPS
AND WHAT DRIVES THEM

As discussed, customer relationships crucial to business results are driven by employee relationships. For most industries, employee costs represent an organization's largest expenditure and its greatest opportunity. In recent years, actions to lower human resources costs—often the disposable asset of choice—has had a bruising and deleterious impact on employee relationships and the value they produce. Many organizations moved their customer-service functions, especially call centers, offshore to lower labor costs.

Yet now a number of U.S. companies are moving those functions back to the United States.[18] According to CFI's 2010 Customer Satisfaction Index, customer satisfaction for calls perceived handled inside the United States was 20 percent higher than those handled outside the United States. In fact, there is a growing segment of customers who refuse to be served by foreign agents due to language and related cultural issues. These concerns impair customer relationships and undermine the brand. Some organizations now promote the fact that their customer service/call centers are U.S. based.

Several years ago a number of organizations like Dell changed their service staff to temporary or contract status in an effort to reduce costs.[19] While temporary employees may have the skills for performing their jobs, they have little or no benefits and so are generally not as committed as permanent workers. As a result, Dell and a number of others have reverted to using permanent employees.

Employee relationships and the experience that goes with them are also crucial to sales effectiveness. McKinsey research shows that sales experience is one of the two most important factors in gaining sales from customers, and that a high-performing sales force can impact sales by 8 to 15 percent.[20] Of the characteristics most valued by customers, empowered employees— those who have autonomy to act on behalf of customers—have the greatest impact on customer relationships by helping them solve problems instead of following rigid scripts and procedures.[21]

Just as employee relationships are key to keeping customers for life, employee relationships are also crucial to product development and innovation—crucial in today's global economy. Often this requires partnering and working in teams with those inside and outside the department or even the company. In a study by IBM, 75 percent of participating CEOs indicated that collaborating was very important to innovation, even though they found it hard to implement, given today's relational challenges.[22]

A real key for management is cultivating employee engagement—much different than gaining compliance. Gary Hamel laments that management traditionally has been very good at extracting employee discipline and tapping employee intellect but not so good at encouraging the traits that required more emotional engagement like initiative, creativity, and passion. In fact, he states that in many cases, those traits were seen as not very helpful in an organization. He concludes: "Creating wealth is going to depend on employees who, every day, are willing to bring those gifts to work. You can command obedience, diligence and intellect, but as a manager, you can't command creativity, initiative and passion . . . people either choose to give to their work or they don't."[23]

Human assets are very dynamic and have a will of their own. Increasingly, employees want to have a say in how they apply themselves. The consulting firm Booz Allen found: "Companies that focus on 'relationship-centric' activities while emphasizing growth opportunities and adapting to a changing marketplace are more likely to be top performers than those companies that focus on decreasing working capital, supply chain efficiency and spinning off non-core businesses."[24] The question is how to build stronger employee relationships and engagement.

One of the important opportunities in enhancing worker performance is in addressing worker burnout. Barsade and Ramarajan at Wharton found that when employees don't feel the organization values or respects them, they tend to experience higher levels of burnout.[25] Demanding, rigorous work environments demand a lot of energy. Effective leaders can be a key source of energy resupply—like refueling an aircraft in flight.

If much of the past 50 years of organizational life has been about wringing the emotion out of business, more recent research shows just how valuable emotion will be going forward. A Booz Allen Hamilton–Kellogg School of Management research study found that how employees felt about working in an organization accounted for 20 percent to 30 percent of that business's performance. And 50 percent to 70 percent of respondents reported that the organization's leadership created the atmosphere to help them work well.[26] (Chapter 13 is devoted to this topic of relational leadership.)

Positive relationships are not just about being nice. They are about the combination of grace, compassion, and conflict mixed with high ideals, standards, and accountability. Some of our most productive relationships have been with bosses who had very high expectations and provided tough feedback without crossing the line into negative territory. Conversely, truly negative relationships can be disabling. Each of us has experienced an environment or boss that caused us to perform way below our capability.

In the fall of my freshman year at Oklahoma State University I played baseball with Jim, a junior college transfer who was also beginning his first year in the program. He was a catcher with a terrific arm, quick feet, and a sweet swing. When winter brought cold weather we worked out in the pitching and hitting cages in the basement of the basketball arena. Often these sessions involved pitchers throwing full-speed to batters, and to protect the pitchers from hard-hit line drives back at them, a four-foot screen was placed just in front of them.

One winter day, Jim was catching me in one of those basement sessions and threw the ball back to me low, hitting the screen. Our head coach, one of the winningest coaches in the country, and who had a national reputation for being hard-nosed and tough, jumped all over Jim for the errant throw. About three throws later, Jim made another low throw that hit the pitching screen. Again, the coach, who would exert pressure on players in practice to toughen them up for game situations, yelled at and ridiculed Jim. Over the next few weeks, Jim's throws got worse and worse and the coach was unmerciful in his wrath. By the time we moved outdoors for spring practice, Jim had devolved into a shadow of his former self. I will never forget the last time Jim caught at practice. As he stood up to return the first pitch back to the pitcher, he moved his arm forward to throw it back and then stopped before releasing it. He tried again—repeatedly—and finally on his eighth pump he threw the ball back about halfway to the pitcher, not even reaching the pitching screen. The coach, who was right behind the batting cage, no longer yelled but in a quiet voice told

Jim to take off his catching equipment and turn it in. Jim cleaned out his locker and left school. I never saw him again.

While his malady, often called the "yips," can have many causes, it appeared to me that this coach, who was so successful at helping a number of players excel under high-pressure situations, brought out the worst in Jim. All of us as parents, friends, and bosses will have our own relational leadership failures, but the bottom line is that those who can bring out the greatest good from the greatest number of people will create the greatest gain.

The Social Economics of Relationships

The world's great disease is not poverty, it is loneliness.

—Mother Teresa

Social economics encompasses feeding the hungry, housing the homeless, protecting at-risk children, healing the sick, treating the addicted, and training the unskilled. Compared to business, some of the outcomes are harder to quantify and see, but the language of economics still applies to the production of social good.

Mother Teresa's quote hits hard. Our core underlying problem is not financial, it is relational. Loneliness is a potent force that often is used as a weapon to oppress and control: think solitary confinement, one of the most powerful punishments that can be meted out. Isolation is often used in abusive relationships to disable, render powerless, and destroy the self-esteem of those controlled and persecuted. Separation from the herd is the first step of the predator in vanquishing its prey.

Whether forced or chosen, prolonged separation and isolation can have a very detrimental effect on people. The Unabomber, Ronald Reagan's would-be assassin John Hinckley, the shooters at Columbine, the perpetrator of the massacre at Virginia Tech—all were isolated and alienated individuals who committed heinous crimes. As humans, we are made for relationships. Isolation and loneliness over time can become dangerous and dysfunctional.

Many of the social problems we experience can be attributed to a lack of relationships. Not only is the toll high on our lives, but so is the amount of money we spend to address these social ills. While there is an ongoing debate as to whether we are spending too much or not enough on the right programs, the expenditure is a significant commitment. Regardless of your politics, this expenditure makes an incredible difference in the lives of millions and the cost is projected to do nothing but grow. Regardless of how much we spend, we will be socially bankrupt until we address our lost relationships.

THE CURRENCY OF *GOOD* GAINS MOMENTUM

Affiliation to a religious community is the best predictor of altruism and empathy: better than education, age, income, gender or race.

—**Jonathan Sacks, chief rabbi, United Hebrew Congregations of the Commonwealth**[27]

After years of focus on financial worth, personal performance, status, and celebrity, there are signs that the pendulum of focus on social good may be navigating its way back to the forefront. We have seen real social leadership in the form of impressive financial contributions from the likes of Ted Turner, Bill and Melinda Gates, Warren Buffett, Oprah Winfrey, and T. Boone Pickens. Celebrities like the late Princess Diana, Bono, Angelina Jolie, and others have supported social causes and spawned a new term: celebrity philanthropy. We have seen organizations such as Susan G. Komen for the Cure and Habitat for Humanity gain greater notoriety, and we have seen the emergence of social entrepreneurs using business skills and innovation to address societal issues.

According to Pew, even before the downturn of the economy in 2008 there had been a growing priority to address the needy in our society but little agreement on how to do it. One camp seems to advocate spending more money, with little insight into how it will help, while the other resists that, with little in the way of alternative solutions for the problem.[28] This divide points to two big relationship issues: (1) the growing partisan rancor that is making it harder to reach agreement on appropriate action, and (2) the limited impact money, technology, programs, policies, and knowledge will have on solving our social problems.

Susan Mayer at the University of Chicago calculates that doubling parental income would have an insignificant impact on the dropout rates of children, have a small effect on reducing teen pregnancy, and barely improve child outcomes overall.[29] Mayer strongly admonishes against promulgating policy that will destroy social bonds. We cannot spend or legislate our way out of a spiraling problem primarily rooted in relationship dysfunction. Relationships—not money—are the crucial missing link.

THE ECONOMICS OF FAMILY RELATIONSHIPS

The social and economic health of our society begins with family relationships. Strong, functioning families are much more likely to be net contributors through the taxes they pay and the positive influence they exert on others. Remember Klausner's quote, "The most important healthcare system in the world is a mother"? If someone needs to be convinced to see a doctor, follow a diet and workout regimen, or get rid of bad habits, relationships are the most powerful sources of positive influence. An example is the recent research that shows that the ability to quit smoking is heavily influenced by friends and family: If your spouse quits smoking, chances increase 67 percent that you will be a nonsmoker; if your friend quits, your chances of not smoking increase 36 percent.[30]

It is hard to overstate the importance of relationships in our lives. A Pew Research Center study reported that 73 percent of respondents spoke at least daily with a family member who didn't live in the same house. A large majority (72 percent) reported being "very satisfied" with their family life while 45 percent turned to a family member for advice and 22 percent turned to a friend, neighbor, or coworker.[31] One of the most defining experiences that lead to homelessness is banishment from one's final safety net of family or friend(s) due to a breakdown in that relationship (assuming such a relationship existed to begin with). Those with the most, best relationships win, and those with the least, worst relationships are impoverished.

THE ECONOMICS OF MARRIAGE

Marriage begets interesting economics. As referenced earlier, research at Ohio State University found that, on average, a couple who marry and stay married accumulate nearly twice the personal wealth per person as someone single or divorced. Those who divorce lose, on average, three-fourths of their own net worth.[32] Research by Olson and Turvey illustrate how this happens: "Because married couples can pool their economic resources, they tend to be wealthier. In fact, the median household net worth for a married couple is $132,000 compared to $35,000 for singles, $42,275 for widowed individuals, and $33,670 for divorced individuals."[33]

Think about that. The cost for a busted marriage is that you potentially give up 75 percent of what you own. That's a steep price to pay. When you consider that the United States has one of the highest divorce rates in the world, that's an incredible loss of wealth attributed to relationship "costs." Think about how much work is involved over a number of years to equal 75 percent of your net worth—after taxes.

In some cases, the very effort of working too hard and long to get ahead contributes to the breakup of the relationship, which then costs more than the incremental work gained. Even for those inordinately driven by economic gain, neglecting your relationships is a poor economic strategy.

Marital status—more specifically, not being married—is strongly correlated with higher unemployment. According to the Bureau of Labor Statistics, the unemployment rate for married men in 2008 was 3.4 percent, and the rate for widowed, divorced, or separated men was more than double that at 7.1 percent. For those who never married, it was 11.0 percent—more than triple the rate for married men.[34]

For married women, the unemployment rate was 3.6 percent, while for widowed, divorced, or separated women it was 5.9 percent. For those who never married, it was 8.5 percent—more than double the rate for married women. This pattern of significantly higher unemployment for the unmarried holds consistently across ethnic groups. Regardless of cause or effect, stable marital relationships translate into significantly greater employment and thus economic advantage.

It's a fact: People who marry, and stay married, do better financially.

Marriage is an efficient arrangement. In the world of business we would say it creates economies of scale. In fact, research shows that if poor single mothers were married to the actual fathers of their children, two-thirds would immediately be lifted out of poverty.[35] Two can live together considerably cheaper than they can live apart: one house, one kitchen, perhaps even one car. In a world concerned about the environment, the consumption footprint for couples is much smaller than for people living alone.

In addition, there are other synergies. David Popenoe, codirector of the National Marriage Project at Rutgers University, says, "People become more economically productive after they marry. They work harder, they advance further in their job, they save more money, and maybe invest more wisely. That's because, one can speculate, they are now working for something larger than themselves. They are working for a family."[36] It seems that marriage or highly committed relationships require us to sacrifice some of our selfishness, and as a result bring out the best in us. In the wry words of Jack Nicholson to Helen Hunt in the movie *As Good as It Gets*, "You make me want to be a better man." We are not fully open for emotional and intellectual business until we are connected.

Recent research indicates that married men fare much better than single men in life expectancy and in health, leading to fewer dollars spent on health care. For males, being happily married is the equivalent of being 18 months younger in chronological age; for women the effect is approximately six months younger.[37] This is another indicator of the cost of single men's isolation.

Better health, a cleaner environment, more disciplined investing, task specialization, and a backup income in the event that poor health deprives a primary earner are all tangible advantages of strong and positive relationships. Certainly it bears pointing out that marriage itself does not cause all of these beneficial outcomes—whether single or married, people predisposed to more committed, permanent relationships have a higher likelihood for these outcomes.

Additionally, the economic cost of divorce is borne not just by the family but also employers. The productivity cost due to divorce is estimated at $6 billion annually, with one study finding an average of four weeks lost the year following an employee's divorce.[38] Divorce also costs taxpayers $30 billion a year due to increases in the costs of housing, food stamps, bankruptcies, problems with children, and more.[39]

Whether or not they end in divorce, broken marital relationships have significant and lasting social and economic impact. For many at the lower end of the socioeconomic scale, the cost of busted relationships will keep them trapped in poverty. Inequality of family relationships leads to inequality of economics. It's a never-ending downward spiral.

The decline in the level of relationship commitment (between the parents and to the child) is producing a level of economic, social, and emotional disadvantage that defies solution. According to the *New Yorker*, "by the time most low-income children start elementary school, they're already so far behind their more privileged counterparts that the educational gap is almost unbridgeable."[40] The primary reason is that their family relationship is damaged or nonexistent.

Foster care provides a microcosm of just how destructive broken family relationships can be. Foster care is the quintessential example of children being taken from parents who are unable or unwilling to love and care for them. Foster parent motives vary from strong, genuine concern for parentless (relationship-less) kids to purely financial. In many ways it combines two unfortunate elements of relationship: abandoned kids and parents for hire. Although foster care provides basic needs, too often the absence of parental love combined with transient care for children already in distress leads to a predictable set of results: As many as 40 percent of adults who were foster children are either on welfare or in jail. Approximately half graduate from high school, compared to 78 percent of the population in general.[41] The consequences of weakened relationships between the parents and children are clearly devastating.

According to research from the University of Wisconsin, mothers who believe their relationships with their partners are likely to last make greater investments in their children's future by the choosing healthier maternal behaviors.[42] Additionally, increased duration decreases the likelihood of poor health behaviors. Sexual partners who lack commitment to each other, yet have kids, increase the odds that both parents and children will suffer economic, health, and social loss.

The facts are clear, but the subject is not easy to talk about because it involves issues of bearing children, religious beliefs, personal choice, individual values, and freedom. No one likes to be told what to do. Yet, there are very real social, emotional, and economic outcomes that impact us all. The Manhattan Institute's Kay Hymowitz pointed out that, as a society, we don't do an adequate job educating young women about the benefits of waiting until marriage to have children. Instead of worrying about stigmatizing single mothers, we need to provide them with the facts about the positive benefits of raising children in a marriage, so they can make an informed decision.[43]

There are innumerable examples of single-parent homes raising smart, educated, successful, and productive children. Single-parent households are not new, nor will they ever completely disappear. Often, generous friends, relatives, teachers, and other individuals and groups step in and help with this challenge. However, what we have never faced in the past is the number of children without the economic, emotional, and social resources and support needed: Their plight has become an epidemic. It is one thing to deal with this relationship challenge as an exception and quite another to deal with it as an intended, manufactured plague. A system designed to handle these circumstances as an exception will melt down when forced to handle them as the norm.

Increasingly, medical research is able to isolate some of the physiological effects of our declining social relationships. Dr. Bruce Perry has looked extensively at the impacts of relationship on the development of the brain in children. He found that as children spend more time watching television instead of interacting with other children, they become "relationally impoverished." He states that far too many children grow up without the number and quality of relational opportunities required to fully organize the neural networks to mediate important socioemotional characteristics such as empathy. The human brain is designed for life in small, relationally healthy groups. He concludes that, unfortunately, many trends in caregiving, education, child protection, and mental health are disrespectful of our biological gifts and limitations, fostering poverty of relationship.[44]

Considering that 32 percent of our schoolchildren are overweight or obese, with the attendant health issues, empty relationships may be influencing our kids to fill up with the wrong stuff.[45] The structure of eating has become less relational: more fast food, eating alone or absent an adult, little portion control. Strong, tenured, functional relationships are not optional—they are required.

THE ECONOMICS OF CARE

On a recent trip to Italy we took a guided tour of some of the Roman ruins. My wife, who runs a ministry for the homeless, inquired about how the government deals with issues of homelessness in Italy today. Our guide commented about how impressed she had been on an earlier visit to the United States with the level of government care provided to the homeless. She said, "In Italy, we would never be able to garner that kind of government support for the homeless—here they are taken care of by their family." My first reaction was to feel good about the commitment we make in this country to those in need. My second reaction was to think how much more personal "family" is over institutions and how much of that experience we have abdicated.

Some alternative organizations have had success in employing strong personal relationships to carry out valuable caring functions. Alcoholics Anonymous is an example of a "relationship-rich" organization that requires relatively little structure or expenditure and yet has touched millions in a life-changing way. According to the *Wall Street Journal*, the nonprofit Alcoholics Anonymous reported total revenue of $13.2 million and total expenses of $12.9 million in 2005. Founded in 1935, AA is a decentralized collection of nearly 53,000 groups in the United States alone, each autonomous and without any membership list.[46] Do the math: $243 per group per year in the United States—talk about a low-cost and high-value solution.

AA runs on a currency more powerful than money, structure, or size. It runs on a set of committed, personal relationships. AA is not in the business of providing health care or housing—which tend to be much more capital intensive—but it stands as a potent, purpose-driven, locally run organization in dealing with difficult problems like addiction. It demonstrates that relationships not only have the potential to heal but they also have the ability to form into organizations that can do great things. It is outside the paradigm of many leaders today to take on a huge problem like alcoholism around the world, with an annual budget of $13 million.

The point is that we have come to see capital, technology, large staffs, and sophisticated organization structures as key to dealing with the social problems we face. Yet often the very institutional nature of these large, bureaucratic organizations robs them of the relational capabilities necessary to provide care and healing.

Several years ago John McKnight wrote a book entitled *The Careless Society*. While controversial, his basic contention about outsourcing of care is hard to refute:

> The most significant development transforming America since World War II has been the growth of a powerful service economy and its pervasive serving institutions. Those institutions have commodified the care of community and called that substitution a service. As citizens have seen the professionalized service commodity invade their communities, they have grown doubtful of their common capacity to care, and so it is that we have become a careless society, populated by impotent citizens and ineffectual communities dependent on the counterfeit of care called human services. Service systems can never be reformed so they will produce "care." Care is the consenting commitment of citizens to one another. Care cannot be produced, provided, managed, organized, administered, or commodified. Care is the only thing a system cannot produce. Every institutional effort to replace the real thing is counterfeit.[47]

Care by its very definition is provided by someone who is in relationship—not a stranger. In this country and around the world we have become efficient at manufacturing things usually by reducing the human component—either by automation or by rote processes or procedures. The move to a service society might look to a visitor from Mars like some higher authority demanded institutions to divest themselves of as many relationships as possible.

Research in intensive care units has validated that the comforting presence of another person not only lowers the patient's blood pressure but also slows the secretion of fatty acids that block arteries.[48] A significant body of research supports the notion that close, personal relationships—whether spiritual in nature with one's God through prayer or meditation, or with others—can lower blood pressure, reduce stress hormones, and slow the heart rate. Relationships alone will not heal those in need, but their caregiving presence surely aids our health.

Our society's transition to trained health care and social service professionals or experts leads to a second, related outcome. As reliance on professionals grows, the responsibility and accountability of the local community declines—as institutions step up, local individuals and groups step back.

McKnight's comments about social service professionals parallel Bogle's financial "agent" society. Whether they're agents of personal financial management or health and human services, the institutional representatives have served as leaky vessels and callous stewards of our health and our wealth.

The larger our social problems, the more money we spend, the more institutional the solution, the more those working on the problem become an industry—the less the role of relationship and local community. Large problems that cry out for relationship are too often addressed by institutions utterly unable to deliver them, further feeding the very cause of the problem that fuels their growth. As providers strain to meet the social services demand, the pressure increases to become more efficient. Human costs in social service organizations usually represent the largest single cost and are the most vulnerable when budgets come under pressure—so it is usually the human, relational resources that get cut.

We now live in a world where relationships and true care are increasingly rationed at home and work, in our government, and in faith-based organizations. The wait time for Section 8 subsidized public housing often ranges from several months to several years. Private-sector systems such as nursing homes avoid taking the very sick because of the unreimbursed cost of their incremental care needs.[49] The public sector tends to ration care based on how much time you have to wait and the private sector tends to ration care based on how much money you have to spend.

* * * *

This cycle would be really depressing except for the fact that the solution is so straightforward and something we have demonstrated we are capable of. Relationships are certifiably a potent force for our development and healing.

In baseball a hit-and-a-half a week differentiates success from failure. In our daily relationship at-bats at home, at work, in politics, and in faith, we can and must elevate our game. That will be the focus of section IV of this book. But first we must understand the underlying root causes that have fed our relational demise.

CAUSES OF RELATIONSHIP DECLINE: UNINTENDED CONSEQUENCES OF OUR ADVANCEMENTS

How did relationships come to be viewed as disposable?

If we are to reclaim relationships, we must first understand key causes at the root of their decline. No one started out to unravel our relationships; that unraveling has been the unintended consequence of advancements. We can't retreat to the past, nor should we. Rather, we must understand how we got here so we can repurpose and redirect our efforts going forward.

That is the focus of this section. We will examine four macrotrends central to much of our progress and, unintended, much of our relational pain: (1) extreme consumerism, (2) extreme commercialism, (3) faceless technology, and (4) extreme institutionalization. Though much has been written on each topic individually, what has been missing is the narrative of how these four macrotrends, collectively, conspire to undermine our relationships and fray the fabric of our society.

Chapter 7

Extreme Consumerism: Me Is Killing Us

What unbridled capitalism is to economics, unfettered indi-
vidualism is to human relationships.

—*David B. Myers*, The American Paradox:
Spiritual Hunger in an Age of Plenty[1]

T he first time I laid eyes on her there was an immediate
disconnect. This tall, beautiful young lady carrying a Gucci
bag and wearing Prada shoes surely did not belong at
this place. She looked much more like a Junior League volunteer,
and, armed with a business degree, she spoke with confidence and
clarity. Yet here she was, waiting to meet with my partner and me at
the homeless ministry where we volunteer as employment coaches.
Kecia had been married to a high-profile professional athlete, lived in
a beautiful West Coast home, and drove an exquisite car. Her circle
of friends consisted of celebrities, and she had worked part-time as
a local television personality. Anything that money and fame could
acquire, she had. And what she "had" became who she was.

She and her two young daughters were at the shelter to escape
an abusive relationship. Kecia's husband got cut from the team, and
the nonguaranteed portion of his contract went away. He began to
threaten her (and the girls), frequent clubs, and gamble and drink
heavily. Rather than leave, Kecia just spent more on clothes and

jewelry. The couple depleted their money, missed several house payments, and were threatened with foreclosure. Her husband became abusive, on more than one occasion in front of the children. Late one Saturday night, in the midst of a melee, Kecia grabbed the girls, put them in the car, and left the town and the state. She drove halfway across the country and eventually showed up at the homeless ministry.

Her ambition was to get back into television, but those jobs were few and far between. The first job she found here paid very little, and she could barely buy food for her kids. She longed for the things she had left behind: the nice home, car, clothes, and her celebrity status. Initially, she held tightly to the symbols that reflected who she had been—the handbag, the shoes, the designer jeans. A couple of times she bought expensive items she could not afford to fill the hole in her identity. But over time, she made the journey to separate who she was from what she had or consumed. Her new community was devoid of celebrities and well-heeled movers and shakers. They were other homeless mothers who, for the most part, had never had anything, plus the staff and volunteers at the ministry. Yet this new community was rich in caring relationships central to Kecia's development.

Eventually, she got a job at a bank, and while her new lifestyle is not extravagant, she is back on her feet and doing well. She currently volunteers at the ministry and willingly shares her journey of redemption from an identity based on possessions to one built on the wealth of relationships.

If we seek to understand the underlying source of our relational decline, there is no better way to begin than to look at the new, rising star of the 21st century—"ME." An ever-expanding culture of consumerism has encouraged us to focus on ourselves: what we want, what we deserve, what we are entitled to, and having it our way. As we have focused more on ourselves, of course, we have focused far less on our relationships.

In many ways, Kecia's story is our story. The *American Heritage Dictionary* defines consumerism as "attachment to materialistic values or possessions." This definition looks at the vagaries of equating personal happiness, success, and even identity with selfish interest and the purchase and consumption of material possessions. Is it true that we are what we consume? In *Trading Up*, Michael Silverstein and Neil Fiske concluded that in America individuals derive their self-esteem not from what they produce but from what they indulge in: $4 cups of coffee, lease payments on cars that exceed their monthly rental payments, $3,000 sets of golf clubs—all on salaries that can ill support these luxuries. The goal? To feel "more rich."[2]

We have been encouraged to consume, and we have obliged in a big way. In 2007, prior to the 2008–2009 recession, consumer credit increased 5.5 percent, the fastest clip in three years, reaching a total of $2.52 trillion.[3] In recent years, while consumer debt reached an all-time high, our personal savings reached an all-time low, traveling into negative territory:

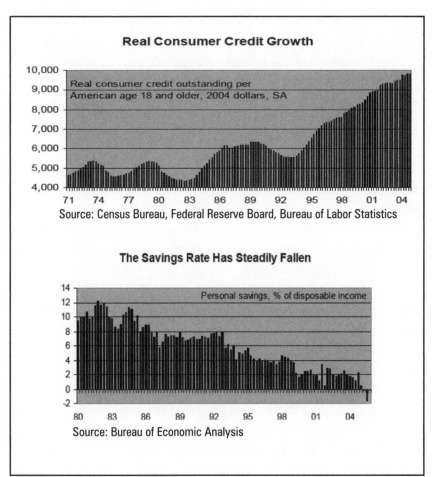

Real Consumer Credit Growth

Real consumer credit outstanding per American age 18 and older, 2004 dollars, SA

Source: Census Bureau, Federal Reserve Board, Bureau of Labor Statistics

The Savings Rate Has Steadily Fallen

Personal savings, % of disposable income

Source: Bureau of Economic Analysis

ME AND MONEY

Extreme consumerism and the accompanying excess of leverage by consumers, government, and corporations (especially Wall Street banks) played a significant role in the financial meltdown and chaos of 2008–2009. The average consumer debt exceeded $9,700 (not including mortgage debt) per individual by the beginning of 2006. The long-term trend has been greater short-term spending and consumption. Post-2008–2009, the pendulum swung to the other side, resulting in a greatly reduced level of spending that hamstrung economic recovery—yesterday's excess created today's scarcity. Our personal spending pales in comparison to recent government spending, where demand for government services greatly outstrips our supply of payments. The U.S. deficit rose from $8 trillion in 2006 to $14 trillion in 2011, which equates to $91,000 per member of the U.S. working population (total projected at $20 trillion by 2016).[4,5] Obviously the consumer debt per individual is dwarfed by the federal debt.

Professor Ronald Inglehart at the University of Michigan found that among the 80 societies he studied, without exception, the higher the level of economic development of a society, the greater the value of self-expression.[6] We have become a society that has often translated this self-expression into purchasing decisions that are a stark reminder of the dramatic difference between the haves and the have-nots.

There have always been big differences between the rich and poor, but that gap has grown in recent years. Greatly enhanced electronic communication means that those with less are much more aware of just how different their lives are from the very wealthy. How we consume has become a significant factor in our relationships; it both unites and divides us. Consumerism represents a triumph for freedom: freedom of markets, freedom of production, freedom of consumption, and freedom from oppressive governments. We are big on freedom. Our country was formed on an explicit appeal to freedom and has flourished because of its productive power.

Most of us are strong believers in the marketplace and celebrate the abundant choices it presents us with. Yet, as consumerism has grown and become extreme, there is the growing risk of unintended consequences that make us relationally selfish and enslaved in a way that deprives us socially, emotionally, and eventually even economically. Self-absorbed and obsessed by what we merely want, we leave little room for what we desperately need— our relationships.

The Rise and Fall of Me

Narcissism and entitlement among college students are
at an all-time high.

—Jean Twenge, lead author of the largest study
ever on narcissism

Few would argue that we have become a society that is increasingly about self. Wherever you turn—the media, personal experience, even university research—pretty much all the indicators are flashing "me." The largest research study ever conducted on generational changes in narcissism reported that 30 percent more college students showed elevated narcissism compared to 1982, making current college students more narcissistic than baby boomers and Gen Xers. In addition, the average college student scored nearly as high on narcissism as the average celebrity from a sampling of actors, musicians, and reality TV stars. According to Jean Twenge, the study's lead author, narcissists are characterized by excessive self-admiration, vanity, and a sense of entitlement. They are more self-centered, materialistic, and attention seeking than the average person is, and they often experience the breakdown of close personal relationships with others. Recent technology such as Facebook and YouTube, whose slogan is "Broadcast yourself," only fuel this trend. [7]

NARCISSISM FEEDS HUMILIATION AND STARVES HUMILITY

As consumerism, self-focus, and the desire to be entertained have become extreme, our amusements often take on a particularly heartless and vicious quality. Our love for drama has made a spectator sport out of humiliating losers, and the popularity of reality television is a prime example. Wanting to win is not the same as trying to beat and demean others.

Elevating yourself is not enough; there is a need to push others down. Those humiliated or excluded may respond by seeking to humiliate others. Much gang violence centers on the relational issue of respect, and small actions of disrespect can lead to shootings. Incidents such as shootings at schools or in the workplace often involve individuals who have been isolated or humiliated by others.

Humiliation is simply a public version of contempt. Humiliation and humility come from the word *humus*, which refers to the soil or ground. To humiliate refers to pushing others down by being condescending or contemptuous. Humility, on the other hand, refers to lowering one's self and thus providing a relational space for healing, growth, and relational development. Nothing squelches humility like humiliation. The end-zone dance performed after the touchdown often shows up the opposition and says "It was all me," which does nothing to build relationships with the linemen who made the block to get you there. The vitriol between liberal and conservative, or religious and secular, often seeks to humiliate. We are a society steeped in an unvirtuous cycle of feeding humiliation and starving humility, which begets more humiliation.

Why does one in three women in America report being physically or sexually abused by a spouse or partner during their lifetime, and one in six report being raped?[8] Why are gangs so prominent? Why does terrorism continue to thrive? Why are religious groups spending so much time disputing the role of women? Why is bullying such an issue? These are all signs of relationship power struggles and dysfunction—and they greatly impact those who are excluded. The narcissistic focus on self leads to a culture of relationship humiliation.

This intense focus on self can have devastating relational consequences and helps explain the reason many of us "bowl alone," have fewer close friends, and treat marriage as disposable. It also provides insight into why CEO and executive remuneration has gotten so out of hand.

Our youth may be self-absorbed, but the "me generation" is a term coined to describe baby boomers. Benjamin Barber's description of that generation's icon, Bill Clinton, sums it all up: "He has the narcissist's gift of making conversation about him feel like conversation about you."[9] Narcissism comes in many shapes and sizes. We all know people, or know of people, who are great as the star attraction but do not know how to be a part of the group; people who drink in adulation but cannot pour themselves out to others. We have observed these traits in others and (if we are honest) ourselves. Addiction to self does not bring out our best—it hollows us out.

It is this inherent human weakness that makes the siren call of a consumer society so insidious. As with individuals, when our whole society succumbs to extreme self-focus, it leaves our collective relational state weakened and inhibits the development that only comes from relationships.

Alone and Longing for Belonging

Our focus on self has left us isolated and lonely. Best-selling author Rick Warren begins his book, "It's not about you."[10] He goes on to say that after a generation of "me-ism," where we have glorified the individual over the community, we are left with an epidemic of loneliness. Whether by choice or necessity, most of us do not remain in the same community for life. The more we move around, the lonelier we become. The result is a longing for belonging.

This view is supported by extensive research. The massive amount of communication enabled by new technologies and a changing culture do not appear particularly fulfilling. Compounded by puberty that comes earlier and marriage that comes later, it appears that while the volume of communication is up and the number of choices has increased, this abundance has not translated into much fulfillment. We may have hundreds or thousands of Facebook friends, but few true relationships.

RADICAL INDIVIDUALISM

It is no accident we are a self-focused, self-reliant society. The United States is a country founded and designed on the ideal of individual freedom. You might say that as a country, we evolved from an abusive relationship—religious oppression, exorbitant taxes, lack of social and economic advancement possibilities. Our country was founded by people so enamored with the ideal of opportunistic freedom they were willing to risk everything to come here.

Our history is replete with rebellion against authority, beginning with the revolution to gain freedom from England's rule and taxes. With a large ocean between us and our mother country, and a large sprawling expanse from east to west, there was both great desire and great opportunity to escape the established group. The move west allowed citizens to experience new levels of freedom and opportunity—at the expense of Native Americans. The Constitution, the Bill of Rights, decentralized state governments, and the Supreme Court all reinforced the freedoms we enjoy today. Anyone who has traveled abroad knows that our country's reputation is both admired and criticized. Our outspoken, independent, and capitalistic ways have rankled many and given us a reputation of brashness, often well deserved.

Several centuries and many iterations later, this founding culture of personal freedom has made for a very attractive marketing platform. "Have it your way"; "Because you are worth it"; and a thousand other "me-me-me" messages drive home the idea that ultimate happiness comes from freedom and getting your way. We stopped eating family meals together and riding in the same car, opting instead to follow our own schedule and tastes. We made sure our kids each had their own computer, phone, TV, and room. By focusing on what we alone wanted, we ended up alone.

We have a new extended life phase for many that is devoid of intimate relationships. At the prime of sexual potency, increasing numbers of younger people are living apart. A number are living together but because commitment is missing or ambiguous, the relationship is limited.

Part of the price and the reward of community is yielding self in favor of others. There is much evidence that in the microrelational decisions of life, as a society we are increasingly coming down more on the side of self and less on others. One tangible is family size, where parents choose the number of family members they will have. Daniel Henninger of the *Wall Street Journal* notes, "Every nation in Europe has a birth rate below replacement, opting for material well-being over the sacrifice of raising two or more children." (Of all industrial nations, only the U.S. birth rate exceeds replacement—by a small margin, and it is heavily driven by our immigrant Hispanic population.)[11] Pew Research reports 41 percent of Americans felt that having children was "very important," down from 65 percent in 1990.[12] Regardless of the reasons, this fits the larger trend of fewer relationships.

Choosing Property Over People: The Wealth-Status-Celebrity Sweepstakes

Consumerism is about choosing things over people, and the facts are not encouraging. By 2005, the average American consumed 6,840 pounds of "stuff" per year, an increase of almost 20 percent since 1998. In 1991, we each purchased an average of 34 garments per year; by 2004, that figure had reached 57 per year—more than a new garment a week.[13]

Clearly, advertisers have become adept at tapping our inadequacies as a means to get us to purchase (the topic of the next chapter). But our relational demise makes us particularly vulnerable to marketers in three ways.

First, our deficient state of relationship makes us susceptible to ads for things to purchase that could fill that emptiness. Shopping addictions, severe obesity, alcohol and drug abuse are extreme examples of potential fillers and poor substitutes for large empty spaces vacated by our relational demise. The more that "stuff" becomes our focus, the less space is left for the very relationships we so desperately need. It becomes a vicious cycle.

Second, for some people, material things are seen not only as the main source of self-worth but also as key relationship enablers. In a material, cool world, not having the right material belongings becomes a powerful sign of unworthiness and an obstacle to relationships with people considered more desirable. The link between what you have and who you are has always existed, but it has gotten stronger and more dysfunctional in this age of consumerism. It is hard to overstate the relationship strain this creates. What if my breath, appearance, tastes, car, phone, or soft drink are unacceptable in the eyes of those with whom I wish to be in relationship? I will be humiliated. Low self-esteem becomes an internalized view reinforced by weak relationships.

AN IPOD OR AN EDUCATION

Consumerism also affects what children aspire to. Oprah Winfrey explains how this impacted her decision to build her school for impoverished teenagers, the Oprah Winfrey Leadership Academy for Girls, in South Africa instead of the United States. "South Africa's students show a greater need and appreciation for education, even though American schools are free. I became so frustrated with visiting inner-city schools (in America) that I just stopped going. The sense that you need to learn just isn't there. If you ask the kids what they want or need, they will say an iPod or some sneakers. In South Africa, they don't ask for money or toys. They ask for uniforms so they can go to school."[14]

While the focus on material things would appear to be worse for those in poverty, it is just as pronounced or worse in families that are focused on money as the ultimate prize—the rich. I heard a school administrator remark recently that rich kids and very poor kids have the same issues: parents physically or emotionally absent because they are obsessed with money. A recent study showed that upper-middle-class girls were more likely to suffer from depression than other socioeconomic groups by a margin of three to one.[15] Affluent parents are more likely to see the child they wish they had rather than the child they have. When the message from parents is that markers like status-enhancing actions and performance trump the value of the bond between that parent and child, the relationships becomes undone and the children suffer.

Third, it is not just about wealth. Anything that can provide fame and celebrity—intellectual prowess, beauty, athletic accomplishment, artistic fame, or even zany behavior—can produce powerful currency. It is telling how these factors are playing a larger role in selecting marriage partners and in admissions to institutions of higher education.

Money and marriage provide a striking example. A nationwide survey asked: "How willing are you to marry an average-looking person that you liked, if they had money?" Two-thirds of the women and half of the men responded that they would be "very" or "extremely" likely. Women in their twenties who indicated that they would be willing to marry for money also indicated that they expected to get divorced.[16]

While money and power have always been attractive, it appears that we are at a point in our society where money has become more dominant in the most intimate of all relationship institutions—marriage. Divorce is seen as the tool of choice to dissolve a relationship that was founded on a false relational base: "for better but not worse, in health but not sickness, and for richer, not poorer." Anyone with wealth has to wonder if his or her relationships are about human connection or money. Conversely, a segment of older men have increasingly been more than pleased to spend their fame, power, or fortune to purchase a "trophy wife." Too often, when it comes to family issues, we have come to behave like consumers.

Whether caused or correlated, as our societal wealth has increased, so has the rate of divorce. At the bottom of the socioeconomic scale, the absence of money may be a deterrent to getting and staying married, but the increase in wealth at the top has its own relational peril. Becoming richer can make us psychologically poorer.

Our extreme consumerism has made us a throwaway society that discards not only "stuff" but relationships as well, in ever-increasing volume. The psychological scarring for being a poor nobody in a society consumed by wealth and notoriety continues to grow and fester. Some have speculated that the aftermath of the recession of 2009 might change all of that, but so far the evidence is scant. We cannot develop the stronger relationships we so desperately need by clinging to this wealth, status, and fame merry-go-round.

REJECTING TRADITIONAL OBLIGATIONS AND COMMITMENTS

When looking out for No. 1 becomes the basic value for individuals, as well as for corporations, traditional community becomes far more difficult to sustain.[17]

—*Alan Ehrenhalt,* The Lost City

This individual focus has affected not just family life, but our roles in business, politics, and religion. No one could have imagined the way capitalism would grow and prosper. It has produced tremendous wealth while contributing to stable government and a free society that is still a source of inspiration. Yet it also has contributed to a society that has less value for loyalty, especially in the workplace. Radical individualism at the expense of solidarity hurts character, as loyalty, mutual commitment, and pursuit of longer-term goals take a backseat.

Self-focus has undermined traditional obligations and commitments in many of our institutions. Too often the exit strategy in business and the prenuptial agreement in marriage are the first thought in creating a union. People seem slower to make, and faster to ditch, traditional obligations involving longer-term commitment and sacrifice. In many ways, investors have become short-term traders who focus on short-term gain.

Likewise in the spiritual realm, faith today has become much more about me and mine rather than us and ours. In response to an earlier age when the state defined religion, we have traveled to the opposite side of the continuum, emphasizing self over relationships and community. We have to ask: Can we survive and flourish where self-focus pervasively and severely marginalizes and undermines relationships and community?

THE SEPARATED SOCIETY: GOING FOR
RELATIONAL À LA CARTE

In our pursuit of extreme consumerism—gated communities, electronic garage door openers, air-conditioning that closes our windows, backyard decks instead of front porches, alarm systems, private swimming pools, private schools—we've lost our villages and become strangers. Today nearly one in five people changes his or her address each year.[18] In both leaving and staying we have become more separated, with a value for privacy and security. As David Brooks puts it: "The story of American development is the story of a contest between privacy and community. . . . In the 1980s, exurbanites wanted golf courses in prestigious new communities. But by the mid-1990s, they wanted Starbucks, Kinko's and walking trails—community spaces to combat isolation."[19] Consumer appetites may take the person out of the community, but they don't take the need for community out of the person.

Much has been written about the reemergence of the town square. Part of Starbucks's success has been the ability to provide a variation on the town square—what they've called a "third place," neither home nor work. Notice the irony—this local place and experience has been brought to us by the quintessential consumer organization. Advertisers these days include words like home, community, local, neighborhood, relationship, and other relational words to tap into our need for community. Is capitalism great or what?

As we have become a more physically separated consumer society focused on self, we have become more compartmentalized emotionally. We have become very creative and at times naïve in attempting to get the benefits of relationship without the commitment and accountability that might encumber us. In so many aspects of our lives we have learned to live à la carte: to disaggregate the whole into just the pieces we want, thus fracturing the relationship into pieces. "You can have it all" has morphed into "you can have only the part you find desirable or attractive."

There are many examples of how our society has altered relationships for convenience. For instance, there is a dramatic increase in the number of couples cohabiting or living their sexual lives as if married, but legally, financially, and perhaps even emotionally they remain single. They have disaggregated the sexual relationship from the other aspects that are associated historically with marriages. As discussed earlier, this arrangement is less stable for couples and their children.[20]

There are many ways to remove relationship from sex. Old ways like prostitution and newer ways like hooking up during college and sex among casual friends—friends with benefits—all have the common denominator of keeping things casual and fun for the short term, but not committed. Yet, this nonrelational arrangement often feels empty. For example, one study found that 41 percent of college students are profoundly upset about their own behavior of "hooking up," with 22 percent using words like "dirty," "used," "regretful," "empty," "miserable," "disgusted," "ashamed," "duped," and "abused."[21]

Similarly in the workplace, contract or temporary worker agreements between employees and employers sacrifice mutual obligation for such things as health care, vacation, sick time, two weeks' notice before leaving a job, and agreement to work solely for the employer. The two sides determine specifically what they want from the other side and design an à la carte arrangement to get that. Either side can generally terminate the agreement at will. The growth in contract workers reflects a value for greater freedom to reduce labor costs and commitment in a rapidly changing world.

While the common thread in these examples is the freedom to get just what you want when aided by new choices, certain obligations in the relationship have been sacrificed. We have not only acted like consumers in regard to the products and services we buy, but also often in our personal relationships, politics and voting, and how we practice our faith. Yet a loss of relationship has contributed to a growing sense of isolation, lack of support, and hidden costs.

There is no free lunch when it comes to relationships. They require an investment of time, money, and energy. When those relationships are messy, don't last, or become dysfunctional, we come to question relational investment in our future dealings. Yet, as we have focused on self we have opted for the benefits of freer relationships without fully calculating the cost.

The more we become focused solely on ourselves and our desires, the more we fall into the trap of lust. Lust is where desire—be it for sex, for money, or even for status—roots out love and relationship. Lust is relationally devoid of love; it's an addictive desire that seeks to separate gratification or pleasure from its "personal" source. It results in little or no regard for the other person(s) involved. When sexual desire becomes the sole basis for one of the parties in a relationship, the relationship cannot be sustained. When desire for freedom and independence become the primary desire between a worker and an organization, rooting out commitment and loyalty, the relationship suffers. Likewise, when price becomes the only consideration for a customer, the relationship is sacrificed.

As a consumer society, we have become so consumed by self and just the part we want, that we have lost sight of the importance of wholeness. We have become masters of breaking things down and inept at putting them back together. Unfortunately, the part left out is often the emotional, relational component we most need, leaving us empty and unfulfilled.

Abandonment: The Most Consequential Form of Separation

Extreme consumerism and self-absorption is about more than just buying stuff. It is a mind-set that leads to extreme separation. While all forms of separation can be painful, abandonment is extreme. The idea of being abandoned and left alone is one of the hardest feelings to endure. Being abandoned by a mother, dumped by a romantic interest, fired from a job, or being ignored by a salesperson all have one thing in common: Someone whose attention you want has said no to you. Loyalty is about relationship; disloyalty is about abandonment.

When we become fixated on ourselves to the exclusion of others, it usually means that someone is being abandoned. Abandonment is the most extreme form of separation because it never stops taking. It is particularly damaging for children. Being left, ignored, and rejected is one of the worst things that can happen to a child. A substantial amount of research indicates that children can tolerate physical abuse better than being ignored. As harmful as physical abuse is, it is even harder to mount a defense for the absence of interest. Abandonment is the act of communicating to someone that they are worthless, therefore making them invisible.

Mary Eberstadt focuses on the feelings of abandonment and hurt in the music of bands like Korn, Linkin Park, and Disturbed. Those group members were raised during a time of extensive divorce and latchkey upbringing.[22] Fractured family relationships and a significant sense of abandonment extracted a price on future relationships—dysfunction often reproduces itself. It is easy to see that fractured relationships are both a cause and an effect of focus on self. For those severely disappointed in relationships, a focus on material, nonrelational things seems safer and more predictable.

Certainly lyrics to a younger generation's music have almost always been a tool for rebellion against authority figures in general and specifically against parents. Yet, as Eberstadt points out, the lyrics from more recent years have a different message than those of the boomer generation: "Baby boomers and their music rebelled against parents because they were parents—nurturing, attentive, and overly present (as those teenagers often saw it) authority figures. Today's teenagers and their music rebel against parents because they are not parents—not nurturing, not attentive, and often not even there." It is interesting that parental neglect rather than parental oversight dominates the message. A generation led by victims of abandonment is unlikely to be a pretty sight. Yet a whole generation of children now becoming parents has experienced firsthand or vicariously, through others, the disabling effects of selfish parental neglect and even abandonment.

Abandoned children make for an abandoned society. Gangs thrive because fatherless boys seek affirmation. Absent the relationship of a strong loving father, society manufactures synthetic versions that may meet some needs but also may prove dysfunctional and costly for those who join.

As segments of men have exercised greater freedom from the responsibility of child rearing, they also have become less integral to the family. Historically and in most cultures, it is considered taboo to purposely raise a family absent a husband or father. Yet this trend continues to grow. The freedom to father children without being in a direct relationship with them increasingly marginalizes the importance of the father's role and thus of men in general, while placing incredible strain on single mothers. Men who trade their family relationships and responsibility for sexual freedom abandon their families, and in return the family abandons them. The result is estrangement that is very hard on children and ultimately hard on those males.

Certain groups of males lash out at women in response to the abandonment they have experienced themselves—their actions represent a futile attempt to receive the attention they covet and the relationship they need. In fact, you can make the same case for some of the terrorist activities in societies where historically men have had a dominant role. The ability of women to succeed without a male present contributes to a sense of diminishment and abandonment. Whether from threats of gang warfare in the Western Hemisphere or sectarian violence in the Middle East, the rise of violent societies is an unfortunate way to heighten the relational role of males.

Abandonment of those relationships that rely on us for support is the utmost in self-absorption and leads to very destructive outcomes individually and for a society.

* * * *

Our consumer society now indulges us beyond what is healthy. In many ways, we are stuck in an abusive relationship with ourselves, hollowed out by our selfish wants while starving to be filled. Perhaps it is time for us to gather the things that really matter—our relationships—and leave the state of extreme consumption and self-absorption. It worked for Kecia, and it will work for us.

Chapter 8

Extreme Commercialism: Influence for Sale or Rent

Wherever I looked there were words trying to take my eyes from the road. They said, "Use me, take me, buy me, drink me, smell me, touch me, kiss me, sleep with me." In such a world who can maintain respect for words.
—*Henri Nouwen,* The Way of the Heart

In the late fall of 1995, I was in Seattle meeting with a large banking client, KeyBank. One of their marketing executives invited me and our regional manager to a Seattle SuperSonics basketball game. That night she shared that the bank had just signed a deal to rename the arena KeyArena. They would be paying $1.3 million a year for these rights even though they had no ownership in the actual building or the team. At the time, I thought to myself that it was probably good marketing, but something about it seemed off: commercial form over business substance. In the years since, naming rights have taken on a life of their own.

For KeyBank, the deal took an unexpected turn in 2008, when the Sonics left for Oklahoma City and left the bank with a contract through 2010—but no NBA basketball team. But comparatively speaking, Key did pretty well. The Houston Astros signed a 30-year, $100 million naming rights deal with Enron, which they wound up buying back when Enron fell. A partial list of organizations who paid big bucks for stadium or arena naming rights but eventually became bankrupt, bailed-out, or bought-out includes: Delta Airlines, Fleet Bank, Air Canada, Quest Communications, Bank One, Pacific Bell, American Airlines (in Dallas and Miami), and Citibank. Citibank agreed to pay $400 million for a 20-year deal to the New York Mets. Some folks derisively concluded post-bailout that Citi Field should really be named Citi Taxpayer Field.

In my gut, naming rights have most often struck a false chord, promoting a relationship that is not quite authentic: There is less than meets the eye. A name does not a relationship make. Typically there has been no ownership relationship between the naming company and the building or the team. When trouble arises, the name is quickly removed and often resold to the next highest bidder. It isn't a marriage and sometimes is little more than a one-night stand: form but no substance.

In his book *Cowboy Ethics: What Wall Street Can Learn from the Code of the West*, James Owen lists a couple of principles that are instructive in identifying commercialism that crosses the line.[1] The first one is: "Ride for the Brand." In the ways of ranching, a brand was a relational device to show ownership and belonging of livestock, but over time it came to mean what you stood for: the quality of your cattle, the competence of your ways, and your character. It was not purchased, traded, or spun; it was earned and it was real. Riding for the Brand meant signing on to a relationship—an identity—that was deeper and more substantive than simply taking a job and a name. Our society hungers for authentic, true brands—a cause, a company, a leader—worth riding for.

The second principle is: "Some Things Are Not for Sale." Reputation is one of those things, and a purchased one is not reputable. Commercial attempts to purchase influence, credibility, and favor for things that have no business being for sale ultimately undermine stakeholder relationships. Never in my memory have people trusted so-called purchased credibility less.

* * * *

A first cousin to consumerism, commercialism becomes extreme when it plies industrial-grade efforts to falsely purchase and monetize relationships. If consumerism is all about individualistic wants and desires to acquire, commercialism is all about the exercise of commerce to convert tangible and intangible things such as beauty or happiness into products and services sold for profit. Commercialism, which has contributed greatly to the bounty most of us enjoy, veers off track and becomes extreme when truth is sacrificed for selfish, short-term, one-sided monetary gains. Truth is the first casualty of extreme commercialism: Deception, in producing, marketing, selling, transacting, or financial accounting, supports extreme commercialism that feeds on and then devours relationships.

So much of the relational carnage we have discussed thus far is rooted in unintended consequences of commercial excess and overreach: children are more interested (to quote Oprah) in the type of sneakers they are wearing than in education; advertising and promotion of fast food, snacks, and sugar-coated everything contribute to a national obesity problem; television and computer games replace family interaction as a source of learning and socialization; commercial-grade celebrities like Lady Gaga and Christina Aguilera set the standard for attire and behavior of young girls; your brand of car, clothes, or sunglasses announces your status or worth; Wall Street banks make money promoting products they are privately betting against; nontransparent financial contributions dominate access to and influence of politicians who spend most of their waking hours raising funds for the next election; and churches preach a gospel of monetary wealth as a primary benefit of faith.

Extreme commercialism is more than just a "business" problem or an accomplice to extreme consumerism. It promotes the false message that financial gain is the ultimate end rather than a potent means. My sister has a saying that provides a more accurate perspective: "Any problem that money will solve is not a very big problem."

The excesses of commercialism go beyond liberal versus conservative or religious versus secular. Extreme desire for commercial gain lobotomizes our collective conscience and cannibalizes the very relationships that are the foundation for commercial success.

THE GROWTH OF COMMERCIALISM

The genesis of our commercial age began as an economic experiment and blossomed into one of the true marvels of the modern world, producing a living standard hard to fathom just a century ago. Keep in mind that for 99,800 of the past 100,000 years most everyone lived on $400 to $600 per year (in today's dollars)—just above the subsistence level. One hundred years ago the average American workweek was 60 hours compared to less than 35 today, 6 percent of manufacturing workers took vacations compared to 90 percent today, and the average housekeeper spent 12 hours a day on laundry, cooking, cleaning, and sewing compared to about three hours today.[2] Even in the worst of times, specifically, in the Great Depression of the 1930s, income levels only fell back to where they had been just 20 years before that.

The rise of the middle class created unparalleled gains for the masses, even though some have fared much better than others. It has been said that socialism made people equally poor while capitalism made them unequally rich.

Winston Churchill pointed to the risk of economic gain run amok when he said, "We are stripped bare by the curse of plenty." We now have converted just about everything under the sun into metrics of money; everything has a commercial value. We know the hourly wage value of our time, the cost to send a child to private school, and the lifetime monetary value of a college education. Corporations recite the fully loaded annual cost of hiring an additional employee and the average annual customer profitability. Governments quantify the daily cost to incarcerate a prisoner or to shelter a homeless person. Commerce has become the dominant cultural force, and its language is money.

Yet many of us question the undue and untoward influence of money and wealth in our society. Philosopher Jacob Needleman made this observation: "Money makes us unjustifiably feel that we're better and more important than we really are. When money can make you feel humble, then I think it's really useful."[3] Feeling better and more important than we are, because of our financial means, usually results in someone else feeling worse and less important.

Commercialism is a relationship game that involves owners, managers, workers, customers, suppliers, partners, and competitors in an effort to create gain. Extreme commercialism crosses the line to exploitation. When relationships are bought and sold, they eventually crumble. When placed above all other interests, extreme commercialism can be more than financially risky, it can be life threatening.

We have learned this lesson the hard way—as we cope with batteries that contain unsafe levels of toxins,[4] wallboard that causes unsafe breathing conditions, and cars that are recalled because of safety shortfalls.

Extreme commercialism doesn't just impact our health. The level of disparity between the haves and the have-nots is also damaging our relationships, especially when we glamorize winners and demean losers.

The finance sector provides a vivid example of the shift. According to Thomas Philippon at New York University, the value added by finance—a measure for calculating the industry's contribution to the economy—rose from 2.3 percent of gross domestic product in 1947 to 7.7 percent in 2005.[5] With all of its contributions, modern finance has become a hog at the trough of commercial enterprise: In 2004, the finance sector provided almost half the corporate profits in the United States (compared with no more than 16 percent from 1973 to 1985[6]), at a time manufacturing slipped to less than 10 percent. While change is expected as we move into a postindustrial economy, this shift further widened the gap between the haves and have-nots, producing questionable real value for society and contributing to a major economic recession.[7]

Money, control, and status keep moving from the many that produce goods and services to the few involved in finance, mergers, and acquisition. According to Stephen Kaplan and Joshua Rauh of the University of Chicago, the top 25 hedge-fund managers collectively earned more than CEOs of the Standard & Poor's 500 companies combined in 2007.[8] The finance tail is wagging the production dog.

A backlash has begun to emerge, and people on all sides now recognize that extreme commercialism is bad for business. By August of 2011, 80 percent of likely voters responded that our country was on the wrong track; beneath issues such as unemployment, health care, and war was a concern that money now rules politics and just about everything else.[9] In response we get private concern and public demonstrations like Occupy Wall Street and political discourse that promotes divisive class welfare—angering and potentially dampening the job-creating efforts of some of our most productive citizens and reinforcing entitlement for some of our least. The unintended consequences of extreme commercialism threaten the very source of commercial gain—relationships.

Marketing, Branding, and Mass Media Overkill

It is instructive to review how marketing plays an ever-increasing role in the advancement and even excesses of commerce and the decline of relationships. Innovative manufacturers have created a growing supply and even glut of products, which further enlarges the need for marketing. In addition to addressing identified needs, organizations have focused on stimulating demand by promoting purchases—sometimes of things customers might not need or be able to afford. Our terminology—hype, spin, getting sold a bill of goods, snake oil salesman, slick, fast-talking, flimflam, used car salesman—reflects a historical and inherent distrust of marketing and sales. We all share a concern about getting duped by someone who might take gain at our expense.

Marketing departments have become more sophisticated at analyzing and understanding segments of the market. Marketing messages are directed not only to our functional needs but also to the unique emotional and social needs that drive our buying decisions. Likewise, politicians, nonprofit organizations, and churches have become big users of marketing. Increasingly, marketing gurus (Karl Rove under Bush and David Axelrod under Obama, for instance) have led political campaigns and played key leadership roles in presidential administrations. All this has led to complaints that governing has now been trumped by endless campaigning.

The role of marketing has changed over the past century as our relationships changed. As provider organizations grew and as their customers migrated to large cities from rural settings, the relationships of commerce increasingly were with customers who were strangers. Marketing stepped into that void with an attempt to create "branded" relationships. You might not know the producer or seller in a personal or "organic" way as in the past, but there could be a "synthetic" or faux relationship and sense of belonging. (Notice how it extended the concept of the cattle brand discussed earlier.) The brand promise was that, even though we don't know each other personally, if you buy our products and services you can trust us to treat you as if we had a real relationship. We will deliver what was promised, whether that is a lawn mower that reliably cuts the grass or a pair of jeans that enhances your image. In other words, our manufactured or contrived relationship will be just as good as the real thing. We will replicate the "knowingness" between us, even though we are strangers. Heck, we will even design a page just for you when you visit our website.

Branding intended that strangers know and trust each other—and feel like a member of the group—absent real relationships. This approach allowed organizations to reach more customers and scale to reduce prices; they also became more removed from the unique requirements of local markets: individual customers and relationships.

Media played a key role. It is easy to forget that in just a few decades we have seen media expand from primarily newspapers to include radio, television, online and print magazines, and social media. Virtually unknown in 2001, there are now more than 30 million blogs in existence.[10] This increased reach marked the beginning of the mass marketing of relationships. Massive amounts of spending on advertising led to the emergence of national and international brands in a number of categories, from detergent to toothpaste to soft drinks to diapers. Between 1980 and 1990 alone, spending on media advertising for food soared 230 percent, from $2.3 billion to $7.6 billion.[11] For each hour of television programming, the number of minutes of advertising has jumped by 50 percent in the past decade—the average American is now exposed to 254 different commercial messages in a day, up nearly 25 percent since the mid-1970s.[12] While spending on advertising in more recent years has remained relatively constant as a percentage of GDP, the number of outlets that support advertising and the efficiency of technology have enabled those dollars to deliver many more messages to many more people.

Talk radio and cable television also have played a role, with programs in which news reporting is mixed with entertainment in an effort to attract more advertising dollars. Accordingly, the network news programs increasingly focus on anchors, formats, and content that tilt to more entertainment in reporting hard news.

These varied talk, opinion, and entertainment formats all have one thing in common: the commercial interests of selling products. As a result, an ever-expanding source of information, wisdom, influence and relational connection has moved from friends and family to strangers who are unlikely to know or care as much about you or your specific circumstances or needs, but are very clear and committed to theirs.

The Influence of Commercial Forces

[Lobbying] rose 5 percent last year [2010], to more than $3.5 billion.
—The Center for Responsive Politics, describing lobbying of Washington officials[13]

The commercial forces of media advertising have dramatically increased influence over us in four ways: (1) what we buy, (2) what we think, (3) how we behave, and (4) who we choose to relate to, and how.

First, media and advertising influence our buying like never before. These "synthetic" relationships are with advertisers who don't know you personally, nor do they understand your individual needs or what might be damaging to you. As we have experienced more commercial influence and less influence from our diminished pool of personal relationships, the odds go up that some of what is promoted will not serve our best interests; for example, we may be vulnerable to specific products that are harmful or overall spending that leads to excess debt. While we certainly can't blame advertisers for turning us into chain-smoking alcoholics who can't buy enough lottery tickets, the sheer magnitude of advertising has made it virtually impossible not to be accosted by messages that attack an individual's vulnerabilities.

The rises in obesity, pornography, gambling, and credit card abuse signal that these messages, along with the ubiquitous availability of commercial products, just might be exerting an adverse influence. There are endless examples. According to research from the Kaiser Family Foundation,

American preteens see approximately 7,600 food commercials every year, 73 percent of which are for salty, sugary, or fatty foods.[14] Consider gambling, which is endlessly promoted on TV and in online promotions; today betting losses represent one-quarter of personal consumer expenditures, up from 5 percent in 1970.[15]

Beauty and gossip magazines have contributed to a $12 billion cosmetic-surgery industry. Breast augmentation for girls 18 and under doubled between 2006 and 2007.[16] At the core of this trend is a commercial message that says your self-image and relationships are based on something that can be purchased. The desire of young girls to be pretty or sexy is certainly not new. What is new is just how much commercial media and marketing firepower there is behind it.

Countering media messages can be tough in a society where relationship time and influence are diminished by work and long commutes and fewer family members and friends. It is a double whammy: greater magnitude and sophistication of marketing messages and diminished relational influence.

Second, media-based commercialism has impacted how we think and interact regarding societal issues, especially through the content and format of news and information. Programming for maximum commercial appeal elevates the importance of drama and entertainment. It places a premium on confrontation, yelling, and fighting at the expense of thoughtful discussion, orderly debate, and consensus building.

Earlier we discussed the commercial appeal of "shock-based" reality TV, along with politically charged commentators on radio and cable news. *The Daily Show* with Jon Stewart has been shown to be a primary source of news for college students, and David Letterman's and Jay Leno's monologues are often comedic versions of news. The major networks have shifted from a fact-based style to a greater emphasis on soft news and entertainment. It becomes increasingly difficult to distinguish between fact and opinion when what gets reported is so heavily driven through the commercial lens of drama and entertainment.

The almost unlimited number of media sources and blogs focused on controversy and highly partisan opinions distorts our reality about how constructive relationships work. As we dial up just the one-sided opinions, drama, and entertainment we prefer, we invariably become more polarized.

News and information have to be paid for in some way. Personally, government-sponsored or heavily regulated news does not appeal to me as a better option because it removes free-market choice and is also driven by the influence of money and commercial interests on politics. Yet, if we continue to be drawn to ever-increasing doses of drama-based news, then we must deal with the negative impact on political discourse and relationships.

It is one thing for this new strain of commercialism to affect what we buy; it is another to let it influence our cultural views and how we think about social policy, politics, values, faith, and relationships. Extreme commercialism, especially involving the media, shapes a culture contoured to the pressures of the highest bidder.

Third, media advertising has promoted and even glamorized certain behaviors that proved harmful or even deadly. Unfortunately, there was a time when we did not know that smoking caused cancer, sugar caused tooth decay, or certain processed foods were unhealthy. Evidently the presence or absence of others even plays a role in how advertising impacts behavior. Interestingly, researchers at the University of North Carolina at Chapel Hill recently reported that children who have a television in their bedrooms are more likely to try smoking than are kids without one.[17] But television ads also promote antismoking aids, fluoride for teeth, and seat belts in cars, and infomercials can warn against behaviors that are detrimental to our health.

Fourth, extreme commercialism damages our connections with those we choose to relate to. Artificial relationships with commercial celebrities are a poor substitute for human ones. People like Oprah Winfrey, Rush Limbaugh, or the hosts of *The View* become so-called friends. These media relationships allow people to feel connected to someone they have never met (and probably never will). As the influence of these media-based strangers grows, more-traditional influencers—parents, relatives, teachers, churches, friends, and colleagues—may wane. We trade close personal relationships for synthetic ones, driven by commercial interests—ones where influence is for sale.

A final observation: Some commercial products, no matter how great, lose their value when experienced alone. A great restaurant, play, or lecture normally enjoyed with family, friends, or colleagues can be ungratifying when you're alone. That fact underscores the point that extreme commercialism—in replacing people with things and personal relationships with strangers—leaves us empty and alone.

Death by Marketing

I recently attended an NBA basketball game where I was reminded that the pros have reached yet another level of advertising excess. The game was one giant ad promotion from the time we entered the arena until we left. There were signs on every cup, tray, and wall, and ads were periodically dropped from the ceiling or floated above the crowd on balloons. The game has now become formatted not only for TV commercials but also for live commercials that emanate from all over the facility before the game and during intermission and every time-out. You can quickly count scores of commercial names, logos, and signs all flashing "buy me." It was an advertising circus interrupted by short bursts of basketball that no longer seemed to be the main event. My wife commented that it was hard to focus on the game.

For a time, businesses that wanted to grow could tap into a simple formula: Spending more on marketing (especially advertising) and sales would lead to more revenue. Sure, the product had to be decent, but if you ran more ads, added more salespeople, and promoted more aggressively, you would usually see an increase in business. Marketing became more creative in finding new ways and places to get the message out. Sports stadiums sold naming rights; "Intel inside" stickers were placed on computers; pop-up ads appeared as you surfed the Web; airplanes flew overhead and trucks prowled the streets brandishing banners or signs; sporting events started branding certain plays, like the "kickoff," to products such as beer; product infomercials began to appear on television screens in airports and on airplane flights; and even public bathrooms became advertising venues. Holidays like Christmas, Valentine's Day, Easter, Independence Day, Thanksgiving, and Halloween increasingly became heavily promoted for gifts, costumes, and food items. We're inundated every day, in every way.

Often, the content of messages has become more controversial, edgy, and counter to our best interests. Beer commercials targeted to the young promote raunchy parties. Victoria's Secret promotes very revealing underwear that would have been viewed as pornographic just a few years ago. The *Sports Illustrated* swimsuit edition has increasingly featured swimsuits sans the tops. All of these are commercially based promotions designed to sell products.

Would most of us think it a good idea to encourage more drinking and wild parties among our kids? Sexier underwear for our daughters? Is that the advice and influence true friend and family relationships would provide? Yet these messages are often promoted by cultural icons, celebrities, and credible publications paid to influence us and our kids. We have invited strangers into our living rooms and given them the microphone to influence us and our children in ways that are counter to our values and beliefs.

Marketing saturation also has occurred in other channels, such as telephone solicitation and direct mail. According to Synovate, a market research firm, credit card issuers hit their peak in 2005 when they mailed more than 6 billion offers, a jump of 16 percent from the 5.2 billion sent in 2004.[18] This translates into about six offers per month per household. Sound like overkill? After the financial crash, that number fell but is now edging back up. Phone solicitation is no different, and even with the do-not-call registry, most of us still receive constant solicitations that interrupt and annoy us. As we are continually blasted by advertising and extreme commercialism, we become immune to it: We ignore junk mail and use caller ID to screen calls.

Immunity to advertising is not just a business problem. The political version of extreme commercialism is also out of control. As discussed earlier, during the 2008 U.S. presidential election, the candidates raised close to $1 billion for their campaigns, more than the size of the economies of several countries in Africa.[19]

The irony is that as we hit saturation, the more spent on paid advertising, the less impact those messages have. As Karl Rove said regarding the 2008 presidential election, "Television ads don't matter as much as they used to. Going on the air with the earliest and most ads doesn't count for nearly as much as it once did. . . . Mr. Romney, who spent $2.4 million on TV ads in Iowa beginning last February, found that out. Voters are discounting advertising. They may be blocking out ads, relying more on personal exposure, information from social networks, alternative information sources like talk radio and the Internet, and local media coverage."[20] (However, his negative ads aimed at opponents in the 2012 Republican Presidential Primary had significant impact.) What? Money won't buy votes. A disturbing trend for politicians if ever there was one.

The goal of marketing is to sell a product or service by positively influencing relationships. However, as extreme commercial efforts promoted by ever more invasive marketing outreach began to compete with and even replace the role of relationships, something had to give.

When Distrust Becomes the Brand

In English-language online social media conversations "false" is the term most closely associated with advertising.

—Nielsen Online, Buzz Metrics[21]

Something did give. As the amount of advertising and promotion has grown, its credibility and impact have shrunk. Recipient receptivity has declined. Recently, Forrester reported that 67 percent of all consumers think there's way too much advertising. A staggering 95 percent of them say that most advertising fails to be "honest and authentic."[22] In some cases, the distrust has become so pronounced that the government exerted pressure to ban some forms of advertising (remember Joe Camel?). Many of us have come to feel that advertising is too pervasive, invasive, and persuasive. To quote Marshall McLuhan, "the medium has become the message." When customers are hounded over the phone and through the mail, yelled at on television, and interrupted on the Internet, there are consequences. Aggressive telephone solicitations, junk mail, and cross-selling efforts in the middle of a service-problem discussion have caused consumers to distrust organizations. Targeting vulnerable groups such as children, old people with failing mental faculties, and the uneducated poor has stirred particular contempt.

In essence, customer-marketing initiatives by both for-profit and not-for-profit organizations have repelled many of us. We've often encountered those whose commercial purpose—whether to sell us insurance or to gain referrals, for example—led to relational distrust. The bottom line is that invasive messages ultimately result in blocked access and possibly destroyed customer relationships. The uptick in permission-based marketing has been an attempt by providers to give customers more control by allowing them to opt in or out.

Divide and Disappoint

A key goal of marketing should be to advance relationships. Yet advertising and promotion most often elevate expectations about a product, service, or organization without improving actual performance. In actually growing the gap between expectations and reality, marketing resources often grow disappointment and then distrust rather than revenue. Customers already have a natural tendency to increase expectations. *Brandweek* says each year the gap widens between what companies pledge and customers receive. For example, in 2005, consumer expectations across 35 major brand categories rose by 4.5 percent, while the average ability of brands to keep up with those hopes decreased 9.2 percent.[23]

Eventually, this gap is lethal. Just as economic inflation lowers the buying power of your currency, message inflation, especially combined with message saturation, means that it takes more and more to get less and less, until everything delivers nothing. In the automotive industry, the marketing cost of relational influence—to get customers to buy—has risen 1,300 percent over the past 20 years, while new vehicle sales rose only 17 percent. By 2005, the industry was spending more than $4,000 per vehicle on marketing and incentives on a product where steel costs were about $700 per vehicle.[24]

This cycle has many of the same characteristics of addiction. In fact, I have heard a chief marketing officer describe their marketing campaigns this way: "Spending more, getting less, and yet dependent on the diminishing revenue growth, we have become addicted to the advertising and cannot make our numbers without them—it's like cocaine."

The gap between what politicians promise when campaigning and what happens once they are elected also disappoints. As referenced earlier, it's no coincidence that the term *politician* refers to someone telling you what you want to hear but not necessarily delivering it. Worse, politicians often segment their constituents, thus conveying different messages to different groups, some of which are diametrically opposed. These wedge issues energize certain groups during the election, but because they trade on deceitful, divisive, mutually exclusive messages, they destroy the ability to build the relational consensus that is so important to governing.

The religious sector also has grappled with commercial messages that promise love, compassion, and moral conduct and then disappoint through abuse, fraud, and mean-spirited attacks on certain groups.

In the private sector, Starbucks avoided these traps, especially in its early days. The company grew its upscale brand and its business with virtually no paid media advertising. It created a value proposition primarily marketed by strong customer relationships.

Conversely, by offering a low-cost product and advertising that stressed an airline run by plain folks offering down-home service, Southwest Airlines lowered and authenticated expectations: peanuts, low fares, fun service, and bags fly free. This was a marked contrast to airlines promising elegant comfort and great food. From inception, Southwest fostered a strong, trusting relationship with employees and customers, making it less likely to disappoint and more likely to live up to its brand promise.

THE FINE PRINT

Hidden or misleading fees have become a huge source of revenue for some organizations, but they are damaging to customer relationships. Fees can be an effective and legitimate way to charge customers for unique or extra services, but they can also prey on ignorance and naivete. The short-term revenues derived from these hidden fees can be sizable and are usually pretty easy to calculate. Citigroup analyst Keith Horowitz estimated that the banking industry was taking in about $30 billion to $40 billion annually in overdraft fees prior to banking regulation revisions of 2010.[25] The hidden cost to relationships is harder to calculate, but it is substantial. In a number of industries, hidden fees have meant increased but hidden marketing costs of selling to a marketplace jaded for life toward the brand and highly resistive to the brand's messages.

Deceit, hidden fees, or less-than-honorable sales tactics have a common denominator: They are designed to get the sale instead of building and growing mutually rewarding relationships. To paraphrase Mario Cuomo, many organizations advertise in the poetry of relationship but behave in the unvarnished prose of transactions. Not surprisingly, the rise in advertising hype and hidden fees correlates with the decline in relationships.

Casualties of Extreme Commercialism

My entry into the world of commerce came in 1973. I was a first-year consultant working for Ernst & Young (then Arthur Young) in Tulsa, Oklahoma. At the age of 25, I decided that the long hours and travel of the consulting business were not enough; I needed more on my plate. I had grown up in the cattle business and it remained a keen interest of mine. So my brother-in-law and I, with some help from my dad, got a sizable bank loan, rented pastureland, and bought 600 head of steers. My brother-in-law worked full-time at the ranch, and I kept my consulting job and worked on the weekends feeding, vaccinating, doctoring, and tending the cattle.

We worked incredibly hard, but prices dropped significantly not long after we bought the cattle. When it came time to sell the steers, we experienced huge losses, which added to our debt. The second year we bought another round of steers. After selling them, we had a small loss, leaving us even deeper in debt. Wisely, the bank was not willing to extend us any more credit, ending our cattle business: We were left with close to a six-figure debt each. Our options were either to declare bankruptcy and walk away debt-free or to spend the next several years paying off the debt. After all the effort we had put into it, the idea of spending years working and scraping for every available dollar to pay the note off was just about too hard to face. I wanted to run away and hide.

Yet the relationship we had with the bankers and with my father made the decision no less painful but clear. We signed up for a schedule that took us five years to pay off the debt. In looking back, the decision came down to a simple but personal relationship question: When I promised to repay the loan the local bank made to me, did I intend to be true to the relationship and to my word?

Indeed, truth and trust are often casualties of commercial-grade self-interest. A lot of renaming and rebranding efforts are simply an attempt to run from a past of broken promises, lost trust, and ruined relationships. Organizations use an alias to avoid being recognized by customers or stakeholders in a marketplace where their soiled reputations impede future business, not unlike someone with a criminal record who operates under an assumed name to avoid the consequences of his past. For example, the Association of Trial Lawyers of America, unhappy with their reputation as ambulance chasers, changed their name to the American Association for Justice.[26] Philip Morris became Altria to disassociate itself from the negative image of promoting and selling cigarettes. Unfortunately, we see too many institutions in need of witness protection from their past because of extreme commercial practices. It explains why renaming and rebranding are increasingly seen as untrustworthy acts.

Sometimes extreme commercialism moves beyond deception to bribery. Financial incentives such as profits, sales commissions, and performance bonuses reward legitimate results. By contrast, bribes are paid for what we know to be wrong. Unfortunately, the old adage that an honest politician is one who, when you buy him off, stays bought, has become too common. Whether we look at Jack Abramoff bribing public officials, Bernie Madoff bribing auditors to aid his bilking of investors, financial firms providing special broker incentives to push poorer-performing stock funds, or mortgage brokers getting paid to bamboozle customers into buying expensive mortgages they cannot afford—they are all bribes. Nothing is more central to extreme commercialism and nothing is more destructive to relationships than when bribes—attempting to monetize relationships to acquire ill-gotten gain—are treated as if they were merely incentives. One of my favorite sayings is "loyalty is what is left when the bribes are all gone." Purchased favor is not loyalty.

Research findings bent to serve marketing are a form of bribery. In addition to the high-profile role of the securities rating agencies and some audit firms in recent financial calamities, there are less notable practices that have slipped into rather common but deceitful business practice. For example, until it was bought by Harte-Hanks in 2006, Aberdeen Group, a technology consulting organization, was tabbed as a provider of "pay-for-praise" reports. The *Wall Street Journal* described how it worked: "If you saw an Aberdeen report saying that Acme MicroMacro sold world-class solutions, you could be sure that Acme had written Aberdeen a world-class check. . . . The potential conflict in this approach, though, is clear. The reports are big business—there were 212 last year—each typically with four or five sponsors."[27] Bribe-based revenue models are hard to break.

The more crucial the mission, the greater the damage when marketing overpromises or deceives. Health care, specifically, pharmaceutical companies and research from medical schools, provides a poignant example of extreme commercialism and its impact on relationships. It's a well-known secret that pharmaceutical companies compensate many of the writers of scientific journal contributions. According to Anna Wilde Mathews, "These seemingly objective articles, which doctors around the world use to guide their care of patients, are often part of a marketing campaign by companies to promote a product or play up the condition it treats."[28] A number of journal editors have acknowledged cherry-picking favorable data to promote certain drugs or treatments, and it is not surprising that the credibility of these reports has suffered as a result.

Are consumers buying and taking medications they don't need simply because, in the short term, a pharmaceutical company's marketing effort has unduly influenced doctors? Setting aside the technical medical arguments, the marketplace has begun to question the proliferation of prescribed drugs at least partially based on the overhyped marketing and sales effort. According to Dr. Marcia Angell, former editor-in-chief of the *New England Journal of Medicine*, 9 percent of Americans surveyed felt that drug companies were "generally honest," compared to 39 percent trusting supermarkets! She felt consumer advertising was actually causing consumers to distrust drug companies, having the reverse effect those organizations had hoped for.[29] There is a line beyond which the practices of extreme commercialism are not only dishonest but also economically damaging to everyone, including the organizations that initiate them. In the extreme, the effect is marketers paying good money to harm and disable their brand, their relationships, and their profits.

Increased focus on fund-raising and endowments at top colleges provides another example of how economic might has undermined the relational landscape. Writing for the *Wall Street Journal*, Daniel Golden reported on how top institutions have increased their giving: "What makes Duke and Brown, among other institutions, stand out, is the way in which they ramped up and systematized their pursuit: rejecting stronger candidates to admit children of the rich or famous."[30] He reports that landing the children of people like fashion mogul Ralph Lauren helped boost Duke's endowment from 25th in 1980 ($135 million) to 16th in 2005 ($3.8 billion). It speaks volumes that this influx of wealth and celebrity has made these places more desirable for top students.[31] It is indeed sad when prospective students place more value on being associated with "cool" celebrity family members than on academic integrity and excellence. The expressed collegiate values—namely, the search for truth, equality, and learning—have increasingly been compromised by forces of commercialism and influence for hire gone extreme.

Extreme commercialism is bad ethics and also bad for business. Certainly, these temptations are not new. But the magnitude of falseness today puts the costs on another level. For consumers, it costs time and money to manage unwanted and distrusted sales and marketing offers, more due diligence for selection of products and services, and peace of mind.

Relationships in the Distrust Economy

Extreme commercialism has, in fact, birthed the distrust economy that runs on a range of new products and services: from spam-blocking software, computer security systems, and shredders for our mail, to unlisted phone numbers and caller ID to protect us from extreme marketing and relational abuse. Consumers caught in this distrust economy first became numbed and immune to the sway of false messages, but now they increasingly seek the refuge of family and friends as trusted sources of information. A Capgemini study into the influences on automotive purchasing found 71 percent of the respondents favored word of mouth compared to just 15 percent for TV advertising. According to the Roper Organization, over the last 30 years, word of mouth has increased dramatically for U.S. consumers in its perceived value as a source of information and ideas about new products (from 67 percent of respondents to 91 percent). Roper points to the 1990s as the period when the change occurred; it was the decade when trust in traditional sources (government, politics, and business) started to slip.[32] To adapt what was said about music the day Buddy Holly died: It was the decade that commercial trust died.

As discussed earlier, word of mouth now drives two-thirds of the U.S. economy.[33] Let that soak in. How ironic that word of mouth, born of relationships, has made dramatic gains over an industry that spent more than $240 billion in 2009[34] to influence us. Extreme commercialism and the purchase of influence have hit the wall; influence for sale devolved into influence for rent and then, finally, to no influence—"sold out."

The response is predictable. In its fifth annual report on trust among the world's opinion leaders, the Edelman company reported that people were trusting each other more and traditional authorities less. Edelman termed this "the democratization of influence," whereby the average person (along with independent experts) was being seen as much more credible than organizations and other groups.[35]

At a time when many entities have crossed a line and become commercially extreme, our trusted word-of-mouth community has become a safe haven. Families, businesses, politicians, and religious groups failing at the business of building and sustaining true relationships cannot endure. Today's technology and media have provided very powerful tools to reach people and build relationships; too often that opportunity has been squandered for short-term commercial gain.

Those abused by extreme commercialism will be slow to recommend anyone or anything with even a whiff of distrust. That is why social networks are so powerful; they rely on highly valued recommendations—one of the ultimate acts of relationship.

* * * *

We are a society that has enjoyed the fruits of commercialism, but we got off track and suffered unintended consequences. Extreme commercialism has impoverished by subtracting trusted relationships and even dividing us. It has promoted a spirit of winner-takes-all that means win-at-all-costs. We have paid the price in broken relationships.

Win-at-all-costs has become the surest way to lose. While not all have practiced extreme commercialism, we have all suffered the distrusting effects of a soulless marketplace. We have become disappointed so often that we reflexively distrust. Unlike at any other time in history, the void created has stimulated a demand for trusting relationships: relationships that are, like the brand discussed earlier, worth riding for, and reputations that aren't for sale.

Chapter 9

Worshipping at the Altar of High Tech

*The scariest thing about Stanley Kubrick's vision wasn't
that computers started to act like people but that people had
started to act like computers . . . it's all about the speed of locating
and reading data. We're transferring our intelligence into
the machine, and the machine is transferring its way
of thinking into us.*
—*Nicholas Carr,* Wired Magazine[1]

We started our company in 1978 as a training and consulting firm dedicated to improving customer relationships. By providing a process, training, information, and coaching for local work teams, we were able to consistently demonstrate measurable increases in customer value. By the late 1990s, we were excited that we had embedded our process, information, and best practices into software that provided a cheaper and more efficient technology-based solution for customer relationship management. We had grown from a staff of three to 200 and our software development group totaled 40 people. The software solution offered better information but fewer in-person group-training sessions and less coaching and change management; this relational stuff took more time and required messy human interactions. Our clients wanted a tech solution that would provide information to efficiently develop changed mind-sets, skill, and desired behavior of local teams. All of us assumed the outcome of improved customer relationships and customer profitability would pour forth as a result.

There was only one problem. The more we relied on the software to deliver the change, the less change we got. In fact, across whole industries, as companies invested more in knowledge-based software solutions to enhance customer and employee relationships, the more the metrics revealed relationship decline. What we all learned the hard way was: bottom line, information and process alone weren't sufficient to deliver the desired behavioral and culture changes. It's a lesson we need to relearn. As one of my colleagues used to say with a wry grin, "If everybody knows the Ten Commandments, how come we still got sin?" As valuable as information and technology are, meaningful behavioral change occurs mostly within the confines of relationships. In fact, technology can steal our attention from the very relationships we seek to build.

The decline in relationships has occurred at a time when the rise and promise of technology has been one of society's defining stories. In so many ways, technology has enabled us to do more—better, faster, and cheaper. We have unprecedented access to information and exchanges with hundreds of relatives, friends, colleagues, and even businesses. *Friend* is no longer just a noun; it has been upgraded to a powerful verb. The hope that technology can cure what ails us comes wrapped in many packages: liberation from ignorance and oppression through access to information; greater harmony from a more informed world; less demanding manual labor through automation; economic wealth from greater productivity; eradication of poverty and disease through technological solutions; and greatly increased communication.

Yet our truly human interactions and relationships—our greatest individual and cultural resources—are more distant, more estranged, and fewer than ever before. Technology consistently and unrelentingly gives us control to separate information and transactions from human interactions and relationships. It is nothing short of a new relational structure. We choose technology-based interactions over human ones, and in the process we spend less time with key people in our lives. Even when we are with those people, many of us are constantly pulled to our smart devices, checking to ensure that we aren't missing out on anything. We're able to screen out those we dislike or find of questionable value. Tech-based marketing enables us to target only those we wish to reach. A growing lament is long days filled by looking at computer screens and constant bombardment by marketers. Commitment and ethical behavior, two of our most treasured resources, thrive in relationships—the very relationships we have unwittingly altered and demoted by our fixation on technology.

The technology that now dominates our lives carries unintended consequences. Nicholas Carr, former editor of the *Harvard Business Review* and author of *The Big Switch: Rewiring the World, from Edison to Google*, elaborates: "Computers are technologies of liberation, but they're also technologies of control. It's great that everyone is empowered to write blogs . . . But as systems become more centralized—as personal data becomes more exposed and data-mining software grows in sophistication—the interests of control will gain the upper hand."[2] He goes on to conclude that as a mechanism to monitor, control, and manipulate people, our computers are the ideal, with no example more chilling than Google Earth. He warns that as artificial intelligence experts rewire our computers, they are in effect rewiring our culture.

It is easy to be under the illusion that we are in control of technology, yet this is a great seduction; in many ways, the technology is addictive and has taken control of our lives and is separating us from our relationships. John O'Neill, director of addiction services at the Menninger Clinic, has said, "We can become overloaded by technology and suffer consequences in our relationships." And psychologists have classified technology addiction as an impulse disorder that can be as socially damaging as alcoholism, gambling, and drug addiction.[3] In fact, research released in 2012 reported that MRI scanners detected similar kinds of brain abnormalities among technology addicts and individuals hooked on cocaine, alcohol, and cannabis.[4]

In business and organization relationships, we have invested heavily in information and software to make us much more efficient and effective. In our organizations, we have developed rules-based systems, like credit scoring, that are likewise efficient and designed to reduce or eliminate human interaction and human error, to objectify decision making, and to reduce bias. Besides, humans get sick, require health care, complain, join unions, and initiate lawsuits—all of which can be costly. The message has come through loud and clear that human fallacy can be remedied by technology. But we have overestimated technology's value in delivering higher sales, better service, loyal relationships, more accurate and secure voting, better employee communication, or more family time. In the process, humans have been downgraded in value and often replaced.

Technology—so powerful in producing things—has mostly failed to deliver on its promise to build stronger relationships. It reminds us of the warning labels on some products: batteries not included, some assembly required. Our experience has confirmed what many already knew: Information technology develops rapidly; the change we hope it will bring us often develops slowly.

In some cases, better information and technology simply increased already-flawed skills and actions in ways that made things worse. As Kevin Martin, head of software development in the early days for my company, used to say, "If you give a fool a faster tool, what you get is a faster fool." We have all had that experience: knee-jerk replies to e-mail, tweets used out of context, unedited and unretrievable messages left on voice mail, or immediate contact with someone by cell phone before we were ready. Some of our most senior leaders have been tripped up by e-mail, voice mail, texts, audio recordings, photographs, or clips on YouTube, doing or saying things that they regret. Technology has documented and archived forever some of our worst behavior.

Patience is no longer a virtue, having been replaced by a preference for the instantaneous and the disposable. Why repair when we can dispose and replace? We have multitasked and traded informational volume for less meaning as we text our way to the top. We leave behind relationships in need of nurturing because we no longer have the patience for them.

Sure enough, the machine is transferring its ways into us and the unintended outcomes are not always pretty. Our affinity for technology has often flowed out of our selfish desires and our commercial interests to control, rather than to build stronger relationships and communities that last. Yet technology is too valuable, powerful, and filled with promise to go away. We must look more closely to understand how it can undermine relationships so we can make it a relational ally rather than an enemy.

The Promise of Technology

The history of technological change and advancement is the history of mankind. Unfortunately, some of the most prominent historical advancements have been in warfare. The ability to develop and deploy improved technology has influenced the rise and fall of nations. The arms race began in early history with such weapons as improved curved bows, longbows, and faster ships. Later came firearms, airplanes, submarines, powerful bombs, missiles, radar, stealth aircraft, and, more recently, unmanned drones.

There are many examples of how new technology has translated into advantage and change. From stylish horse-drawn carriages to automobiles, to just the right iPhone or iPad, technology has bestowed not only functionality but also status that has conferred favorable advantage in the form of social standing, dating, and winning a mate. In agriculture, the advancement of technology—from John Deere's prairie sod-busting cast-steel plow to tractors, to new pesticides and genetic developments—transformed productivity such that most of us don't give a second thought to having enough to eat.

The array of scanning technology such as MRIs available to the medical profession is a shining example of how technology has enabled longer, healthier lives. Technology has elevated our safety and prosperity and protected us from potential catastrophe by enabling us to predict the weather. Personal computers, online shopping, cell phones, and now smart phones, wireless connectivity, cable/satellite TV, iPods, and even online dating services have all provided us with greater freedom, new options, and a greater sense of connectedness and even security.

The savings in time and cost for companies who no longer need to provide offices and even workers has been significant, as has the time employees save by not having to commute to a remote location. Electronic bill paying, banking, research, commerce, job searching, and employment application are a few of the ways that time and money are being saved thanks to technology. Technology has made it possible for business and personal interactions and transactions to take place around the clock.

In my work with homeless families, I have been amazed at the lengths they will go to keep their cell phones. Computers, high-speed Internet access, and even cable/satellite television are increasingly seen as necessary for the basic functions of life.

In commerce, technology has stunningly transformed the speed and ease of business analysis and communication. Technology continues to drive business efficiency while doing things thought impossible just a few years ago.

Relationships and Technology: Generational Differences and Divide

Typical kids ages 8 to 18 spend an astounding 7 hours and 38 minutes a day consuming entertainment media, drinking deeply from the fire hose of TV, computers, game consoles, cell phones, music players and other devices.

—Kaiser Family Foundation[5]

One of the profound ways that technology has impacted relationships is by providing a new model for interacting, collaborating, and working as online communities. Facebook, Myspace, eBay, Craigslist, Twitter, LinkedIn, and Wikipedia are all examples of a new paradigm driven by large, highly participative social networks. These sites have grown rapidly and changed how relationships, communities, and the world work.

Who could have imagined just a few years ago that something called social media would give voice to freedom and play a role in pressing entrenched autocratic leaders in places like Egypt, Libya, and Tunisia to step down? Or how about soldiers in Iraq or Afghanistan being in daily contact with spouses and loved ones via e-mail and Skype from the battlefield halfway round the world? Closer to home, social media has connected friends, classmates, and family members more than ever before. The price of these technologies has plummeted rapidly, providing access and benefit worldwide. Technology has enhanced the speed, frequency, and ease of communication, all of which have the potential to aid stronger relationships.

Yet these technological advancements do not come without relational baggage and generational differences. Often, discussions about the upside and downside of technology and especially social media slide into a debate between the young, who are sophisticated in its use and inexperienced in a world without it, and the old, who remember the pretech world but struggle to fully grasp today's tech capabilities.

The older crowd, of which only 40 percent over age 65 (70 percent, age 50 to 65) use the Internet, worries that the younger groups spend too much time passively glued to screens and not enough time engaged in physical activity and face-to-face interactions with others.[6] They also worry about identity theft, techno-predators, cyberbullying, sexting, and postings on Facebook that can be used against them by prospective employers or others. At a more personal level, they often feel excluded by comments from the young like "Don't call me; just e-mail or text me." Their lack of techno savvy in using e-mail, text messaging, Facebook, or Twitter leaves them feeling separated and left out.

The younger crowd—dubbed by Booz & Company as generation "C," which stands for connected, communicating, content-centric, computerized, community oriented, always clicking—was born after 1990 and by 2020 will represent 40 percent of the U.S. population.[7] Fully 93 percent of teens and 90 percent of young adults (ages 18 to 29) within this group use the Internet.[8] They are baffled by anyone's resistance to the efficiency and effectiveness of these great new tools. They see the benefits of technology to meet, visit, shop, collaborate, trade information, and apply a thousand other uses that are immensely convenient and powerful. To them, failure to use this is Luddite-like, antisocial, and frustrating. In their view, tech enhances their relationships.

What is particularly worrisome is how social media is contributing to the relational gap between the generations. The young, seen as much more multicultural and inclusive of diversity in race, ethnicity, gender, and sexual orientation, are increasingly less open to older generations, and the dividing line that most firmly excludes them is technology. In their study "The Rise of Generation C," Booz & Company described it this way: "Older people will also continue to lag in the intensity of their digital behavior. Generation C will distance itself further, particularly in the development of its own pervasive culture of communication. That culture has led some observers to dub this group 'the silent generation.'"[9] For them, digital communication channels have replaced much of the physical interaction typical of older generations. So the language of choice for this new generation or tribe is audible silence. In a relationally challenged world, technology with all its pluses is yet another source of divide—a generational one. Change has a way of doing that.

Recent research from Pew helps us understand the magnitude of the shift to technology among the young.[10]

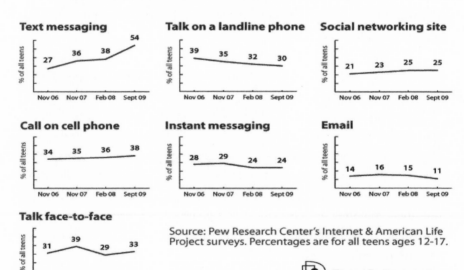

Texting takes off, while use of other communication channels remains stable over time
the % of all teens who have used each communication method to contact their friends daily, since 2006

Source: Pew Research Center's Internet & American Life Project surveys. Percentages are for all teens ages 12-17.

The most significant recent trend is the rapid increase in text messaging among teens. Concerns about diminished interaction seem unfounded, as use of cell phones and face-to-face talk have held their own. In earlier research, Pew found that, overall, Internet users have larger social networks and get more out of them. People who e-mail their close friends and family regularly also speak to them 25 percent more than do non-e-mailers. They also are more likely to meet their social contacts in person.[11] Larger social networks and frequent and more fulfilling contact would seem to be a plus for relationships. Those growing up with this technology are particularly adept at staying in touch and building relationships and communities via technology.

However, early research raised concerns that people who spent a lot of time on the Internet were at greater risk of isolation and even depression. Subsequent research tempered that concern but did reinforce that introvert Internet users tend to become more isolated.[12] In 2011, researchers for the American Academy of Pediatrics coined the term *Facebook depression,* defined as depression that develops when preteens and teens spend a great deal of time on social media sites such as Facebook and then begin to exhibit classic symptoms of depression.[13] These preadolescents and adolescents at risk for social isolation sometimes turn to risky Internet sites and blogs for "help" that may promote substance abuse, unsafe sexual practices, or aggressive or self-destructive behaviors. Technology can help build and maintain relationships, but for some it can also become a destructive substitute.

I remember speaking in the late 1990s at a conference in London where the speaker who preceded me, a technologist, spoke excitedly about the capability to do all sorts of things—banking, buying, conversing, researching, and more—without ever leaving home. (Much of what he described has since taken place commercially on a routine basis.) The message: We can do just about anything without engaging in human interaction. I remember thinking at the time: *Disengaged may not be so good.*

We have removed the human element from much of what we do, and the relational effect is mixed. But one thing is clear. There has been a shift: The role of technology has been elevated and the role of human interaction has been diminished. For some, technology has become a new deity, worthy of adoration, and for others a source of concern and fear.

Technology: The Power to Corrupt Relationships

The shift that technology has brought offers the promise to make us healthy, wealthy, and wise. Yet here we sit with families falling apart, fewer close friends, weaker local communities, and organizations with diminished stakeholder relationships. At a time when technology is king, what is driving these unintended relational consequences?

Among the many ways to view technology, its role as new source of relational power is perhaps most illuminating. Technology allows us to know and do things in forceful and often effortless ways that did not previously exist. Throughout history, the desire to acquire territory, wealth, dominance, or status has often rested on translating technology into power and control—over adversaries or even irritants. All too often the hope of technology was about creating a power advantage that removed the need for the give-and-take of relationship. The goal was to defend, conquer, and control.

Today we are locked in a battle over control of our lives. Technology is highly valued because it has consistently given us greater influence and power over our time and priorities. Yet most of us have learned to question and distrust the concentration of power. Power corrupts and absolute power corrupts absolutely. In our exercise of technology-based power and control, we have in many ways corrupted relationships. Let's examine four unintended consequences of the extreme use of faceless technology.

INFORMATION OVERLOAD: BLURRED VISION AND FALSE CONFIDENCE

The hope has been that in a world where information is more universally available, we would better understand each other, and that sensitivity and tolerance would be the result. The assumption was that many of our problems are rooted in ignorance. It turns out that more knowledge can produce new, different, and in some ways more resistant strains of ignorance and arrogance.

While more information is often beneficial, research has also shown that we are sometimes blinded by more information. Nassim Taleb, author of *The Black Swan: The Impact of the Highly Improbable*, cites an example of giving two groups a blurry image of a fire hydrant. For one group, the resolution increased slowly in 10 steps, and for the other group, it is increased more rapidly in five steps. The members of the group that saw fewer intermediate steps identified the image more quickly. Too much information increased the noise. People faced with a higher number of blurred images tended to develop opinions based on weak data, which can create bias in interpreting subsequent data.[14] We see so many trees we lose sight of the forest.

Worse, research shows that beyond a certain point, more information fails in helping us draw better conclusions, but it succeeds in falsely increasing our confidence. Bookmakers were asked to predict the outcome of races using 10 key statistical variables. Then they were provided substantial additional information and asked to predict again. The additional information did not improve their accuracy but did improve their confidence.[15]

What does this have to do with relationships? A lot. The family, ethnic, organizational, political, and religious strife so tough on today's relationships occurs in a technology-enabled society too often blinded and biased by information, false confidence, and arrogance.

This unfounded confidence also affects our ability to communicate and be in relationships with others who are less informed. According to McKinsey research, the more we know, the harder it is for us to assume others don't share our knowledge.[16] Think about the last time you called your company's IT help desk and you'll know what I mean. We have all dealt with people who know a topic inside and out, but they turned us inside out trying to explain it. This creates stress on the relationship because both parties are frustrated. Contempt creeps in.

For relationships, technology-enabled information overload can reinforce the worst of all worlds—less insight and greater confidence and even arrogance.

CONVENIENCE THAT DISTANCES

Internet users . . . are 40 percent less likely to rely on neighbors for help in caring for themselves or a family member and are 26 percent less likely to rely on their neighbors for help with small services, like repairs and lending tools.

—Lee Rainie, Director of Pew Internet and American Life Project [17]

Technology can serve to distance us from each other in ways that disregard relationships. Relational disregard is an act of control for reasons such as avoiding conflict, saving time, getting more done, or doing what we want. There are many ways, both intended and accidental, that technology has moved us further apart.

When I was growing up, most families had one automobile. Families traveling to eat out, shop, or attend a recreational activity or church were likely to all ride in the same vehicle. That meant that everybody left at the same time, were part of the same conversation, listened to the same radio station, arrived at the same destination, and returned home together. There were no cell phones, headphones, or TV in the back. Everyone pretty much shared the same experience.

Contrast that to today. We are more segmented: There are fewer family events and more specialized events or programs designed just for kids (and adults), such as children's movies, athletic events, and date night for parents. For most events, unless the parents are involved as sponsors or the like, mom or dad drives the kids to the event and later picks them up. The kids may have headphones on, and mom or dad is likely to be on a cell phone.

It's not just new technology that changes us but how we use the old tech (like a car). George Bullard, a noted consultant on church issues, found that historically a parking space would be needed for every 2.5 people attending a congregational worship service.[18] Now that figure is as low as 1.5, requiring over 60 percent more parking spaces for the same number of people. It is not uncommon for a family of three to have three cars in the church parking lot.

Spontaneous relationship-building time has been traded for convenience and segmented activities. Research on propinquity or proximity reveals that more than half of what is learned in an office environment is learned through spontaneous interactions like bumping into someone at the water fountain. Researchers at the Stanford Institute for the Quantitative Study of Society lament the loss of family time and workplace interactions, warning that the Internet is replacing face-to-face interactions without replacing the benefits.[19] We drive alone, we surf the Web alone, and we don our headphones as a signaling device that we want to be left alone. Franklin Becker, a social and environmental psychologist who directs Cornell University's International Workplace Studies Program, describes growing distant from each other this way: "If you essentially put yourself in an auditory cave, you're going to miss opportunities to learn by observing what others are doing, by overhearing."[20] It's ironic that the more our workspaces become open, the more we use technology to become isolated.

Headphones, DVDs in cars, computer games, television as babysitter—we have invented many ways to replace human interaction and in the process distance ourselves from each other, ignoring the need for relationship. Research from Stanford has shown that heavy Internet use extracts a significant cost of time with the family: Those in the U.S. population who use the Internet frequently spend 70 minutes less a day interacting with family. In 2010, Facebook reported that its average user spent over 55 minutes per day on its site.[21] The loss of 70 minutes of family interaction is huge when you consider the total interaction left after a day of work, school, and other activities for parents and their kids. For many families, that could represent a loss of 30 to 50 percent or more.

Technology has made us more informationally connected, but according to research, the quality of those interactions has gone down substantially.[22]

When it comes to relationships, distance is replacing closeness. Quantity, efficiency, and convenience trump quality, meaning, and relationship. Many are more electronically connected but less personally related. As we are less related and more isolated from each other, we become more dependent on technology, which exacerbates the situation. It is the perfect storm for addiction, serving both as cause and result of a misplaced reliance that, instead of filling, empties us. John O'Neill, director of addiction services at the Menninger Clinic, referenced earlier, warns that technology might be just as addictive as alcohol and drugs and can wreak havoc with personal and work relationships. In the clinic's Internet/computer addiction services program, which runs treatment programs and provides therapy, they estimate that 6 to 10 percent of the approximately 189 million Internet users in the United States have a dependency on technology. As he says, "Some people are drinking a bottle of technology and some people are able to drink a glass."[23]

Nothing isolates us like addiction. Just as alcohol, drugs, and gambling addictions can become synthetic sources of short-term pain management, technology has become the source of synthetic relationships that moves many of us further from the very resources we need. Television started us down this path and now an array of technologies has further enabled our isolation like never before.

It is not just our personal time with family and friends that has declined. Many things that used to require human interaction now can be done independently. For example, the frequency of visits to a bank branch dropped from an average of 4.4 per month in 1995 to 2.9 visits in 2002[24] and, according to the research firm Celent, have fallen another 10 percent in the past 10 years.[25] The number of ATMs increased from 139,000 in 1996 to more than 400,000 in 2008.[26] This is part of a larger trend of replacing human transactions with automated kiosks or related automation. In 2006, about $300 billion in transactions moved through kiosks. That figure is expected to be more than $700 billion by 2014. Likewise, employment in office and administrative support declined 8 percent from 2007 to 2009. Voice mail, e-mail, and PDAs have automated and replaced the role of secretary.[27] Elevator operators, gas station attendants, tollbooth agents—the decline in human contact is legion. While very efficient, the combined effect is a dramatic decline in relationship interactions and jobs.

As we have increased our information and ways to communicate, we have lost ground in the realm of spontaneous social interaction—the kind that builds bonding relationships. As an example, TeleParent Educational Systems provides teachers with a menu of 600 canned messages for communicating with parents: anything from "your child is a pleasure to have in class" to "your child has been late to class five times."[28] Talk about authenticity taking a sabbatical. Could there be a clearer message to a parent that her or his beloved child is just a number, warranting no personalized communication? It is no wonder that handwritten notes are making a comeback.

The sheer volume of tech-based communication overwhelms us. About. com reports that in excess of 294 billion messages are sent each day.[29] E-mail is a detached, insulated way to send information. It is efficient, clean, recorded, and nonengaged, and it is sometimes relationally dehumanizing. In one extreme example, RadioShack Corporation laid off 403 employees at its Fort Worth headquarters via e-mail.[30]

E-mail and texting are so low-cost, easy, and efficient that there is a temptation to over-distribute information. Because e-mail is devoid of visual cues and messaging, ambiguity often results, and the e-mail exchanges go on and on. Ironically, what used to take a few minutes to resolve in a quick conversation can now take hours, days, or weeks.[31]

PARTIAL TASKING AND IMBEDDED INTERRUPTION

With technology came a new term, multitasking, a word that feeds into our need to be productive, efficient, self-important, and stimulated. It implied that in this busy world we would be much better off if we could do several things simultaneously: drive while talking on the phone, visit while doing e-mail, send or receive text messages while eating dinner, or play solitaire while participating in a meeting.

A more accurate term for multitasking would be "partial tasking," which means diverting attention from the business or interaction at hand and reallocating it elsewhere. The effect of partial tasking during interactions is that we often miss the most important part of the conversation—the very slight smile or the near tear that wells up in the eyes. Research on human communication has shown that nonverbal communication is much more accurate than verbal communication. Granted, with voice mail we do get some of the nonverbal cues such as voice inflection, and people are getting more adept at using words and signs in e-mails to express emotion (smile, frown, LOL). But technology that enables us to disrupt the already diminished face-to-face or even phone interactions may increase the overall volume of communication but lower our capacity to process it. Given the technology of today, communication production is not the problem—consumption and absorption are.

Due to technology's ubiquitous nature, those of us in the technology club are both perpetrators and victims. As Thomas Friedman said: "Technology is dividing us as much as uniting us. Yes, technology can make the far feel near. But it can also make the near feel very far." Friedman quotes technologist Linda Stone: "We're so accessible, we're inaccessible. We can't find the off switch on our devices or on ourselves. . . . We are everywhere—except where we actually are physically. I was much smarter when I could do only one thing at a time."[32]

Partial tasking is like announcing our power to be partially present to a friend or colleague: "Look, I am going to devote 50 percent of my focus to being here with you, but I have decided to devote another 35 percent to several other people who aren't here right now, and the rest to whomever else might text or call me." In the new world of technology, we have made it acceptable to be absent when we are present.

In many ways, the interruption has become the main event. I was at a nonprofit fund-raising event that successfully targeted a number of 20- and 30-somethings. There was a terrific band, and a number of them were dancing and enjoying the evening. After dancing for two or three songs, however, they would return to their tables, pick up their smart phones, and check their messages. Their facial expressions became serious and even pained as they scrolled through the text messages. They were transported from a fun, friend-filled atmosphere to some other place. It took several minutes for them to complete their tech chores and then to emotionally and relationally return to the event.

As we become more attracted and even addicted to constant interruption, we are weaned from present relationships. This means that any time there is conflict, boredom, or an issue to face, we are bailed out. We structure our relationships and our lives for planned interruption. We eschew organic things for a system and lifestyle that invites and requires synthetic disruption.

We have mastered technology except for turning it off. How do we create sanctuaries for our relationships, safe from invasion, interruption, and distraction? Knowing sooner and knowing more has become our default position. Sometimes knowing later and knowing less may be the path to truly knowing more. The very technology that has given us so much control to send and receive information has also taken that control back by putting us at the receiving end of a never-ending barrage of messages. Power gives, but power also takes away and oppresses.

SEGMENTING, SORTING, SEPARATING—AND SHEDDING RELATIONSHIPS

Technology is a powerful tool for doing the heavy lifting of segmenting, sorting, and separating relationships. It gives us the ability to choose with whom we will interact and to repel the rest (think caller ID). The risk is that we exercise extreme control that narrows and even isolates us in the choices we make; we might call it the "new narrow." In genetic terms, this narrowing of relationships represents a less diverse gene pool, thus exposing us to limitations of inbreeding and limiting advantages of mutated hybrids. A very narrow gene pool has not been kind to most species trying to evolve and adapt. When sameness oppresses, diversity, innovation, and evolutionary change suffer.

> I will never forget my first night of volunteering with the homeless. I was CEO of a rapidly growing company surrounded by smart, highly motivated employees, sophisticated Fortune 100 clients, and ambitious investment bankers intent on taking my company public. As the homeless residents straggled in, it struck me how the control I exercised kept me separated from their world. Because of who we hired, the clients we worked for, where I lived, the people I exchanged e-mails with, where I attended church, there was virtually no chance for me to interact with those at the bottom of the socioeconomic ladder until I decided to volunteer. Yet I would find over the next 10 years that sitting face-to-face with the homeless was one of the most enriching, enlightening, and developmental experiences of my life. Being in relationships with those in need—those we otherwise might avoid—is sometimes the very thing we most need.

Separation is one of the most compelling things we do in a relational society. Separation can range from a temporary form of discipline for children in a "time out" to solitary confinement. It is ironic that one of the worst fates we can bestow on someone who breaks the law is to separate the offender from society by placing him in a prison with other separated people. Yet, removing that prisoner from his cell and fellow inmates into solitary confinement is exponentially more punishing. Technology used to separate and segregate strikes at the heart of relationship.

Technology has enabled us not only to avoid specific people but also to avoid thoughts or opinions not to our liking. As discussed earlier, in this new frontier of on-demand information, we get the news we choose. With powerful search engines, customized home pages, and favorite bloggers who communicate with the world at virtually no cost, we can dial up just the commentators and the points of view that suit our fancy and block out those we don't want to hear. In essence we can choose not only the ending of the story but the story itself. On the surface, the increase in the amount of available information would seem to broaden our perspective, but in reality it has enabled information bigotry that gives us control to narrow and block out the unwanted. More has morphed into less.

Technology has enabled greater divide, and it has often put more of an edge in the discussion by falsely elevating our confidence while lowering diversity and tolerance. In opting for the news we choose, we are getting the divide we deserve.

Technology has empowered our view that we know what is good for us and that we know what in fact we don't know. Often what we most need is something we do not know to ask for. Our ignorance is often of the pooled variety—shared with others who are of like mind—which makes us feel smarter than we are. The things we do to narrow our views may ease our efforts and reduce our dissonance in the short run, but over time they often lower our ability to innovate and make the best decisions. There is a cost for the comfort and efficiency of narrowing our scope and becoming insular from a world that is constantly changing. While I doubt it was anyone's intention 10 or 20 years ago to say, "I am going to have fewer and less-diverse relationships," for many that is what has happened. Until we decide differently, this will only get worse.

I am certainly not advocating the removal of freedom of speech or the marketplace of information. What I am advocating is that we need to give more weight to relationships in the choices and controls that technology now offers.

Remember Tom Peters's admonition a few years back to manage by walking around? It was valuable advice for executives insulated from the real world of customers and frontline employees. The same is often said about politicians isolated in the "bubble" of the nation's capital. Relationship is a team sport with shared give-and-take. When technology affords us too much control and distance, there is less to receive and narrowness triumphs. It helps explain why rich, diverse, messy relationships are left starving for oxygen. The extreme control that technology can bestow is a gun pointed at our most precious and life-giving resource—our relationships. Let's adopt a new slogan—live by walking around. Technology, used properly, is a great tool to help us do just that.

* * * *

In an age of extreme consumerism and commercialism, it is not surprising technology has so often been focused on making us more self-fulfilled, hip, and rich. Technology is a new form of currency that operates much like the old currency; it can make us feel more important, confident, and powerful than we really are.

While many of the technological breakthroughs are breathtaking, when it comes to social changes like eating habits, sexual practices, child rearing, education, business relationships, governing, and faith, we struggle to meld social policy, morality, religion, and financial incentive to affect useful change. Too often we look to technology for the answer—a pill, new software, or a new device—with little success.

The key is to become more intentional about reaping tech's relational potential. The growth of social networks reflects the pent-up demand for people using technology to better connect. Mark Zuckerberg, Facebook's founder, has said he wants his site to be a "social operating system" for the Internet.[33] Yet, the technology is still more informational and lacks some of the more sensitive capabilities of face-to-face or even phone interaction. A thousand friends on Facebook may not equate to the relationship infrastructure and support at the core of our human needs.

As technology has advanced in our society, we struggle to find the right role for human interaction that has been edged out. The love of sports and reality shows; the growth in tabloid news; the increasing partisanship of politics—all point to a pent-up demand for emotion, even the dysfunctional variety. While we feed our desire for the detached power of technology we are left with a void for relational emotion.

The good news, however, is that we now have enough experience to see both the promise and the unintended relational consequences in our use and overuse of technology. Technology is at its highest and best when it enables rather than replaces relationships. It is neither a god to be idolized nor an evil to disdained; rather, it is a force to be used for a greater good. To build on Nicholas Carr's quote, with which I opened this chapter, we must now be very intentional about transferring the ways of relationship building into the technology. That is a worthy goal and part of a larger vision that we will address in section IV, where the focus is on revaluing and reclaiming relationships.

Chapter 10

The Institutionalization of Relationships—Growing Care-less

There's a combination of anxiety and loathing. There's a sense that every single one of these institutions is totally out for their own betterment, versus the public they serve.

—Peter Hart, pollster[1]

T he board chairman of a small private school called to tell me the school's executive director was leaving the organization. The chairman asked if I would lead the school board through a process to reassess their direction before they started searching for a new director. The school had been a small, very hands-on institution that provided personalized attention to students. It had developed a great reputation that fueled its growth; in fact, it was just about splitting at the seams and had a decision to make. The school could either remain at its current enrollment, in keeping with its vision for a highly personalized experience, or it could implement plans for scaling up and expanding, with the risk of losing some of the personalized attention students were accustomed to.

As we explored the school's options, I asked the board to consider the words of the late Dr. Henri Nouwen, a former Yale professor who had spent his last years living with and helping the severely disabled at the L'Arche residence near Toronto.

> Nick, who works with four handicapped men in the wood shop, spoke about his joys and frustrations. He explained how hard it is to do a job well and at the same time keep the needs of the handicapped men uppermost in mind . . . it asks for deep inner conviction that a slow job done together is better than a fast job done alone. I found this out myself this afternoon when I went apple picking with Janice, Carol, Adam, Rose, and their assistants. My attitude was to get the apples picked, put them in bags, and go home. But I soon learned that all of that was much less important than to help Rose pick one or two apples, to walk with Janice looking for apples that hang low enough so that she herself can reach them, to compliment Carol on her ability to find good apples, and just to sit beside Adam in his wheelchair under an apple tree and give him some sense of belonging to the group. We finally collected four bags of apples, but eight people took more than an hour to do it. I could have done the work in half an hour. But efficiency is not L'Arche's most important word. Care is.[2]

As a society, we have faced these decisions countless times over the past century and have mainly opted, as did that private school, for efficiently gathering more apples over care. The decision to institutionalize by growing, amassing resources and power, and increasing economies of scale has been a consistent trend—whether it was President Franklin Roosevelt's expansion of government under the 1930s New Deal, the massive growth of Microsoft, the continual expansion of Walmart, or the evolution of the megachurch. Our individual focus on extreme consumerism and the economic focus on extreme commercialism pave the way for extreme institutionalism.

The result is that big government, big business (especially banks), big unions, big oil, big schools, and big churches, purposely or not, dominate by too often placing their own needs and survival over those they serve. The response? The Tea Party takes on big government, Occupy Wall Street takes on big business, Bank Transfer Day (movement to move deposits out of large banks) takes on big banks, state governments take on public-sector unions, environmentalists take on big oil, and so on. Peggy Noonan, a columnist for the *Wall Street Journal*, opines that many of the great institutions we rely on to hold us together have forgotten their mission and their purpose—what they existed to do. She laments: "And as all these institutions forgot their mission, they entered the empire of spin. They turned more and more attention, resources and effort to the public perception of their institution, and not to the reality of it." She then cites how this attitude plays out in the public schools, where too often the mission of teaching and guiding the young gets lost and instead teachers come to think the schools exist for them—to give them secure jobs to meet their needs.[3] As the world increasingly is ruled by institutions growing larger and more powerful, this loss of mission and relational serving sucks the life out of relationships; it institutionalizes them.

Yet it is simplistic and unhelpful to just condemn these institutions that have made such significant contributions to our lives. Some of the large jobs of society require the size, scale, and order of large organizations. We need to better understand how large institutions have unwittingly become adverse for relationships, so we can identify ways of restoring their relational capacity.

The Growth of Big

Much of what used to be offered locally and purposefully on a smaller scale by family, friends, or neighbors is now done by institutions—strangers. This is having a material impact on the DNA of society's relationships.

Put the word *big* in front of any organization or industry these days—big pharma, big labor, big government, and so on—and it makes their appeal smaller. Why are such successful organizations viewed so negatively? These organizations are ineffective in growing, developing, and sustaining relationships. Institutions are good at forcing compliance but not winning commitment; maintaining status quo but not innovating new approaches;

detailed analyses but not quick market responsiveness; one-size-fits-all transactions but not individual relationships; and cutting cost but not growing revenue.

How are institutions eroding the depth, breadth, and duration of our relationships? As former BBC writer and broadcaster Sir Antony Jay points out, we are often one-sided in our fault-finding, by either taking the viewpoint of the institutions, looking down and seeing the dangers of the organism splitting apart, leading to anarchy; or taking the side of individuals, looking up from the bottom and seeing the dangers of the organism growing ever more rigid and oppressive until it fossilizes into a monolithic tyranny. This latter vantage point tends to be preoccupied with the need for liberty, equality, self-expression, freedom of speech and worship, and the rights of others. Jay's conclusion: "The reason for the popularity of these misunderstandings is that both are correct as far as they go and both sets of dangers are real . . . sometimes society is in danger from too much authority and uniformity and sometimes from too much freedom and variety."[4]

Regardless of your point of view, large institutions such as government, the military, health care, financial institutions, churches, education, and large corporations are central to who we are and what we enjoy as a society. Many of us work for large institutions, and all of us rely on them for key services. Yet, as with dysfunctional relationships, we have become too dependent on institutions and they have become too independent of us.

Diminished Confidence and Care

The pain of dealing with institutions has increased our desire for communities of local, responsive, and caring members—the kind that come from our families, local businesses, and self-governing organizations where relationships have greater importance and accountability.

From businesses to churches to government, survey after survey finds that confidence in large institutions is eroding. According to the General Social Survey, since 1976, across 13 institutions, only the military has experienced an increase in confidence. The five groups at the bottom in 2008 were organized labor, the executive branch, Congress, television, and the press, with less than 15 percent of those surveyed expressing a great deal of confidence in them.[5]

We have lost confidence in the very institutions on which we rely; we are still living together, but we're estranged. Like the abused spouse, we lack the will or confidence to leave but are unable to fully survive and thrive. Starved of basic nutrients, relationships have become malnourished and cannot grow and develop properly. Yet we keep expanding the role of institutions to efficiently gather apples at the expense of care and relationships. We need both, but institutional efficiency has overwhelmed compassionate care, not only affecting us in personal ways but also eventually crippling apple production. The two—care for people and apple production—are interdependent and relational.

Societies migrate toward what they value. Today that means we have chosen to have large institutions prepare our meals, provide nursing care, and take care of our children—to the detriment of smaller, more local communities and groups. Close personal relationships have lost ground to large institutional ones. While these changes have occurred gradually, cumulatively they represent a monumental shift in the depth, breadth, and duration of personal and organizational relationships that have become part of the larger pattern of outsourcing relationships.

Larger institutions evolved for a number of good reasons like better national defense, more social services for an expanding population, and economies of scale to make things more affordable. They produced the Union Pacific transcontinental railroad, the Hoover Dam, victory in two world wars, highways spanning the country, space exploration, and the computer hardware and software industries. These feats were accomplished by large groups of people working together.

However, these new organizational capabilities did not come without a price. Mass production and the industrial revolution meant that family members moved away from home, leaving their local communities. In many organizations such as IBM (aka "I've Been Moved"), you were expected to relocate often if you wanted to succeed. Community, friends, and work relationships were less permanent, more disposable, and not a priority—we became a land of strangers.

As discussed earlier, in many ways, the organization replaced the community and family as the primary support mechanism through which we received benefits: health care, child care, and retirement. As more mothers moved into the workforce, and more families became dual-income, incomes rose significantly. Families were now in the position of paying for what used to be the domain of the extended family—child care.

In the realm of health care, child care, welfare, mental health, and assistance to the elderly, government took on a much stronger role. Programs like Head Start, Medicare, Medicaid, Aid to Dependent Children, Welfare to Work, and Social Security evolved to fill the void. In spite of the tremendous safety net that these programs have provided, they diminished the role of personal relationships.

Private and public institutions that provide health care, education, and social services, among others, are highly organized and can hire and develop specialized workers with a deep understanding of specific fields like specialized medicine, social work, engineering, finance, accounting, research, and technology. However, as institutions have grown larger and more specialized, separation occurred due to the sheer numbers, geography, and specialization among workers. The understanding of the breadth of tasks performed most often declined as breadth was traded for depth. Employees and customers or those served are less likely to know the people they interface with in a company, school, or government entity.

Inevitably, decline in the role of personal relationships was an unintended consequence of these organizational advancements. We kept stacking additional responsibilities on organizations that have limited relational capabilities. Institutional "experts" often lack the commitment that family members and friends have. The signs of societal fracture that we have discussed throughout this book all increased as we placed more relational responsibility in the hands of faceless organizations. Enamored of their scale and efficiency and how they took us off the hook, we lost sight of their corrosive impact on relationships.

After decades of downsizing, rightsizing, reengineering, and mergers designed to gain ever-increasing efficiency and scale, there is a growing realization of the considerable damage inflicted on employee, customer, and other stakeholder relationships. Louis V. Gerstner Jr., former CEO of IBM, provides a colorful example in describing the impact of reengineering: "[It] is like starting a fire on your head and putting it out with a hammer."[6]

A steady stream of postmerger failures and disappointments led thoughtful people to question this newfound hope of unlimited size. Geoffrey West, president of the Santa Fe Institute, compares the equations for the growth of biological organisms—like the relationship between their mass and their energy use—to the equations for the growth of a corporation or a city. He states: "In organisms, there are clear limits to growth. There are good reasons why there aren't creatures bigger than a whale or a sequoia. We're wondering if there might be fundamental laws that constrain the growth of social organizations regardless of what they do."[7]

Yet these deals were usually cheered on by Wall Street as investment banks got rich on them. In fact, it became common for the brains on Wall Street to claim that the only organizations that would survive would be those who grew large enough to attain massive scale. In industries such as banking, insurance, telecom, automobiles, oil and gas, and airlines the mantra was "acquire or become marginalized." The problem is, the numbers don't support the claim. According to the *Harvard Business Review*, over 65 percent of acquisitions have destroyed more value than they create.[8] Mergers stacked on top of mergers began to behave like dinosaurs with indigestion. "Too big to fail" had a new bookend: "too large to manage."

The forces opposing size are not just confined to the private sector. Considerable evidence shows that places like New York City are making impressive strides toward the goal of replacing large and often dysfunctional factory-style high schools with smaller schools where children have closer contact with faculty members.[9] Also, mainline Christian churches (Methodist, Presbyterian, Episcopalian/Anglican, United Church of Christ), with their traditional hierarchical structures and established doctrines, have seen significant declines, while nondenominational congregations grew substantially (from 194,000 in 1990 to more than 8 million in 2008).[10]

Eventually, the projected math of financial economics must submit to the actual performance erosion of declining relationships. I have purchased and sold companies, and I have lived through being acquired. I have worked with scores of merged and acquired companies and have consulted in the planning and integration of mergers. The most predictable outcome is eroded relationships. Regardless of the spin you put on it, employees in most acquired companies feel vanquished. The message from acquirers is clear: "We won and you lost, so we are going to do it our way." Nonetheless, usually the acquiring company spends an inordinate amount of effort trying to salve bruised relationships. Usually customers feel less important and often neglected. Stymied by their inability to grow organically, many organizations choose to grow through acquisition. As in blended families, it takes a lot of work just to get back to abnormal.

Institutional Dysfunction and Marketplace Distrust

> [People are] "in a kind of lostness," in which we destroy the source of our own lives . . . [that is] what you get when the economic destinies of community fall into the hands of financiers and money men who have no connection to local folks and are not sharers in their fate.
>
> **—Rod Dreher, discussing writer and activist Wendell Berry** [11]

The very process of creating large economies of scale and competitive advantage often sows the seeds of stagnation. Too often that evolution has stunted our growth—Dinosaurs "R" Us.

We have a lot to learn about how to facilitate relationships that are functional and productive. Former prime minister Tony Blair of Great Britain has said that one of the tests of a country is whether more people are trying to get in or get out. This is a simple but profound measure. We can use the same metric for our relationships: Are more people trying to get in or get out? In most of our institutions—family, business, politics, and religion—substantially more people have been trying to get out.

In Japan, half of the respondents to a survey of full-time employees in their 20s and 30s responded that they would quit if they had the chance.[12] That is a staggering number in a country where loyalty and commitment are traditionally so high. How hard is success in an organization where half of the workers want out? How hard is it to raise children in a society where half the marriages end in divorce, with one or both parents trying to get out? The answer is "very."

What is it about how organizations have grown and evolved in recent times that has made relationships increasingly less attractive to stakeholders—employees, customers, constituents, parishioners, party members, or congregants? If becoming more efficient is so attractive, why has there been such an exodus? Rather than being one-to-one, institutional relationships have increasingly become "un-to-un":

- Un-known: As relationships degenerated, we moved apart and became strangers.

- Un-valued: Relationships have no residual value, no benefit for remaining together.

- Un-served: Our skills and commitment are not sufficient for the need.

- Un-connected: Isolation and divide grow between those who serve and are served.

- Un-powerful: Institutional control feeds feelings of powerlessness and oppression.

Intended or not, stripped of relationships, our institutions have reached a tipping point.

Why the Status Quo Can't Survive

The very intention of getting larger sends a message about what is valued. It says we want each individual to have less importance and say in what goes on. It may enable a large and worthy cause, but the math says that a one-person proprietor has more relative importance to that enterprise than does an employee in a 100,000-person organization. The very nature of growth trades away the control and impact of those involved for the higher purpose that can be accomplished with greater size and scale.

It would be like a family saying, "Let's make our family larger by adding several more husbands, wives, and children." In our culture, most would say that the economies of several adults and their children living under one roof would be more than offset by the loss of freedom, control, and personal intimacy—chaos unchained. Family is an obvious example where we usually place a higher value on personalized relationships than we do on economies of scale, even though the family itself is considered an efficient entity.

As organizations grow, they behave differently. They become more bureaucratic and eventually more institutional. They move to a more institutional style that changes worker and other stakeholder relationships. Institutional requirements to act more uniformly take away employee freedom and creativity. The institution of marriage is often cited for these pejorative characteristics.

As organizations grow, people within them increasingly interface with those they do not personally know (where there is no relationship at all). Whether it is a company, church, government agency, or volunteer organization, relationships and behaviors change; as the organization grows, those relationships become secondary. Most often, the significant financial rewards for the growth of organizations accrue to top management and shareholders. They are much less likely for lower-level employees and customers.

Innovation, also, is often a victim of growth. Small businesses and entrepreneurial organizations are the ones who provide most of the innovation that makes a major impact on a society. As Robert Litan notes, it is the innovators who matter most: "Their enterprises are the ones which create the jobs and industries of the future . . . The automobile, the airplane, the telephone, air conditioning, the personal computer and its software, and Internet search engines—all were launched by innovative entrepreneurs rather than large companies."[13] There is something about how relationships work, or don't work, in large organizations that dampens innovation and invention. The same goes for loyalty of relationships. In the banking industry, only 15 percent of large banks' customers are loyal, compared to 24 percent for community banks and 26 percent for credit unions.[14] Small community bank customers are over half again as loyal as those of the largest banks, even though the smaller banks typically are less efficient and have less sophisticated products and technology. Their marketplace has consistently voted for personal relationships over efficiency.

The impersonalized nature of large, efficient entities often creates relationship diseconomies. As organizations grow and become more dominant, their energy and focus often shift away from those they serve. Unwittingly, institutions create a form of narcissism in which they become mirror images of the consumerism we discussed earlier. Part of this is the natural evolution of institutions: The survival of the whole trumps the intentions of the few. It is this behavior that has led to such low trust scores and why we see trends toward homeschooling, smaller private schools, and home-based churches.

The result is "reverse branding." It used to be that if you could show you were a large, well-known national company you were branded as reliable and trustworthy. As early as 2003, Forrester began reporting on polls that showed consumers were gravitating away from big-name companies because of a lack of trust.[15] Think of some of your favorite providers: restaurant, bakery, flower shop, a place where you volunteer, your church, or a study group. Do you find yourself thinking, "I wish they would grow rapidly; maybe become 10 or 100 times their current size?" Neither does anyone else.

I can remember when my own organization had about 60 employees, with a history of growing 20 percent to 30 percent annually; our growth rate jumped and we began growing in the range of 50 to 100 percent annually for several years. We met with our largest client at that time, and were excitedly sharing that our growth had taken off and we had doubled in size in the previous year. Surprisingly, their reception was cool. I later found out from one of their top executives that they were concerned that our size might change the relationship by making us less focused, less attentive, and unresponsive. In looking back, I must admit that his concern was legitimate. Even though our relationship remained strong and our growth added stability and a broader range of capabilities, their perception was accurate—bigger was not better. They moved from being our most important client to being one of our most important clients.

Don't get me wrong. Growth is a sign of and crucial to marketplace success. I'm not anti–big business or –big organizations. The concern is how to sustain growth by growing relationships rather than shrinking them. The math of relationships may not be as tangible or linear as the math of efficiency, but make no mistake, relationships matter measurably.

As organizations become larger and more institutional, they often move further away from stakeholders, both physically and psychologically. This separation may be expressed in miles, hours, time zones, hierarchy, rules, unfamiliarity, or arrogance. This creates both the perception and the reality that individual relationships have less influence.

Hierarchy creates its own form of "strangership." A saying I heard a number of years ago captures it: "Rules without relationship equals rebellion." Meager investment in relationships fosters rebellion. In his book *Out of the Question . . . Into the Mystery*, Leonard Sweet looks at this issue in the context of marriage: "Consider the statistics that indicate Southern Baptists—the denomination that went on record supporting wives' submitting to their husbands—have the highest divorce rate (29 percent) of any Christian denomination and are more likely to get a divorce than atheists and agnostics." He then wonders how a more relational approach to Christian faith, versus a rules-and-principles approach, might affect this tendency toward divorce among Christians.[16]

In medicine we see loss in the core relationship between the doctor and patient. The number of primary care doctors has dropped by half in the last decade, and their income is a third less than what most specialists earn.[17] The primary care doctors who are left see more and more patients, and spend less time with each one. The priorities are money, control, and specialization, resulting in fewer relational resources for burdens like taking care of sick kids and needy seniors.

Since revenues aren't generated by wellness, or even doctor/patient relationships, doctors continue to be pressured by the metric of number of patients "seen"—not to be confused with "engaged" or "related to." We have all experienced a doctor who seems to be operating off a stopwatch where "seen" (and no more) was an apt description. This behavior puts patients on the defensive and is a barrier to disclosing and discussing sensitive issues that may be important. This relational distance leads to poor medical practice and does not promote wellness. Its surface efficiency is easy to calculate, but its hidden and growing costs are not.

The Bottom Line

In a world of instantaneous and global communication, the speed and cost of institutional relationships gone bad has greatly accelerated. Consider the images of prisoner treatment at Abu Ghraib; or rats running rampant in a New York restaurant; or photos of congressional politicians' private parts and prurient messages circulated around the world.

The ability to shape and spin relationship illusions is losing ground to reality. Institutions are increasingly playing out their relationships with stakeholders via online chats, instant messages, blogs, and YouTube. Like the fall of the Berlin Wall a couple of decades ago, the wall that protected institutions has fallen. The strength, quality, and duration of relationships are now playing explicitly and in real time at a computer screen near you. If information is power, then there has been a shift in power to family members, employees, customers, and shareholders that means a new level of relationship accountability to institutions. To date, this change has lowered our trust and regard for institutions.

Younger people have responded to this lost ground by changing how they relate to institutions. They wait longer to enter the institution of marriage and have children, and are more deliberate in choosing a career. Mike Malone, writing for the *Wall Street Journal*, reports that half of all new college graduates now believe that self-employment is more secure than a full-time job. He warns: "An upcoming wave of new workers in our society will never work for an established company if they can help it. To them, having a traditional job is one of the biggest career failures they can imagine."[18] While money still matters, relationships have grown as a priority. Younger adults want to avoid the "chew them up and spit them out" experiences their parents went through. They value egalitarian structures that are more relational and less hierarchical. This approach relies on stronger stakeholder commitment as a path to growth and profitability. Many newer tech organizations— Facebook, Amazon, Google, Apple—stand in stark contrast to older, more structured organizations like General Motors, IBM, General Electric, Citibank, and Exxon Mobil.

Nothing will impact the success of our society like the ability of our key institutions to excel at attracting, growing, and building committed relationships. In a world where the demand for stronger, more productive relationships is surging, the competition is changing. We have to recognize that while technical and scientific skills have been very important, this new world requires more relational skills. Whether we think of the global risk of nations armed with nuclear weapons and that have dramatically different worldviews from us, or of the domestic challenges of distrusted and dysfunctional institutions, the ability to develop and grow relationships will be the new, old requirement. This skill set will be harder to acquire and just about impossible to outsource. Organizations that can foster this skill set will reap rewards; those that cannot will pay a heavy price.

* * * *

We have moved from a hard-asset economy—of plant, equipment, and raw material—to an information-based one. Now we are moving to a relational economy where our connections and ability to work together constructively will make or break us. Relationships are the new risk, and relationship management is the new risk management. Intangible relational assets have become the most valuable ones regardless of where they are found—at home, at work, in government, or at your place of worship.

We have spent the past decades creating efficient and protected organizational institutions that now leave our relationships dispirited, unprotected, and ineffective. Unwittingly we invested heavily in purging relationship dependencies by standardizing processes, centralizing brands, using workers as interchangeable parts, and minimizing the human touch as much as possible. The result is institutions built on detached individual relationships. Short on emotionally committed and loyal stakeholders, institutional efficiency and detachment now carry increasing risk.

The big lie was that large-scale efficiencies could replace or at least offset the need for relationships. We have tilted to the extreme by pouring resources into large schools, churches, companies, unions, government, and businesses, while ignoring the attendant diseconomies of relationships.

The truth is, if our institutions are going to survive and thrive, they must cultivate a stronger form of relationship. If our relationships are going to prosper, we need to grow a more prolific form of institution. Institutions can no longer be the places where relationships go to wither and die; they must become the places where relationships are born and nourished. The way to gather more apples is to develop stronger teams of committed apple growers and gatherers. And that will be our focus in the final section, about realizing the Age of Relationship.

THE AGE OF RELATIONSHIP: REVALUING AND RECLAIMING RELATIONSHIPS

W hat will it take to reclaim relationships?

There are some societal challenges that only stronger relationships can successfully address—at home in our personal lives and in the organizations where we work, govern, and worship. Reclaiming relationships will require a new set of priorities and leadership that moves us forward. The good news is that there is hopeful and compelling evidence that a number of these changes are surfacing in this, a new forthcoming age—the Age of Relationship.

In these final chapters, we will discuss three key priorities for reclaiming relationships: (1) revaluing relationships, (2) reclaiming small and local, and (3) embracing relational leadership. Along the way, we will report on some of the encouraging evidence that these priorities are reemerging across our society.

Chapter 11

Revaluing Relationships

But the big change came when the officers running these wars understood that R.B.'s ("relationships built") actually matter more than K.I.A.'s ["killed in action"]. One relationship built with an Iraqi or Afghan mayor or imam or insurgent was worth so much more than one K.I.A.

—*Thomas L. Friedman,* The New York Times, *describing the shift away from body counts (à la Vietnam) in Iraq and Afghanistan*[1]

L ast year, over the holidays, we were sitting at the dinner table when my wife casually mentioned she was in the market to buy a new laptop. Our older daughter, knowing her mom had never owned anything but PCs, responded immediately, "Mom, you have to get a Mac." When my wife inquired why she felt that way, our daughter effused over the "genius bar" where you can walk into a store and get instant, in-person technical support. I had already extolled the virtue of Apple's highly trained and motivated roving in-store checkout clerks who sold me a Mac the previous year, completing the transaction on the spot with a mobile device, eliminating the trip to the checkout line.

How ironic: The leader in the technology revolution that is a catalyst for enabling online purchases, slowing foot traffic in stores, and reducing face-to-face contact is also leading a renaissance in human interaction, local retail stores, and customer satisfaction. According to the University of Michigan's American Customer Satisfaction Index, Apple's nine-point lead over other PC makers—its highest rating ever—was the largest lead for any company in 2010 over its competition across 45 categories, including airlines, autos, and financial services.[2] By the end of 2010, Apple surpassed Microsoft and had the largest market capitalization of any technology company and was number two among all companies.[3]

Certainly the popularity of the innovative iPhone and iPad, along with the Mac—considerably more expensive than most PCs—played a key role. Apple charted a different course and made relating to customers a new priority. Erica Ogg, writing for C-Net News, describes the strategic role of their stores: "Apple stores are the best example of what makes it different from its peers and are illustrative of the company's approach. The retail stores are one of the most important ways people interact with Apple."[4] The organization now has 300-plus stores with upward of 50 million store visits per quarter and annual per-store revenue of $40 million—truly the highest-performing retail stores in the history of retailing. Half of those who make purchases are first-timers. Apple has built not only a global community but also a local community with local relationships where people can return and receive support for using their products. Ron Johnson, the builder of the Apple Store, in an interview with the *Harvard Business Review*, explains that the deeper rationale for the Genius Bar wasn't just: How do we fix people's computers? It was: How do we restore and enhance customer relationships that may have been damaged by problems with the iPod? He concludes: "It's not just the product that's broken but also customers' trust in Apple. Apple is in the relationship business as much as the computer business. And the only way to really build a relationship is face-to-face. That's human nature."[5]

Several years ago the conventional wisdom was that the PC market was a mature, commoditized industry that would duke it out on price, with most purchases made online, and that stores were obsolete and face-to-face interactions would mostly go away.

Yet Apple designed a human, face-to-face experience for selling, servicing, and providing technical support that pulls millions of young, hip retail and small-business customers into their stores. Who says stores are dead?

Finding Our Way

Alone is much better together.

—*George Strait*[6]

The evidence of a worldwide movement under way toward stronger, more lasting relationships is hard to miss. David Cameron, prime minister of Great Britain, said while campaigning in 2008 that the great challenge of the 1970s and 1980s was economic revival. He quickly added: "The great challenge in this decade and the next is social revival. . . . We used to stand for the individual. We still do. But individual freedoms count for little if society is disintegrating. Now we stand for the family, for the neighborhood— in a word, for society."[7] Given the recent financial upheaval in countless countries, including our own, it is accurate to say that social revival will also be crucial to sustained economic revival.

Forward-thinking organizations are finding ways to expand family-friendly policies. For example, Parkland Hospital in Dallas is doubling the size of its ICU rooms from 160 to 330 square feet and outfitting them with a full bathroom, a sleeper sofa, and a chair to accommodate a patient's family members. The hospital cites research that shows the advantages of a family's bedside presence: social interaction between patients and families can distract from the pain and solitude of being hospitalized; better observation of the patient's condition; more frequent communication between hospital staff and family members who will share the information with the patient; and improved planning for the patient's discharge from the hospital. The net is that it allows the family to provide relational care and attention to the patient that a nurse doesn't have the time to provide.[8]

Likewise, more businesses have made it a priority to choose CEOs from within, to focus on longer-term value over short-term gains, to be more transparent in financial reporting, to emphasize local markets, and to focus on the importance of culture as a defining variable for success. Both organized religion and the military (as we will discuss in the next chapter) increasingly use small, local efforts to build stronger, more lasting relationships with the local community.

Even in our schools we see glimpses of progress. In the fight against child obesity in Maine, administrators and teachers have rallied parents to adopt 5-2-1-0: five vegetables a day, two or less hours of screen time, one hour of exercise, and zero sugary drinks. By changing how meals are eaten, increasing group exercise, and decreasing TV and computer time, relationships have been elevated. The result: a measurable drop in child obesity.[9] The popularity of the Waldorf school model and similar models reflects a focus on organic relationships by keeping the homeroom teacher with a class of students for several years, encouraging heavy parental involvement, and discouraging electronic media such as television.

Finding our way to more valued relationships does not start with others—relatives and friends or leaders of businesses, government, churches. It starts with each of us. We can't single-handedly change the world, but if we strengthen our relationships, the world will change.

Not Just the Relationships We Like

What key changes will be required to support this emerging and needed emphasis on relationships? How do we move from dividing and subtracting to adding and multiplying? Recall that when we talked earlier about relationships we included competitors, critics, and even enemies because they help define us and can be instrumental to our development. Our network of key relationships is—and must be—much broader than just friends and those we feel comfortable with.

And developing and supporting relationships involves more than just being nice to people, of course. Simply being nice to others can prevent us from confronting issues that are important. Respecting others, including those with whom we have differences, is a crucial component of relationships. Critics can be particularly hard for us to stomach and can drain us of our energy, but they can also help us adjust, grow, and deal with issues that are central to our development. The ability to accept that even our worst critics and enemies have valuable information that we can use is a precious gift.

In many cases, we have attempted to structure our lives to reduce our dependence on relationships because of the work involved. Much of the recent excitement regarding technology has been the hope that it might deliver us from the mundane and even the pain of certain relationships— using the ATM to avoid the teller at the bank or using e-mail to avoid the person at the office who drives us up the wall. Many of us live in a world where status, power, and organization hierarchy buffer and insolate us from feedback, criticism, and challenge, yet these interactions are essential to our growth and success.

Not Just What We Have

Medicine is the art of engagement with the human condition rather than with the disease.

—Dr. Bernard Lown, author, medical doctor, and Nobel Peace Prize recipient[10]

Relationships are our richest source for healing, growth, and development. When we are in strong relationships with strong families, vibrant places of work, healthy organizations, spiritual mentors, and even challenging competitors, we are able to develop and flourish. When we are isolated or surrounded by disabling social forces such as low expectations, groupthink, hopelessness, short-term thinking, immediate gratification, and negative role models, growth is stymied. You are the relationships you seek and keep.

Placing a higher priority on relationships means making them central to what we value. For those tempted to make money the center of their lives, financial writer Scott Burns shared this wisdom from one of his readers: "You know you are rich when more money won't change where you live, what you eat, what you drive, or who you sleep with."[11]

It is easy to interpret that quote to mean that you have enough money when, even if you got more, you would not change your life. I think a more substantive interpretation is that when we give relationships a higher value, we are less likely to be subordinated and twisted by worship of money, status, or power, which so often leads to destruction. We live happier, more productive lives when relationships are a key source of our riches. Longer-term it may be better for us economically, to boot.

You have probably heard the adage "the person who is rich is the person who knows he has enough." Making relationships a priority means being full of gratitude for who—not just what—we have.

For many of us, this gratitude translates into a call to reclaim this most precious gift—our relationships. In the movie *Freedom Writers*, Erin Gruwell, played by Hilary Swank, tells her father of her difficult but exciting calling to help a group of inner-city kids who want to stay together with her as their teacher as they complete their last couple of years in high school. "You've been given the gift of a burden," her father responds. Reclaiming relationships in our families, business, politics, and religion is nothing short of the gift of a burden.

Relationships and Human Capital

Reclaiming relationship is central to developing incremental human capital. Everyone from Adam Smith to Karl Marx has taken a swing at defining human capital—I define it as our human abilities.

Incredible progress has been made in the past several hundred years in freeing human capital to govern itself and pursue economic independence and success. For instance, analysts estimate that from 1950 to the present, the average annual income per capita in the world has increased to $7,000, from $2,000, with poor countries growing at about the same rate as the rich ones. This growth gave us the greatest mass exit from poverty in world history.[12]

Yet the current state of our economy in the United States and around the world points to severe inequality. Although this is a very complicated problem with no simple solution, it is hard to refute that the growing chasm between the relational "haves" and "have-nots" is making this problem worse. Our problem isn't too much or too little capitalism; it is developing relationships that grow human capital that in turn produces economic, social, and emotional well-being. The rub comes because developing relationships is messy and requires hands-on efforts.

In attempting to solve the human capital problem, we have tried top-down government social programs that are bureaucratic. We have tried tax credits, subsidies, and technology that were designed to add money or information to the equation but unfortunately failed to build stronger relationships or success. When the British government redistributed large amounts of money from rich to poor regions, for example, regional inequality accelerated. As David Brooks has noted, inequality in income mostly results from inequality in human capital—which cannot be so easily taxed and redistributed.[13]

In reality, human capital is primarily developed through relationships, from the bottom up. If we are committed to making a difference, we must pay attention to what really develops us: the caring, coaching, and accountability of competent healthy relationships. The inconvenient truth is that people need people. It is a truth more complicated that just sending money or hired guns, or providing tools such as technology. Democracy, freedom, and economic opportunity—all key tools for developing productive relationships—have delivered great wealth, but these advancements have now become weakened as they cannibalize the very relationships that produced them.

Some believe the financial incentives that drive capitalism by themselves are enough. Yet we see the same limitations in society that are apparent with organizations regarding incentives. Too many of the incentives have become "winner take all," available only to a few. Those who no longer believe they have a chance will be immune to such incentives. In fact, they will most likely disengage and oppose. We must become more intentional about developing more team-oriented financial and nonfinancial incentives that reinforce productive and accountable relationships.

Relational Capacity

If we are serious about further developing human capital, it will require the development of enhanced relational capacity. I use the term *relational capacity* to define the potential of relationships, working in concert, to be highly productive. For families, it means environments that create functional households, strong parental support for productive children, stable workers, recovery from adverse conditions such as illness, payment of taxes, support of other family members as needed, or volunteer efforts to support those in need. For organizations, this productivity can mean manufactured products, new customers, new markets, or better social services.

The very concept of a family, business, or nonprofit organization assumes that some level of synergy exists. Whether that synergy existed to reproduce, to band together to avoid predators, to hunt, or to build, it is basic to relational economies of scale that a committed, competent, accountable group can do certain things quicker, cheaper, more reliably, more often, or with higher quality. Research shows that two parents are more productive in raising children than one. A manufacturing plant can build a car faster, cheaper, and of higher quality than a single person can. Some tasks are so complicated or massive that it is humanly impossible for an individual to know or do everything necessary to perform all of the tasks. Relational capacity is the capability to capture the inherent productive potential of a group in performing important work. This applies just as much to parents working to provide and care for children as it does to workers in a factory.

Relational capacity requires the commitment and competence of stakeholders to build strong, functional, lasting relationships that then bear fruit. Relationship capacity is all about attracting, motivating, developing, and then retaining these targeted relationships. Attraction requires some level of affinity, causing relationships to initially form. Motivation involves building commitment and energy. Development involves advancement through learning, feedback, and accountability to increasingly produce over time. Retaining relationships requires a level of cohesion and glue that helps the relationship stay together even in difficult circumstances.

In an organization, relational capacity means forming, staying formed, producing, and advancing key stakeholders: employees, customers, management, owners, suppliers, partners, and others. Each stakeholder gives enough to the others that the relationship not only survives but also grows. It involves dealing with disagreement, conflict, short-term failure, and unwarranted success in ways that make relationships stronger and more productive over time. The energy and excitement that relationship capacity creates are very apparent; we have all walked into a store or a restaurant, for example, or visited a family where the relational energy points to the presence (or absence) of relational capacity. It is not surprising that IBM's study on the global CEO showed that team-oriented cultures were more profitable than were more segregated ones, producing nearly three times the average operating margin.[14]

Family relational capacity is no different; it also means forming, staying formed, and producing more output together than apart. Organizations and families operating with an ample supply of relational capacity are much better equipped to deal with relational or related challenges because they have reserves to draw on. Conversely, those operating on empty cannot withstand adversity because they are vulnerable, and a little adversity can put them under. Think of the personal and organizational relationships in your own network: Where is there ample relationship capacity and where are you running on empty?

The relational models deployed by organizations in biblical times, such as the use of slave labor that built the pyramids, were driven by a one-sided power-exercising force. Likewise, family relationships historically have placed a premium on control and compliance, most often with the male in the role of authority. More recently, we have moved from the power of force and oppression to one of freedom and reciprocal relationships. Yet we seem to have let go of the former without fully mastering how to deal with the latter. The list below is an instructive reminder of how relational capacity helps us make this shift and contributes to personal and organizational productivity.

- **Relational capacity generates energy.** Increasing relational capacity increases energy. Some of the people and organizations we interact with add to our energy while others drain us. Those adept at building and sustaining strong relational capacity by valuing and obtaining value from others build the energy supply to get important and difficult things done. Leader arrogance toward those in lesser roles chews up large chunks of relational capacity.

- **Relational capacity translates conflict and diversity into influence and innovation.** Poorly managed or suppressed conflict drains relational capacity, while differences handled effectively can be sources of influence, innovation, and risk taking. In families and organizations, dealing with conflict prepares children and workers for a diverse world.

- **Relational capacity enables learning and development.** Strong relationship cultures are very intentional about promoting learning, while organizations that focus on short-term productivity to the exclusion of learning atrophy. When learning stops, energy and innovation decline and productivity suffers.

- **Relational capacity requires accountability.** Accountability is the way individuals and organizations correct past mistakes and avoid future mistakes.

Building relational capacity means making relationships a top priority. It requires being attentive to decisions and actions for their impact on stakeholder relationships. As the marketplace becomes more global and competitive, our personal freedoms expand, work becomes less physical and more knowledge based, and we become more partisan—the importance of relationship capacity grow exponentially.

Making the Change: A Model for Cultivating Growth

A civilization flourishes when people plant trees under whose shade they will never sit.

—Greek proverb

Building relational capacity requires intention. When something is in a state of decline, outflow exceeds inflow. For relationships, this means they are being harvested at a faster rate than they can be grown. We will now examine how the prevalent model of premature harvest must be shifted to one of cultivation and development.

PREMATURE HARVEST

The harvest of relationships becomes premature when selfish, short-term interests get in the way of development, maturation, and longer-term realization of potential. You could argue that Wall Street is a "harvest machine" in that it converts business interests into cash through events such as public offerings, sales, divestitures, and private equity deals. Harvesting is big business, which helps explain, as referenced earlier, why major banks and securities firms get paid such large sums.[15]

Harvest is an important season that is part of the cycle of life. Having a market for what is reaped is a good thing and drives owners to invest. It delivers accountability to business leaders in the same way farmers and gardeners plant with a future harvest in mind. The problem arises when there is so much attention focused on the harvest that it subverts the operation and development of the business by shrinking its relational capacity. Too often the exit strategy has come to dominate and overwhelm the planting, growth, and development. Sooner or later this reduces relational capacity, thus decreasing sales and profits by lowering the weight of what is harvested. Recent years have been defined by organizations and their executives overdeveloped in harvest capability and underdeveloped in organic growth and development.

I have experienced this harvest mania firsthand. In the spring of 1998, at my company's quarterly meeting, prompted by a couple of shareholders eager to cash out, we decided to start preparation to take my company public. We had doubled our revenue the previous year and were on track to grow over 50 percent the following year. Southern Methodist University's Cox School of Business had recognized us as one of the fastest-growing companies in Dallas, and I had been a finalist for Ernst & Young's Entrepreneur of the Year for the Southwest region of the United States. We selected investment bankers and were off and running.

I was not prepared for just how profoundly it would alter the very fabric of the organization. In order to show a strong and predictable level of growth each quarter, it was imperative to get deals closed in three-month increments. Because of their size of our deals, one or two closing a little early or late could materially change our numbers. I found myself trying to orchestrate activities and harvest outcomes in very short intervals. Quarterly accountability was certainly not new, of course, and it can be very helpful in improving discipline and decision making. However, in retrospect, it is clear we crossed a line; it became extreme.

In trying to get deals done on our schedule, we frayed relationships with some customers, made short-term decisions, and shifted our strong relationship culture into a "premature harvest" mode. Compounding the challenge, we found ourselves in the early stages of the tech bubble. I learned up-close and personal just how debilitating it was when customer and employee relationships took a backseat to short-term financial "harvest" targets. Our growth slowed to 25 percent, and in 2000 we sold to a public company.

In personal relationships, the one-night stand has become the quintessential example of a short-term relationship designed specifically for harvesting, which can lead to outsourcing the parenting of kids. Among the wealthy, prenuptial agreements can reflect a relationship designed with a "harvest" end in mind—convenient parting. Steve Jobs, the late founder and CEO of Apple, expressed it this way: "I hate it when people call themselves 'entrepreneurs' when what they're really trying to do is launch a startup and then sell or go public, so they can cash in and move on. They're unwilling to do the work it takes to build a real company, which is the hardest work in business. That's how you really make a contribution and add to the legacy of those who went before."[16] Likewise, empty political promises fall into the same category.

Media messages now play a significant role in the abuse of harvest. Your new best friend is really a poorly disguised ad person trying to sell you a car, fast food, beer, cellular service, or otherwise shape your wants, needs, and buying behaviors. These messages usually promote spending but not investing. We have turned over a great deal of our relational and instructional resources to those in premature harvest mode, and that has undermined the very essence of relationship.

CULTIVATING GROWTH AND DEVELOPMENT

If we are to reclaim relationships, we must make growing and developing relationship capacity a much higher priority. A mind-set of growth carries a specific set of assumptions, beginning with a unique view of time. Growth involves a sequenced process in the same way planting precedes harvesting, giving precedes getting, and investing precedes return. Nurture and care are a part of the growing process. We sometimes forget that the food for the meal we are enjoying was grown and cared for over a long period of time.

We must seek relationships in which to become invested. Personal, business, political, and religious entities in the age of relationship will choose to be in communities where investment and growth are prized and linked.

Organic growth is most productive when cultivated. This is true whether you are talking about plants or humans. Farmers and gardeners know that planting is not enough. There is ongoing investment of time and effort in order to support growth that involves planting, cultivating, pruning, and harvesting. Just like the maintenance required for machinery, long-term and proactive upkeep and repairs are necessary for relational development.

Sometimes we plant and invest in places where great relationships and great returns spring forward, exceeding our highest expectations—and other times, not so much. However, giving is often its own reward. Research has shown that those who give to charity are 40 percent more likely to report that they are "very happy" than are nondonors.[17]

YOU ARE WHAT YOU GIVE, NOT WHAT YOU GET

For two consecutive weeks, the same guy slipped into the back row of the class for a summer series I was teaching on relationships at a church in a neighboring town. His was the look of a person in deep despair. The second week, as I was heading out of the classroom, he was waiting at the door. He asked if I had a minute and we ducked back into the vacated room. Seemingly out of nowhere, in short, non-emotional phrases, the dam broke: This man's marriage was teetering on the edge, he had lost his job, and his teenager had drug addiction issues and was on the verge of being expelled from school. The only thing sadder than his words was the hollow look in his eyes and the emptiness in his voice. I listened but couldn't muster a single word of advice other than to see a counselor. He was. The next week, we had a similar discussion after class.

Over the following weeks we had lunch several times. The issues were overwhelming and there were no easy answers. I suggested he find a place to volunteer locally with the homeless. Nothing puts issues in perspective like working with people who have lost everything yet who often retain a strong sense of faith, gratitude, and hope. He found a local shelter and began to serve food on Wednesday nights.

After several months of volunteering, we got together for lunch. My class had ended and I hadn't seen him since those early conversations. He looked like a different person. The light had returned to his eyes. His voice had energy. We laughed. He had several new ideas regarding ways to feed the homeless. I asked him about his family. He had found a job. His marriage was still a struggle and his teenager was barely getting by. His circumstances were less volatile but still troubling. Yet he was dramatically better. It has now been 10 years and we stay in touch. He is still volunteering.

I wasn't surprised. About a fourth of the volunteers I work with who desperately try to find jobs for residents are themselves unemployed. There are other issues. Amy, one of the volunteers I partner with, is an attorney who lives alone. She started to volunteer when she started chemo treatments for cancer. Amy continued to show up despite being tired and worn out, losing her hair, and having to undergo unscheduled brain surgery. Why? Nothing heals pain, emptiness, and loss like helping others. Unlike anything else, relationships are the solution to the relationship problem—self-focus, separation, and abandonment are treated by relationally giving to others.

The good news is that society is beginning to recognize the downside of self-absorption and how it separates us. When we are self-absorbed, it not only creates abandonment for those we are close to, but we become abandoned as well. Because of what they experienced growing up, younger generations are more deliberate about marriage than their parents, in trying to avoid divorce and relational divide.

Winston Churchill's relational admonition holds true: "You make a living by what you get; you make a life by what you give." The almost unlimited possibilities in today's consumer economy may make getting more tempting, but we are defined by what we give. There is something that is tangibly unbecoming when getting dwarfs giving, and we forsake relationships and serving. It is why helping the homeless, if they are able, to find jobs is so important. Sure, it reduces welfare cost, but the act of contributing and giving is what we desperately need to feel alive and whole.

There are a million ways to abide in constructive, productive, contributing relationships. I have recently worked with a partially disabled, elderly woman who has had a difficult time making ends meet in a government-subsidized apartment. When I first started working with her, she required someone (funded by a government program) to come in and help prepare her midday meal. As her health improved following surgery, she called to tell me she had a job: She was going to help take care of another lady four hours a day, four days a week. Her whole countenance changed when she knew she would be able to work, create, help others, and yes, earn some additional money that she really needed. Giving, working, and producing gave her life.

If the joy and benefit of giving is so apparent, why do we experience so little of it? We all know that some of our toughest work is in relationships where we get no return. I attended a talk by Milos Forman, the Czechoslovakia-born director of such movies as *One Flew Over the Cuckoo's Nest* and *Amadeus*. Mr. Forman was asked to comment on the political implications of his movie *Goya's Ghost*, which tells of the French invasion of Spain by Napoléon during the last years of the Spanish Inquisition. His response was, "Sometimes very good seed—freedom, liberty, and the early strains of democracy—is planted in unfertile soil." Relationship disappointments can be so painful that they discourage future planting and engagement.

In the world of relationships, planting must be followed by cultivating, which means committing to giving of our time, attention, and focus. Meeting, talking, coaching, supporting, encouraging, and providing honest feedback are ways we cultivate relationships.

Pruning and weeding are particularly tricky aspects of cultivation. In the midst of growth, there is the need to get rid of undesirable or superfluous growth because it is not purposefully aligned and absorbs precious, scarce resources. The ability to prune and weed in a way that promotes purposeful growth versus cuts that destroy is both art and science.

Arie de Geus, the father of scenario planning at Royal Dutch Shell, describes the choice that rose gardeners face each spring, which greatly influences the long-term fate of the garden: "If you want to have the largest and most glorious roses of the neighborhood, you will prune hard . . . if you are in a spot where you know nature may play tricks on you, you may opt for a policy of high tolerance." Hard pruning with little tolerance may beget bigger roses in the short run, but higher-tolerance pruning enhances your chance of having roses every year.[18]

The bureaucratic growth of organizations requires regular and purposeful trimming. Much of the radical downsizing of organizations was required because proper pruning had not been performed periodically, at the right time. The larger an organization gets, the harder it is to trim. In our personal relationships we are also confronted with relationships that have moved outside of boundaries, migrate to abusiveness, or exhibit other problems. Often it is in confronting attitudes and behaviors detrimental to a relationship that some of the most important trimming takes place. And sometimes we find ourselves in relationships from which we must remove ourselves. Pruning or being pruned can be painful because no one wants to be identified as the weed in someone else's garden.

Harvest is a crucial time. Timing and conditions can have a huge impact on the results. Ultimately, the best stewards take the gains from the harvest—seeds, money, insights—and use them for the next planting. It is a never-ending cycle.

The bottom line is that building relationships is an organic process that requires placing a high value on planting and cultivating first, with the harvest a more distant, yet bountiful, outcome.

Goals and Metrics That Support Relational Growth

Placing a higher priority on growing relationships and building relational capacity means altering the goals, metrics, and incentives we currently use. Organizations have fallen in love with metrics that provide financial and operational insights. As Friedman said regarding Iraq, we historically counted KIAs (killed in action) but not RBs (relationships built). Likewise in our personal relationships, we know how much money we have in the bank, the mortgage balance on our home, and the cost of braces for our children but are in denial about the state of our relationships. What we need are goals and metrics that will enable us to manage our relational capacity and lower the considerable costs of broken, dysfunctional, or nonexistent relationships.

Relationship goals are simply a way to identify what you relationally aspire to. What are the goals that can help us prioritize relationships? The answer is different for each of us. Take, for example, budgeting specific time each week to nurture relationships with family and friends, which we say are very important to us. There are indications that this is beginning to happen.

Smart organizations are providing more time and flexibility to parents for child-related activities. Executives are given more flexibility to decline positions so they don't have to move their families. While this clearly doesn't help the majority of workers who are not executives, it's a start. When I went to work for Arthur Young & Company (now Ernst & Young) in the 1970s as a consultant, we would typically fly out on Sunday afternoon or evening and return late on Friday night. Today, a more typical arrangement is to fly out on Monday morning and return Thursday evening. We followed the same practice in my own company when possible. While this may not seem significant, it actually doubled the number of nights at home from two per week (Friday and Saturday) to four (Thursday through Sunday), which really improved the lives of our consultants and lowered the hotel expenses charged to our clients. More and more families are setting aside family nights, which was the norm for every night 50 years ago.

The values and desires of young people coming into the workplace reflect a growing emphasis on family relationships. For example, in 2007 a network of more than 125 top law graduates from places like Stanford e-mailed hiring partners and recruiting coordinators at the top 100 law firms asking them to sign on to principles promoting a more sane work environment. They hit this issue head-on: "We are working to ensure that practicing law does not mean giving up a commitment to family, community, and dedicated service to clients."[19] They went on to acknowledge that changes in work structures would come with an economic cost and that they were willing to be paid less in exchange for a better working life.

This reflects a changing dynamic: giving up money for family, community, and client relationship time. Yet the law-grad petition was circulated prior to the 2008 recession that saw a number of law firms rescind offers to law grads, thus making it harder to win these kinds of concessions. In the real world, economic conditions impact relationships.

As we assess where we want to grow relationships in our lives, there are four key relational goals all of us should keep in mind:

- **Retention**: investing in key at-risk relationships in order to save them

- **Expansion**: targeting existing relationships for growth or advancement in a specific way

- **Attraction**: identifying new relationships to add to our networks

- **Cost management**: redirecting energy away from costly or time-consuming activities that prevent focusing on key, targeted relationship building

Setting goals to strengthen and redirect relationships is a first step toward making them a priority, and it requires a new set of metrics—relationship metrics.

Most organizations have a number of revenue, investment, and cost goals associated with key relationships: revenue per customer, average cost per employee, average donation, or holdings per shareholder. A number have progressed to track the tenure of relationships: average tenure per customer or customer group, average tenure per employee, or average holding period per shareholder. The next level is to better understand the leading indicators that inform and predict success. What are we doing to develop metrics that will tell us we are on track to building deeper and higher-quality relationships?

Harrah's in Las Vegas has focused on how to create a set of relationship metrics. They migrated their metrics from how much people spent in their casinos during a single stay to their value over time. They focused on improving customer service and the overall experience by training everyone from housekeepers to slot attendants, from valets to stewards, and from receptionists to chefs. The goal that is reinforced each day they come to work is this: "If your service can persuade one customer to make one more visit a year with us, you've had a good shift. If you can persuade three, you've had a great shift."[20]

Relationship metrics hold up a mirror that forces examination and accountability. In our families, it is increasingly important to track our relationship time with spouses, partners, and children to ensure that we are aligned with our priorities. We need to protect the one-on-one time we have with those most near and dear to us—time when we are not distracted. It is interesting how this plays out with kids. I once missed a very important client meeting with a CEO and his team in Canada to coach my daughter who was pitching in the finals of a junior high softball tournament. To this day this is something she still mentions. It made an impression on her precisely because I had given up an important priority in the business to put her first (full disclosure: I had also missed my share of her games). It conveyed that our relationship was really important. As children grow older, time for closeness has to happen when they are ready. In addition to setting aside time in advance, we have to stand by in a rigid state of flexibility so that when they need us, we can be there for them.

We allocate time to relationships every day—sometimes on purpose and sometimes by accident. While we do not have complete control over relationships, we do have control over how we allocate our relational resources. It comes down to this: Relationships require cultivation. Relational goals and metrics, whether formal or informal, track our alignment with what we say we value. What gets measured gets done. Metrics help make us accountable for living our relational values.

Good News: The Age of Relationship

Mounting evidence indicates that people are making relationships a renewed priority. Some of the specific indicators are quite compelling, beginning with parents recognizing how important relational time with their children is. In 1965, mothers spent 10.2 hours per week primarily dedicated to tending to their children (defined as feeding, reading, playing games, etc.). While this dipped in the 1970s and 1980s, it is now higher than ever at 14.1 hours—a 38 percent increase. Certainly, many parents today were children of parents during the period when the amount of time spent was much lower. It's likely that their experience influenced this renewed commitment to relationships. The one exception is the time that single mothers, our most rapidly growing parent segment, spend with their children, which has declined significantly, from 50 to 44 hours, as they juggle roles as wage earner and parent.[21]

As parents are finding ways to invest in more relational time with their children, city planners and architects are beginning to design communities more conducive to building relationships and relational capacity. These towns include more community space such as town squares, trails, and parks.

There is growing evidence that relationship efforts across our society are paying off: The divorce rate has declined from its peak in 1981 of 5.3 to 3.4 in 2009 (per 1,000 of the population—partially due to fewer marriages and more cohabitation).[22, 23] The crime rate, incarceration, and drug use of teenage boys has declined.[24]

Younger generations, including the 75 million members of Generation Y, are more relationally and socially conscious. They are more than twice as likely as other generations to report that consulting with their family members was the most influential factor in the decisions they made. Eighty percent have donated their time to a nonprofit cause, and 69 percent consider a company's social and environmental commitment when deciding where to shop.[25]

Business practices at some of the country's top companies are being designed to foster longer-term, committed relationships:

- Costco strategically pays higher wages than other discounters do.
- Starbucks provides health benefits for part-time workers.

- Google has moved to grant employees greater say in selecting their work projects.

- The Container Store hires its best customers and sets a workday for some workers that runs from 9:00 AM to 2:00 PM to accommodate their children's school schedules.[26]

Faced with research showing that 62 percent of women who graduate from Harvard Business School leave the corporate world after having their second child, Deloitte & Touche has developed a program that allows employees to leave for up to five years and return. During the time they are away, those employees receive training to keep their skills current. As a result of this program, the difference in employee dropout rates between women and men has been erased.[27]

There is also evidence that process improvement initiatives such as reengineering, Six Sigma, and outsourcing are slowing as organizations get smarter about their impact on longer-term relational capacity, so vital to their growth.

Organizations are placing greater emphasis on 360-degree feedback to obtain key relational insights from all angles, to better understand how attitudes and behavior impact performance. We even hear organizations these days talking about a "no jerks" culture and taking action to dismiss dysfunctional employees from the workplace, no matter how talented they may be.[28] It is refreshing to see companies adding weight to the long-term relational view.

On the political front, the growth of independent voters reflects a desire to move toward more relationally functional discourse and constructive political action. While we may lament the relational outcome, George W. Bush, Barack Obama, Arnold Schwarzenegger, and Michael Bloomberg all campaigned on the platform of bringing people together, which seems to reflect an electorate hungry for relational progress.[29] The 2010 midterm elections were an about-face back to the right, just like the 2008 election was a move to the left. The relational carnage of these swings only reinforces the need to reclaim political relationships that can function and address crucial challenges.

* * * *

Relationships are the key source of organic growth. And organic growth requires a series of steps—planting, cultivating, and pruning—that ultimately produce bountiful harvests. Social relationships must be nurtured in order to develop and grow. If we are serious about making relationships a priority and claiming the fruit of a new age where relationships rule, we must do things differently.

There is a little exercise we called "Big Rocks" when we used it with branch or store staff to demonstrate the importance of making their customer relationships the highest priority. We took a jar along with a bunch of small marbles and two or three large rocks several times the size of the marbles. First we would fill the jars with the marbles and then try to add the big rocks, and there was not enough room left to get the big rocks in the jar. Then we would empty the jar and put the big rocks in first and then fill in with the small marbles, and all of them would fit in the jar. The point is that if you start with the big priorities—put them in the jar first—the smaller things would fill in around them and there was room for all. Relationships, including the difficult ones, are the big rocks of our lives. Put them in the jar first.

Going all-in for stronger, more functional, lasting relationships is not a spectator sport; it requires active effort and engagement. It reminds me of the way Anglican priest and author Nicky Gumbel describes European football (soccer): "22,000 people who desperately need exercise watching 22 people who desperately need rest." For the cause of relationships, each of us must get on the field.

Chapter 12

Reclaiming Small and Local That Is Bigger and Better

A nationwide survey of more than 1,800 independent businesses by the Institute for Local Self-Reliance (ILSR) found them outperforming chain competitors . . . independent retailers in communities with active "Buy Independent" or "Buy Local" campaigns reported an increase in holiday sales three times stronger.

—*Jeff Milchen, cofounder, American Independent Business Alliance*[1]

I n the 2008 National Basketball Association first-round playoffs, the home team won 64 of 86 games, a winning percentage of 74. In the second round, the home team won 22 of 25 games (88 percent) over the road team.[2] While this represented an unusual home court advantage, and the teams with better records had a slight edge in the number of games played at home, home teams have won 60 percent of their NBA regular-season games for 20 years, consistent with the edge to home teams in other sports. Same ball, same rules, same-size court, same opposing players and coaches—yet playing at home yields a measurable and recurring double-digit advantage. What is the source of this advantage? It is the spirit of community—local, known, and championed—that flows from relationship and cultivates better performance.

The spirit of small and local is an invisible, relational force that breathes life, animation, and energy within and among us. Small and local is a structure that nurtures relational capacity in the same way the home team feeds off the energy of the crowd. It is a marked contrast to loneliness, which, as discussed earlier, signals starvation and danger. Whether we are talking about kids, pro basketball players, or ourselves, community triggers and feeds growth and development.

Our quest for relationship is nothing less than the desire to live more of life as the equivalent of the home team rather than the visitor. Home teams win more often because having people root for them is a potent force or gift—making them more committed and accountable. In his book *Community: The Structure of Belonging*, Peter Block says the small group is the unit for transformation.[3] And although the transformative power of small groups is not always good (misguided peer pressure or gang influences are negative), they almost always effect change. Small groups present a place where every voice can be heard, where belonging resides, isolation is overcome, and accountability is real. Small and local is the infrastructure of relationships, where rebuilding takes place.

The spirit of small and local is making a comeback, not unlike the parable of the prodigal son. It does not mean returning to a simpler past, shunning advancements that have improved our lives, or even eschewing large organizations. Rather, it means discovering how to reclaim local community in a relationally challenged era.

Just as the declining physical demands of the workplace have not diminished the need for exercise, the relational shortcuts available to our society have not eliminated the need for relationships. The workout center for building and growing these irreplaceable relationships is the local community. In this chapter we will examine how that is occurring.

The Resurgence of Small and Local

The balance of advantage—in nearly every aspect of society—is shifting from big organizations to small ones. Economies of scale and scope matter much less in the information age than in the industrial one.

—Glenn Reynolds, An Army of Davids

When I was a boy, one of my jobs every spring was to mend the fences on our ranch before we turned the cattle out to pasture. For several weekends in March and April, I would saddle up and ride horseback alongside the several miles of fence, repairing broken barbed wire and washed-out water gaps so the cattle would not wander off. The spring that I was 10 years old, I was riding the fences on the back side of our largest pasture, which we called Coon Creek. There, a large, heavily wooded area surrounded a natural spring that ran year-round and produced cool, clear water. As I made my way through the trees down the slope toward the spring, something startled my horse. I looked up ahead to see a number of empty sugar sacks and several large barrels and some copper tubing—all out of place. Then it hit me: I had ridden up on a bootlegger's (so named for concealing illegal flasks of whiskey inside boots) still. My heart pounded.

I knew of a couple of people around the area, including the father of one of my classmates, who had gone to prison when they got caught making and selling illegal whiskey. They were tough, typically armed, and drove fast cars with heavy-duty overload springs for hauling the whiskey and outrunning the sheriff.

I looked around to see if anyone had seen me. I did not see anyone but wondered if I was being watched, if a bootlegger had a gun aimed at me. (Maybe I had seen too many Westerns.) I was sure whoever owned this still would be determined to keep me from turning him in to the sheriff. It felt as though I had walked into the middle of a robbery. Fortunately, no one materialized, and I quietly eased my horse down the slope, past the still, by the spring, and out of the woods into an opening. Then I ran my horse the couple of miles to the house. I breathlessly told my dad what I had found. I asked him if he was going to call the sheriff and was I at risk because once the owners of the still saw my horse tracks, they would know they had been discovered. My dad paused in his quiet and confident way and said he thought he knew whose still it was, and that before he called the sheriff, he was going to go talk with the man. He went that very night. Sure enough, the guy admitted it was his and, shaken up, promised to remove it immediately. As quickly as the episode began, it ended.

In looking back, I can't help but be intrigued at the efficiency of the process by which this local problem was resolved. No sheriff, no deputies, no jail, no lawyers, no legal action, no paperwork—enforcement happened overnight. Granted, the crime of producing contraband whiskey was not prosecuted, but the illegal trespassing and violation of property rights were elegantly addressed. (Word spread, incidentally, that the bootlegger quit making whiskey.)

In community there exists a form of local, relational scale or proportion that can exert influence efficiently and very effectively. Today we are hungry to restore some of that unique local relationship scale that enables us to cut through the crap with both grace and accountability to get things done.

If the loss of local is something valued and worth reclaiming, then it is important to focus on what the essence of "local" is and the relational value it can restore to our lives. Distant, large, impersonal, alien, inauthentic, separated, uncaring, selfish, mechanical, bureaucratic, mercenary, uncommitted, indifferent, and one-size-fits-all are all descriptors of life in a land of strangers. By contrast, strong local communities are described as close, small, belonging, personal, authentic, connected, caring, giving, warm, altruistic, committed, attentive, customized, accountable, and trusted. While the economies of scale can be attractive with the former, local or human scale is part of an emerging advantage that can be holistically and synergistically more productive, fed by greatly needed growth and development.

Home is the place safe from strangers. It is the place you know and where you are known. It is where you count the most and are supported. It is a place where you have influence by knowing and being yourself. No home is perfect, of course, and some are downright dysfunctional. It is the ideal of home that we are addressing here. Home is the place where your weaknesses, foibles, and past mistakes are most likely to be known and where you are loved in spite of them. Home is located in a place called "local," where we are surrounded by people and relationships that grab our heart, cure our loneliness, provide support, and positively influence us. Many of us have lost our sense of belonging. When someone says, "I want to raise my family in a neighborhood where kids can play together and where we know our neighbors," they are expressing a desire for "local," or what in earlier times was called the village.

Communal influences are rising. For most of us, membership in the right local community (be it physical or virtual) brings comfort, influence, and protection from a separated world. We have come to live too much of our lives apart and estranged. A new world is emerging that is attempting to crack the code on how relationships—fed by a spirit of small and local—can rise and become more productive and effective.

The Rise of Small Scale

Carnegie made it abundantly clear that the centerpiece of his gospel of wealth philosophy was that individuals do not create wealth by themselves. . . . The creator of wealth in his view was the community, and individuals like himself were trustees of that wealth.

—*David Nasaw,* **Andrew Carnegie**[4]

Wealth creation—economic, social, emotional, or spiritual—is a community endeavor requiring a host of innovators, producers, supporters, and consumers. Whether at home, at work, or in social organizations, the whole issue of leadership and management is about how to make the community productive, profitable, and valuable for everyone involved.

The good news is that the world is taking notice of the loss of and the need for local. It is occurring on a number of fronts: family, business, government, military, and religious. Large institutional models reliant on hierarchy and bureaucratic rules have struggled to respond to educated, highly informed stakeholders with instant and unlimited access to information along with the ability to organize and mobilize. Think of the recent customer backlash to Netflix's pricing policy; HP's overturned decision to exit the PC market, costing its new CEO his job; or the Tea Party and Occupy Wall Street movements. A new and prolific local model is emerging, where small groups can wield strong influence, power, and consequence. Organizations, communities, and families are returning to their roots to claim the local, human scale that created the value that got us here.

Perhaps there is no more compelling example of the rise of small scale than the 9/11 attacks carried out by a small group of radicals who used box cutters and duct tape to wield incredible destruction. Despite its military might, the United States was unable to prevent it. In Afghanistan and around the world, we are opposed by a decentralized but highly committed terrorist organization made up of locally based groups. Even though the United States' armed forces have superior weapons, organization, and resources, we are finding it hard to compete against smaller and more local groups. The events in both Afghanistan and Iraq illustrate just how powerless commanding power and resources can be when we lack the ability to influence hearts and minds through local relationships. Reporting for the *New York Times*, Rory Stewart observed in 2007 that "Our officials are on short tours, lack linguistic or cultural training, live in barracks behind high blast walls and encounter the local population through angry petitions or sudden ambushes." He concluded that this separation is a significant obstacle to acquiring the sense of values, beliefs, and history needed to create lasting changes, and certainly to leading a political, social, and economic revolution that we initially hoped for.[5]

Short of an enforced permanent military state, sooner or later military power must translate into local political and social influence. Lasting, sustainable political and social influence is driven by relationships. When you are not invested locally, and are perceived as inaccessible and distrusted, there is little likelihood of exerting influence for change. This helps explain why the subsequent surge strategy under General David Petraeus, which relied on a much more local and relational approach—more troop time in the local villages, more relationship building with local leaders, more effort to address local issues like availability of clean water or electricity—has been more effective in Iraq and became a key component of the strategy in Afghanistan. The newer, more relational goal is not only to win the war but also to win the peace.

Whole Foods has taken the mature grocery industry to a whole new (sometimes controversial) level of "local." Each store has the autonomy to carry different local products, something the much larger chains have not traditionally done (though this is starting to change). They promote their efforts on their shopping bags: "Go Local," "Good Stuff from Around Here," "We Support Local Growers and Producers." Whole Foods is so successful it's been one of 13 companies to make *Fortune* magazine's Top 100 Companies to Work For for 13 straight years.[6]

The benefits of small and local now feed a movement. Jessica Prentice, a food writer in San Francisco, coined the term *locavores* to describe this trend. "The local foods movement is about an ethic of food that values reviving small scale, ecological, place-based, and relationship-based food systems."[7] Relationship-based food systems feed our yearning for local and organic connection. Farmers' markets have more than doubled in the past decade, to 6,132 nationwide, according to the U.S. Department of Agriculture.[8] People want to have a relationship with the person who produces the food they eat.

In fact, some have eliminated grocery stores altogether in favor of going direct. As reported in the *New York Times*, more "people are skipping out on grocery stores and even farmers markets and instead going right to the source by buying shares of farms."[9]

Local Harvest, an organic and local food website that has the largest directory of these "Community Supported Agriculture" entities in the country, underscores the point. In 2000, it started with 374 listings and that number has jumped to 4,100.[10]

In another area, more of us are moving our money to smaller, more local banks. Disillusionment and anger at large institutional banks have spilled over into a formal movement with liberals, conservatives, religious, and secular depositors alike pledging to move their money from large banks to small ones. The *Huffington Post*, which has helped lead this movement, provides a website where you can enter your ZIP code and up pops a list of local banks, prescreened for soundness by the group Institutional Risk Analytics.[11] It all culminated in November 5, 2011, with Bank Transfer Day. The natives are getting restless.

And the beat goes on. After spending the last few decades consolidating a bunch of small agencies into a handful of superfirms, the advertising industry has sought to reorganize into new, smaller structures that foster more creative cultures. Paul Lavoie, cofounder of the ad firm Taxi, a leader in working in small units, estimates that as an ad firm approaches 150 people it begins to lose its unique culture.[12] And speaking of advertising, you have probably noticed more ads promoting the local angle. I just saw the following example from a local maker of luxury leather couches. Main heading: "Made in Dallas, Texas." Subheading: "You've seen our sofas, but you may not have known your neighbors made them."[13]

The trend to smaller and more local has a number of large organizations working hard to adopt a more local model that builds greater commitment from customers and employees. Large organizations are recognizing that they have alienated certain groups, especially customers and prospective customers. McDonald's, in attempting to gain acceptance in Europe, advertised that it used local produce and created local jobs.[14] Even Walmart has moved in this direction by undertaking a program to tailor stores to unique local-market needs over a one-size-fits-all approach.[15]

This behavior occurs at a time when a number of local communities are in a running battle to block Walmart, Home Depot, McDonald's, and others from entering their neighborhoods. Locals argue that these behemoths are too large and distant to earn a presence in the local neighborhood. This backlash is the ultimate assertion of distrust by the local communities they hope to serve.

The move to local does not eliminate the need for large, highly efficient organizations (we will talk about the trade-offs later in this chapter). Rather, it means the market is shifting by valuing small and local in new ways. One executive from a large organization told me their strategy was to "out-local the nationals and out-national the locals." In essence, they were going to leverage the advantages of being a large national firm while localizing—market by market.

Small and Local Is the New Big

[The] aim is clear: to shift control of England's $160 billion annual health budget from a centralized bureaucracy to doctors at the local level.

—Sarah Yall, The New York Times[16]

There are many examples of big success from smaller or more regional firms. Chick-fil-A in the fast-food business and Hillstone (formerly Houston's) in the upper end of the casual dining category have strong followings and enviable results. J.D. Power and Associates found that customers of smaller financial institutions such as credit unions and community banks tend to be more satisfied than are customers of those institutions' larger competitors.[17]

Oil exploration is no different: Small wildcatters have discovered about 80 percent of the oil found in the United States; the bigger companies then extract it.[18] The dramatic increase in recoverable reserves of cleaner-burning natural gas in this country was not driven by major oil companies but by innovation, new technology, and know-how of much smaller companies focusing primarily on gas exploration and production.

The public sector is also winning with smaller, more local structures. Since 2002, more than 20 large high schools in New York City—with enrollments of about 3,000 mainly black and Hispanic students and graduation rates as low as 40 percent—have been closed. They have been replaced by much smaller schools with typical enrollments of about 400 students. The results reported in 2010 are impressive: "The average graduation rate for students in the small schools was right at 69 percent, nearly 7 percentage points higher than the rate for students in the traditional schools. That means that the small schools erased about a third of the 20-point graduation-rate gap that currently exists between white students and students of color in New York City."[19] A student population of 400 students or less is designed around a key relational goal: Ensure that the principal knows every student, every teacher knows each student they teach, and students know most of their fellow students. Anonymity disappears. This strong relational model thrives because of relational connection and accountability.

Research conducted in New Mexico schools has shown that smaller schools strengthen relationships between classmates and teachers and can have a profound effect on achievement, particularly with low-income students. In a pilot program conducted at Santa Fe High School, students who started the year below average in math and reading ended the year scoring above average. The improvement was attributed to the relationships that developed between the students and instructors.[20] I recently spoke with an educator I greatly respect who said that, in her opinion and based on her review of available research, the greatest organizational enemy of education is size. Large "dropout factories," a derisive term for schools with less than 60 percent of entering freshman graduating in four years,[21] are not conducive to building the relationships crucial to learning. It explains a key advantage of private schools; they tend to be smaller. Smaller size is not a panacea, but it is one key variable.

Likewise, in our social programs, the Local Nurse–Family Partnership is an example of a more community-centric hands-on model. Started in the 1970s and lauded for its proven effectiveness, the program has been adapted around the country. The partnership provides ongoing home visits by local registered nurses to low-income, first-time mothers. It provides care and support aimed at a healthy pregnancy, competent care for children, and making participants more economically self-sufficient. In the *New Yorker*, Katherine Boo describes how it places nurses who are able to relate to the locals: "They know the environments, and also the values, that shape the choices of young, poor families. When they push young mothers to finish high school, or to talk to their crying babies instead of slapping them, that familiarity can be part of the leverage."[22]

True, this form of relational care is very expensive, but so are the consequences of the no-care alternative. Government programs are in many ways attempting to replicate the role of a parent and stable community—a very tall order. Yet this approach is not just service, but care. Peter Block describes the commitment required: "True commitment is a promise made with no expectation of return—such a promise delivers true care."[23] Care is relational. Money is necessary, but it's not enough. The good news is that we are seeing a growing awareness of the power of this local, relational, and influential form of care.

The emotional and relational nature of care touches our hearts in a way compelling statistics cannot in evoking change. In 2006, researchers conducted a simple behavioral experiment with prospective donors that validates the point.[24] One-third of study participants read about and saw a picture of a poor, starving seven-year-old girl from Africa named Rokia. Another third viewed a statistical snapshot of that part of Africa: 17 million severely hungry people, plagued by food shortages, and another 4 million without homes. The final third read both Rokia's story and the statistical information. Surprisingly, the group that heard only Rokia's story gave the most money. The group given only the statistics gave the least, and the group given both was only slightly more generous. Even a remote personal connection can greatly trump statistics that depersonalize or overwhelm and thus immobilize. Our passion and our accountability are stirred by a relational connection that becomes "localized."

Many megachurches today have found a way to become more local. They have adapted cell groups, small groups of eight to 12 parishioners that meet in their homes several times a month—often sharing a meal, fellowship, personal challenges, and study—to build relationships at the local level. As one person put it, "Ours is not an impersonal thousand-person congregation; it is really one hundred congregations of ten friends each who meet, break bread, study, and discuss topics, then share their joys and concerns."

Likewise, Barna estimates that the house church movement—small home-based churches where people meet in one another's homes and conduct their own programs and study—has grown from 8.8 million to 11.5 million since 2008. "They are turning to small, regular weekly gatherings where they pray, worship, study Scripture and support each other's spiritual lives without all the trappings of a building, a budget, an outside authority or, often, even a pastor . . . they 'do church,' rather than 'go to church.'"[25]

It is a very relationship-centric, local model. "Love your neighbor" is about embracing your local community. It is what successful churches do well. It is interesting that when local relationships form and develop around helping those in need, the power of the relationships grows much stronger. Neighbors helping neighbors: There could not be a more basic message about organic growth and development for churches.

Dealing with the uncommitted and relationally empty makes us tired, whether it's neighborhoods or churches full of strangers. Our need for relationships is driving us toward small and local. It is nothing less than a strong gravitational pull to come home.

Family: Small and Local Begins at Home

The journey to fill the void of small and local begins at home. More than anything else, what divides the haves from the have-nots isn't just money; it's the presence or absence of strong relationships that undergird them. Families are the foundation of society, and how we think and act regarding family relationships dramatically affects outcomes. As we've discussed, many today—mostly haves—are waiting longer to get married and have children, in part because they desire more stable relationships with their children than they experienced with their parents. No one is more aware of the pain of broken homes than those raised during this period of rising divorce and relationship decline. Premarital counseling, discussion of roles during the early child-rearing years, greater sharing of household duties, focusing on establishing more desirable settings for children—all are indicators of a growing relational awareness. Their childhood pain can translate into more committed adult relationships.

The movement to re-embrace family relationships starts with you and me. It means unplugging computers, turning off the television and cell phones, clearing schedules, and making time to be connected. It means more conversations, family meals, and time spent together experiencing life as this most crucial, intimate local community.

This precious time connects us in a number of ways, including embracing where we've come from. While sheer information can translate into knowledge, it is stories about our past that are more potent in building context, wisdom, and positive emotion. Research is revealing what many of us already know: Our family history establishes a relational link that anchors our past and directs our future. Sue Shellenbarger, a columnist for the *Wall Street Journal*, reports on a growing topic of research at Emory University about the impact of family stories on children's development: "What they're finding is that a sense of family history is linked to self-esteem and resiliency in kids. And, contrary to what adults may assume, happily-ever-after tales aren't always best. Instead, stories of relatives grappling with sad or difficult events may give children the wisdom and perspective [needed] to thrive."[26]

A family's story is its historic and social DNA that tells its members who they are and gives them confidence about what they might become. It is this need for a sense of history that often moves adopted children to seek their biological parents. Peter Block describes a deeper motivation: Therapy and healing are really the process of re-remembering the past in a more forgiving way.[27] The story is a powerful device for instructing us in our relationships.

Investment in local communities means growing relationships with neighbors. It means making the time to cultivate relationships with those who live nearby and finding ways to support each other: picking up each other's mail during vacations; cooking meals for an ailing neighbor; taking walks together, forming book clubs, or hosting periodic get-togethers; joining in at block parties and local street parades. And yes, it even includes sharing news by e-mail or website to support face-to-face interactions. It means getting to know, supporting, and purchasing from local merchants, giving them the benefit of the doubt when their prices, selection, and quality are slightly less favorable than the big box store's across town. Local merchants may not have the lowest price, but the added value of a relationship (service, flexibility, trust) can result in an overall lower cost to own. All of these examples are pretty obvious; a century ago they were the status quo. Today we need to be more intentional about investing our time. Time is more than money; it is the core to building relationships.

In a world where relationships hold greater value, families think differently about career advancement and mobility. It is a trend that has been gaining steam for a while: Many of us are willing to pass up promotions and pay increases because of the value attached to current relationships and the estimated relationship cost to family and friends. Some of us are sacrificing opportunities in order to move closer to family members and the experience of smaller communities and local relationships we can't enjoy when we live a long distance away. In some cases it may mean seeking out jobs that require less work-related travel and commuting. When relationships are our highest priority, we pursue decisions and actions that appreciate rather than depreciate relationships—which is especially trying in tough economic times.

Back Home to the Future

Recently, friends of ours were in Italy on vacation. As they were hiking near Monterosso, in the northwestern coastal region of Liguria, Kathy became very ill. She wound up being rescued by helicopter off the side of a mountain and taken to a hospital. By the next morning she was feeling much better. Having gone nearly 24 hours without food, she was famished. When her minimalist breakfast arrived, she was disappointed. What Kathy later learned was that the hospital provides meager food service because the local custom is for family and friends to bring food from home to hospitalized loved ones. Needless to say, this doesn't work very well if you are a guest of that country without local family and friends; however, it can lower the cost of health care while keeping members of the community engaged and accountable in a personal way. Breaking bread together is a time-honored way to share a relationship.

Home is the place where our relationships are most rich, which explains why cocooning, or hibernating at home, is so popular. Home health care, working from home, home nursing care for the elderly, home births, home-based churches, home hospice, and homeschooling have all risen dramatically in recent years. According to a report by the U.S. Department of Education, homeschooling increased 74 percent between 1999 and 2007,[28] with estimates of up to 2.5 million children being homeschooled as of 2008.[29]

Community: Small and Local Fosters Learning and Innovation

This morning 10 of Archie's adult Sunday school students loaded into the church van and came to the hospital so he could teach. They stood around his bed and he went at it despite all of the tubes! He had laid off the morphine pump for four hours to be lucid, and he was wearing a tie with his hospital gown. He was in seventh heaven!

—Linda LeBron (in a note written a few days before her husband, Archie, passed away)

Living local—whether it is a group of students with an engaging teacher, a parent raising a child, peers working together on a team, a customer dealing with a local provider, or a citizen working in a local community or church group—can be the richest environment possible for learning and growing. Living local means being enveloped in an environment of attentiveness. The tools of distraction we have become addicted to—smart phones, computers, iPads—mean attention is in short supply. Yet these tools also enable a new kind of local. According to Google, 73 percent of online activity is related to local content.[30]

Psychologists tell us that one of the most difficult conditions for humans to counter is indifference. We all know what it feels like to be invisible or of no consequence—it feels lousy. Our defense mechanisms seem more sharply tuned to deal with being treated badly through physical or emotional duress.

Indifference is the silent but intrusive weed in society's garden that smothers us. The swing back to local community reflects the need to be invested in accountable relationships where each individual member matters. Living locally involves the hard work of building the trust that enables us to function.

Local community has a big impact on innovation. Whether it was Steven Jobs's garage that birthed Apple's first personal computer or Millard Fuller's vision of the need to build houses for the poor that became Habitat for Humanity, these innovations came from an off-the-beaten-path locale. The idea of an individual or group with a different viewpoint from everyone else's is at the core of local community innovation. Nassim Taleb, author *The Black Swan: The Impact of the Highly Improbable*, describes examples of schools of thought that formed around new ways. "You hear about the Stoics, the Academics, Skeptics, the Cynics, the Pyrrhonians, the Essenes, the Surrealists, the Dadaists, the anarchists, the hippies, the fundamentalists. A school allows someone with unusual ideas with the remote possibility of a payoff to find company and create a microcosm insulated from others. The members of the group can be ostracized together—which is better than being ostracized alone."[31]

Community is also a place of sweat, pain, failure, and even injury. It is a place of setbacks and disappointments, where our efforts don't always pay off. Yet community is our most productive source for development and breakthrough innovations—its absence surely retards both.

Organizations: Re-building Small and Local

Small businesses, defined as employing anywhere from one to 49 people, account for 48 million jobs in the U.S., and medium-sized businesses, between 50 and 499 employees, account for 42 million jobs. Large businesses account for just 17 million.

—Ann Lee, Wall Street Journal [32]

Many of our organizations are built by strangers, for strangers, to serve strangers. Repurposing and revitalizing the relationships of customers, employees, and other stakeholders is a daunting task. It is tempting to simply wait for "them"—the board, executives, the marketplace, or others—to demand better relationships, but there is no "them," only "us." If we are to be a force for more responsive, innovative, engaged organizations, we will have to choose where and how we will do that.

The trick is to optimize the mixture of central and local, much as in war, when air cover is used as a central resource and ground troops are deployed both for combat and to establish local peacekeeping efforts. Strong families, winning teams, and successful organizations understand that both competencies—local bottom-up and central top-down—play a key role.

We have talked about what happens when centralization becomes too large and oppressive. There is also a set of challenges when local becomes too dominant.

Purely local capabilities can be inadequate, overly skewed to community prejudices and even the corruption of local authority. This can play out as cronyism among community politicians or powerful drug lords, mafiosi, or clan leaders. Unchecked local power can be just as corrupting as unchecked central power. Like the intended balance of power between national, state, and local government, the challenge is to optimize the scale and objectivity of central governance with the intense ownership and commitment of local autonomy, insight, and control. To regain our balance we must revalue central and local, but especially local.

Let's look at three types of organizations that can elevate the value of local relational capacity.

Purely local. These organizations are betting on a marketplace of employees and customers with a growing appetite for products and services delivered close to home via a local relationship: independent coffee shops, restaurants, banks, and dry cleaners, as well as churches, synagogues, and mosques, in city neighborhoods and sparsely populated rural areas alike. For example, the *Wall Street Journal* reports that the number of independent cafés in the United States grew from 9,800 in the year 2000 to 14,000 by 2005.[33] Independents are giving Starbucks a run for their money. For a society overdosed on strangers, the future is bright for serving those ready to come home and do business locally. Investors, customers, and employees tired of the corporate world of nonrelationships will increasingly migrate to local organizations to apply their trade and energies. The current high unemployment rate nationwide, coupled with the younger generation's distrust and even disgust with large institutions, provides additional impetus to this form.

Central-local. The mantra is "think global and act local." Today, more than 3,000 franchisors and 500,000 franchisees testify to the powerful growth of this structure that dates back at least 2,000 years.[34] In addition, a number of nonfranchise organizations today operate under this central-local structure, in which the local stores, branches, offices, churches, or other units operate in a decentralized fashion. This model provides a common vision and strategy; centrally driven brands with advertising designed to drive customer traffic; centrally managed product development and standards; and common operational and administrative systems. All of these make for efficient use of shared resources and division of specialized tasks and responsibilities. Yet, this model also promotes local management and even ownership to tailor each location's offerings to the unique needs and opportunities of local markets.

Moving to a central-local way of doing business usually means shifting power and accountability from headquarters. That is often a fight worth having but nonetheless a fight. Having worked with more than 100 public and private organizations attempting to enhance their local capabilities, I can say it takes special leadership, vision, culture, and processes to support this more local approach. Yet, many larger organizations have identified additional opportunities for improving their success through greater localization. For example, ESPN has announced local websites in New York, Los Angeles, and Dallas in what the network's executives labeled only the "first inning" of their effort to provide hyperlocal sports coverage in cities across the country. This type of strategic shift cries out for the passion and competence to make it happen.

Purpose driven. Credit unions, nonprofits like Alcoholics Anonymous, and user-based, open-source software developers like Linux are examples where shared purpose brings people together to build strong relational organizations. The Internet makes the formation and work of these types of groups easier, but many have been around longer than the Internet has been in existence. Shared purpose combined with strong local relationships serves as a form of organization currency that can be much more powerful than money. Purpose-driven organizations provide the potential for rich, relationally meaningful work.

* * * *

Good news. Small and local, the source of our relationships and our communities, is making a comeback. Individuals and even organizations have surveyed the loss of local and are moving to fill the void. In many cases, we are finding ways to create the kind of scale or advantage in local that has been missing. Small and local not only fulfills us emotionally but also adds to society economically, socially, and even militarily.

The resurgence of the spirit of small and local is really about coming home to the place where we have the advantage of others—knowing, supporting, advocating, and rooting for each other. Coming home is not a matter of simply returning to the past; the journey home is also a journey forward in a changed culture and an evolving landscape where a global economy, greater wealth, more sophisticated organizations, and gee-whiz technology are now staples of our existence. Elevating relationships means reembracing the spirit of small and local by reclaiming our families, business, government, and religious organizations. Getting there requires a different form of leadership, the final piece of the puzzle, which we'll explore in the next chapter.

Chapter 13

Embracing Relational Leadership: Where Do We Go From Here?

To save a community, you must first serve the community. To lead a community, you must first love the community.
—Unknown

In his mid-20s and with his GED in hand, Mike joined my company as a warehouse laborer, packing and loading boxes of training materials. When I met him for the first time, he seemed a little rough. Tall and ruggedly handsome, he was nevertheless tough looking with his tattoos and ever-present jeans. His looks and manners reflected the travails of his early years: an alcoholic mother, tumultuous home life, victim of abuse, gang member, drug user, and homeless teen. In fact, Mike had been living out of his car prior to joining us. In a company of polished consultants with advanced degrees, Mike stood out. Yet there was an enthusiasm about him that was magnetic.

Mike was a hard worker who constantly solicited feedback regarding how he could improve. Although inexperienced, he was soon promoted to warehouse manager when the incumbent left. Mike promptly revamped and improved our whole shipping operation. At company meetings, Mike was notorious for asking disarmingly simple but penetrating questions. His drive, eagerness, and intelligence were infectious. He sought advice from our human resource manager (my wife) about how he could advance. She coached him on his writing, speaking, and people skills and advised him to spend more time reading the *Wall Street Journal* rather than the sports page and comics in the local newspaper. He followed her advice and eventually enrolled in evening courses at an area college.

Mike unabashedly asked me how he could advance to become a member of our management team. At the time, I thought it a long shot, but I coached him informally. Not too long after my first book was published, Mike casually said to me that he was going to write a book and that he had already started on it. By the time I sold my company, he had become senior vice president of operations and a member of the management team. He secured a similar role in the company that acquired us.

I had been out of the business for a couple of years when Mike called me one day out of the blue to share his devastation. Another person had been selected to run the division he had just spent two years turning around. Over lunch, we were discussing his options when he mentioned that the division might be sold. That was it! I suggested he was the perfect person to buy it, and we strategized over the next few weeks as he prepared the business plan, identified potential investors, and presented his case. One of the people he met while doing his research wound up hiring him to run his company, and then together they bought his former division.

Today, Mike is CEO of this growing records-management company that has tripled in size in the five years he has been there. The book he wrote and published about his life's story is called *Rock Bottom—From the Streets to Success*.[1] Mike started volunteering with a housing ministry when my wife was named its CEO so he could share his story with and coach and mentor homeless families. Today, Mike speaks frequently to inner-city kids, prison inmates, and families. He is a shining example of how relational leadership that loves and serves community can unleash people's potential and enable growth and development that then reproduces itself.

Not everyone is as hungry, focused, or talented as Mike is. But across our society, in large ways and tiny, there is raw potential in families, communities, workplaces, ordinary citizens, and places of worship waiting to be nurtured, developed, and empowered. There are millions of Mikes; in fact, we are all Mikes. Each of us has parts of our lives that can be upgraded and restored by strong, caring relationships. This leads us to a crucial question: What kind of leadership will be required to change our culture to one that values and builds stronger relationships?

No one sat down 50 years ago and plotted a strategy to create a culture where we are hemorrhaging relationships—and yet we are. We are on the brink of "generational" relationship decline, which means the damage is ingrained and being passed culturally from one generation on to the next. Stopping the bleeding will take more than simply having a strategy to restore relationships. As Louis Gerstner, former CEO of IBM, said, "When strategy and culture clash—culture always wins."[2] The word *culture* is derived from the Latin *colere*, which means "to cultivate or till." In spite of attempts to apply government policies or even private-sector incentives to strengthen relationships with stakeholders such as voters, customers, and employees, the net effect to date is a culture, judged by results, that continues to cultivate relational demise. Brink Lindsey provides an example of how culture is trumping financial incentive. She reports that the wage premium associated with a college degree has jumped to around 70 percent in recent years from around 30 percent in 1980. Meanwhile, the rise in the percentage of people getting college degrees is growing only modestly, and as we have discussed, the number of high school dropouts remains stubbornly high, all but guaranteeing socioeconomic failure. She concludes: "Something is plainly hindering the effectiveness of the market's carrots and sticks. And that something is culture."[3]

Culture is the primary means of change in both our personal and organizational lives. Gerstner described culture as the central focus: "I came to see, in my time at IBM, that culture isn't just one aspect of the game—it is the game. In the end, an organization is nothing more than the collective capacity of its people to create value."[4] So many policy changes in companies and legislative changes in government are an attempt to impose bureaucratically what is desperately needed culturally.

Something has to give. How do we reclaim a more relational culture that expands relational capacity and human capital? Certainly, making relationships a priority and emphasizing small and local are important. However, those will require a different kind of leadership.

Leadership That Builds Relationships

Leadership is the single most important variable for turning schools around and influencing students.

—*Wendy Kopp, founder and CEO, Teach for America*[5]

To reverse what has become both destructive and expensive, we need a specific form of leadership that reinvigorates our culture with productive relationships. Wendy Kopp, who proposed Teach for America in her undergraduate senior thesis in 1989, now leads this national organization as its founder and CEO. Teach for America recruits top college graduates to teach disadvantaged students. In 2011 it had 9,300 members who reach 600,000 students across 34 states.[6] Kopp's model focuses on local leadership—in the classroom—and has demonstrated remarkable results with students in low-income, challenging schools.

What seems so obvious often isn't. Leadership that builds strong relationships involves the head and the heart. The authors of *Primal Leadership* describe the role of leaders as bringing positive emotion to "inspire, arouse passion and enthusiasm, and keep people motivated and committed."[7] Ample research supports the notion that our emotional intelligence, which guides us to tap into feelings of those with whom we relate, may be the most important quality for leaders.[8] It is one of the reasons that charisma has been so highly valued. (Yet, we have also seen misguided charisma acting as a catalyst for negative change—think Hitler.) When large groups of workers become starved for positive relational energy across an organization, motivation, innovation, and commitment all suffer—the relationship economy goes into recession or even depression.

This ability to lead with positive emotion that creates better outcomes is the hallmark of what I call *relational leadership*. Relational leadership is needed because we are increasingly a society that responds to invitation rather than force or coercion. Quoting Gerstner again: "In fact, in the end, management doesn't change culture. Management invites the workforce to change the culture."[9] Control in the form of dictators, lifetime employment, state-ordained religion, and arranged marriages has been replaced by democracies in which citizens are invited to choose leaders, marriage partners, employers, investments, and faiths. In this world of invitation, relational pull—rather than push—is a magnified source of power or energy for forming or disbanding. Brute force is still a means of change, but the cost in this connected world, where information flows like water, is a prohibitive loss of stakeholder commitment.

This is where it gets personal. Each of us is a leader. We must ask ourselves: How can I be a source to bring out more relational capacity—that is, more like Mike and Wendy—in myself and those in my path? Now, honestly, as we have talked about all of our society's relationship challenges, have you found yourself wishing the president, Congress, CEOs, religious leaders, and all those dysfunctional families out there would get their relational act together? We cop out if we look to others for that. It begins with our own relational leadership in our homes and neighborhoods, in work and social groups. So let's take a closer look at how we can become a relational leader, wherever we are.

Relational Leadership: What It Looks Like

Netted out, relational leadership is leadership that builds relational capacity. It cultivates, releases, and levers the inherent productive potential of a family, team, group, or organization in producing purposeful outcomes. Over time it reinforces and reproduces itself by contributing to a relational culture. Leadership is a complex subject; much has been written about participative and related styles of management. Yet often what has been missing is the full relational, cultural context that now makes this shift so necessary. Here, we'll focus on three key components of leadership that are inherently relationship oriented and central to building relational capacity.

RELATIONAL PURPOSE

Relational purpose reminds me of a story I once heard. A traveler came across a group of stonemasons. He asked the first worker what he was doing. "I am busting rocks," was the answer. The traveler asked the second mason, who responded, "I am cutting stone. It is backbreaking work, but I earn two shillings a day." When the third worker was asked the question, he paused, raised his eyes to the heavens, and said, "I am building a cathedral."

Worthy purpose is relational because it engages and invites our hearts. It is what transports us beyond self or our task and unites us with others around something higher. Seeking higher purpose in small things and large is where relational leadership begins. As leaders become more wealthy and powerful, purpose can become more elusive. For example, making enough money to feed your family can be a worthy purpose, but as you become rich, making as much profit as possible any way you can drains purpose. The relational leader is continually clarifying and refining purpose as a force for growing the connection among stakeholders and the organization. Why are the late Steven Jobs and Apple Corporation so revered even though they became very rich? They remained committed to their purpose—designing really cool high-tech products—which trumped the quest for profits and in the process actually contributed greatly to them.

The single most important relational act of a leader is translating a worthy purpose into meaning that invites and inspires shared effort and productive outcomes. Years ago, research uncovered that "more successful" salespeople are able to appeal to a broader range of customers than are "less successful" ones. I think a similar formula applies to leadership. The more effective leaders engage and influence a broader range of constituents, who may have different opinions, styles, and needs—to work together. Relational leaders are highly intentional and persistent in selecting and connecting the task at hand to the larger purpose in a way that produces relational connection and capacity.

Most of what we do has inherent purpose, but often much of its worth has leaked out. We need reminding in the midst of trying work such as busting rocks, cutting stones, and working with others that we are building a cathedral. Relational leaders constantly battle to shift the attention from narrow, inward-looking, selfish interest to make purpose the prevailing shared thought of the organization. Purpose serves as the lubricant for reconciling disagreements, the energy source to overcome fatigue, the glue for splintered groups, and the point of focus for the bored and distracted. It does not make everyone agree, be best friends, or even like each other; rather, it elevates the mission so group members do not allow differences to subvert it.

The evidence of relational leadership can be seen in groups—be it a family, a community, or a corporation—where commitment is high, focus is clear, and actions support the longer-term purpose over short-term, self-focused goals. It helps explain the research of Rüdiger Fahlenbrach cited earlier, that founders of companies, who usually have a longer-term relationship with all stakeholders and a closer connection to their company's purpose, are better stewards of value.[10] One founder expressed it like this: "There's no way a babysitter can feel the same way about a child as its parents." Or remember the biblical story of the two women who approached King Solomon, fighting over a baby. The birth mother was willing give up the baby rather than have it cut in half. Relational leaders engage and connect members of the family, the community, and the society in purpose and thus bring out our best.

You are a leader at home, in your workplace, in various groups. How are you doing on the "purpose" test? Where have you been unclear, neglectful, uninviting, or uninspiring in translating purpose into meaning for the groups you help lead? It is so easy to drown in the minutiae and bile of daily life that we lose sight of why we are here and what we stand for. The goal is to prevent fear or greed from causing selfish wants and desires to be placed above the group's purpose. Relational leadership starts with purpose that unites and moves us.

SERVANT LEADING

Sacrifice authenticates purpose. The litmus test for followers to gauge their leaders' devotion to purpose is this: How do they serve, and what are they willing to give up? The widening compensation chasm between top-paid executives and frontline workers has become relationally toxic because it undermines purpose. "To the winners go the spoils" is a precept of conquest and pillage, not relationships. Surely, receiving fair pay for contribution is a shared belief for most in a capitalist society. But asking everyone in the organization to sacrifice time and effort on behalf of purpose when leaders appear focused on exorbitant remuneration undermines the ability to galvanize the troops. Much of the grief these days about congressional leaders' health care and retirement benefits comes from a feeling that these leaders have protected themselves with much greater diligence than they have those they represent. You may or may not think it immoral, but its relational drag on purpose is clear. Leaders who take on the trappings of power—excessive money, status, perks—trap themselves and subvert purpose by separating from the very relationships they rely on for success.

Sacrifice is relational. Shared purposeful sacrifice is a powerful uniting force. A classic example is military leaders who spurn fancy quarters to eat and sleep with their troops in conditions of danger and squalor so as not to be "separated" from them. This sacrificial style of military leadership may help explain why their leadership scores are so much higher than are those for corporate CEOs and political leaders.[11] It is why a relational leader like John Mackey at Whole Foods has been praised for capping the CEO's pay at no more than 19 times the salary of frontline workers.[12] Relational leaders know that talk is cheap and thus they repeatedly find opportunities to serve and give sacrificially—a point equally relevant for highly-paid entertainers and athletes.

Sacrifice comes in many forms. Teach for America received 48,000 teaching applications in 2011, including 12 percent of all seniors at Ivy League schools.[13] It is inspiring to see this level of interest by these young people for a job with low pay and rejection rates of nearly 90 percent. Its mission of helping disadvantaged students shows the power of purpose to attract sacrifice. As the familiar adage reminds us, "You can give without loving but you cannot love without giving."

This leads each of us to ask: How are we doing on the "sacrifice" test? Are we overcoming our human temptation to be self-focused, to feel victimized, or to act entitled? Because positive attitudes are infectious among our stakeholders—at home and in the organizations where we serve—and so are negative ones. Serving and sacrificing is the leadership gold standard for authenticating purpose that boosts team members and builds relational capacity.

LEADING THAT INVITES AND ENGAGES

Commitment must be won. Relational leaders continually invite and engage stakeholders to be fully and mutually present and committed. They continually ask others their opinion, listen to and consider suggestions, provide forums for open discussion, seek feedback, and pursue more participative decision making. All of these aspects of the process sustain engaged stakeholders around purpose. Ironically, rather than let the information bog them down and delay or even prevent their making decisions, collecting information from different sources can be a source of conviction for relational leaders to act decisively.

Achieving the right level of engagement is challenging. In organizations there often has been an oppressive patriarchal presence that is short on invitation, maternal nurture, grace, and care. Conversely, in too many of our families there is an oppressive absence of paternal protection, goals, boundaries, and accountability. Regardless of gender stereotypes, abandoned absence or oppressive presence leads to the same problem: emotional disengagement that kills relationship capacity.

Being a relational leader in larger organizations that inherently rely more on command and control is especially important but also challenging. Yet it can be done. Geoff Colvin has made this comment regarding *Fortune* magazine's 100 Best Companies to Work For: "These firms are highly successful. The average American business lasts less than 20 years before it fails or gets bought. The 100 Best Companies, on average, are an incredible 85 years old. Bottom line: Being a great place to work pays."[14] Workers who feel invited and engaged stay more connected and committed to their workplace, their leaders, and their company's purpose.

A number of thoughtful corporate leaders like John Mackey, CEO of Whole Foods, Kip Tindell, founder and CEO of the Container Store, and Doug Rauch, former president of Trader Joe's, are part of a movement called Conscious Capitalism. It focuses on four tenets: higher purpose, stakeholder orientation, conscious leadership, and conscious culture.[15] They emphasize the importance of inviting employee input and mutual stakeholder value-exchange as core to success for more resilient business cultures. It is their mantra that if we can get the relationship right, for-profit does not have to be a dirty word to so many. Their kind of thinking and acting provides promise for an Age of Relationships.

How is each of us doing on the "invite and engage stakeholders" test—at home or in organizations? We live in a world desperate for relational capacity that helps stakeholders bring their highest and best. Are we enlisting those who seem invisible, different, or difficult to be with? As relational leaders we must be very intentional to invite and engage, because the cost of uncommitted, absent followers is just too high.

Engaged Leadership: Four Keys

It is easy to be in favor of engaged leadership, but relational leaders encounter some especially trying challenges. As a CEO who has made my share of mistakes, as a coach of numerous corporate and nonprofit leaders, and as a mentor of broken families, I have identified four key issues that are uniquely difficult and valuable in engaging stakeholders.

1. **Engage failure constructively.** Failure is a painful fact of life, but it is also our greatest teacher and best source for innovation. The big temptation is to ignore it or its source. Relational leaders engage failure, which is not the same as condoning it. Engaging failure means confronting it, openly discussing it, understanding it, and acting on it. The greatest opportunities and the greatest risks for relational leaders occur around their own or others' failures. While failure can be risky, a culture too fearful to innovate and learn exchanges the risk of failure for the certainty of stagnation and death.

2. **Foster bottom-up innovation and change.** Relational leaders invite informal leadership and bottom-up innovation and change. Think of the many wonderful benefits in our lives that started at the grassroots level: the Reformation in the 16th century, American independence,

the Apple computer. It is interesting that viral marketing—a bottom-up phenomenon—has become the "it girl" of marketing. It is a way to unleash viral forces at the most local of levels to accomplish what top-down force or incentives have proven unable to do.

3. Productively engage doubt. Is there anything more relevant to understand than the doubts of the faithful? Productive engagement of doubt activates the early warning system for failure and is the first step in warding off victims and reclaiming purpose. Flight or fight—either often the preferred form of denial—keeps leaders from addressing this irritating but invaluable friend of success. Relational leaders protect a space for the doubting and dissenting to ensure that inconvenient truths come out and questioning stakeholders stay engaged. Relational leaders go to great lengths to keep doubters in the conversation, in the game, and accountable. Sometimes you have to separate from them, but nothing builds strength like constructive engagement of doubt and dissent.

4. Secure peer commitment and accountability. Much of our leadership lore revolves around subordinates committing to their leaders. (Remember the phrase, "Win one for the Gipper"?) But astute coaches have learned just how powerful and lasting commitment to peers can be. These coaches talk more about commitment to the team, not the coach. Phil Jackson, the all-time leader among coaches in the NBA, with 11 championships, often refrained from calling time-out in the middle of an opponent's run because he wanted the team, not the coach, to be accountable for turning the game around. Followers often express commitment to leaders and their causes, but compliance, not commitment, rules much of the time. Fear of reprisal can produce counterfeit commitment. Like rebar in concrete—commitment helps hold everything together.

In the demanding marketplace of leadership, relational leaders who can embrace these four engagement challenges will produce more because they invite insight and commitment from a broader set of stakeholders, and not just the positive or pleasant ones.

A frequent misconception is that the move from authoritarian control to a more relational model is a sign of weakened or abdicated leadership. In reality, the problem today is that traditional authority often exerts diminished impact because stakeholders ignore it or rebel. Strong relational leadership is a force for increasing order and accountability by engaging those involved through input and commitment. With it, the odds go up that we will not only retain our best talent but also the best ideas.

I recently witnessed the power of engagement with a mother struggling to restore her family from their bout with homelessness. Several times I suggested that she take steps to get child support from the estranged father of her child. She always resisted, claiming it took all of her energy to focus on finding a job and getting settled into her interim housing. She finally got a job, and a few weeks later, at our weekly meeting, she said: "You know, if my ex were making his payments, it would help me get back on my feet and it would make things better for my young daughter. At the end of the day, he would be more connected to her—that would be good for both of them in the long run." Her epiphany had arrived.

We then discussed, in practical terms, the unpleasant task of engaging the father regarding child support and his role in his daughter's life. She had no interest in getting back together with him, and the prospect of broaching the topic yet again with him took every ounce of energy and leadership she had. But several weeks later she came into our weekly meeting wearing a broad smile that just lit up the room. She had received her first child-support check. Her relational leadership act of engaging, confronting what up until then had been failure, paid big dividends.

Relational Leaders: Coaching and Mentoring That Invite Growth and Development

Coaching and mentoring are central to how relational leaders invite and engage growth and development. A coach or mentor is someone who imparts and facilitates insight for the purpose of developing another person. Coaches or mentors can be a formal authority—such as a boss—or an invited "authority" that is not part of the hierarchy. Coaches and mentors provide more than just information; they also encourage, provide feedback, set stretch goals, and may help impose discipline or accountability.

Many aspiring companies and individuals have hired professional coaches to help improve performance and, ultimately, success. The *Harvard Business Review* reports that executive coaching is now a $1 billion business,[16] and a Marketdata report estimates that more than 40,000 people work as either life or work coaches in a $2.4 billion industry that is growing at an annual rate of 18 percent.[17] In recent years, I myself have coached a number of corporate and nonprofit CEOs and executive teams on both strategic and leadership effectiveness issues.

In the social services arena, providers have increasingly incorporated coaching to help individuals and families navigate through challenging times. Examples include Big Brothers or Sisters, surrogate fathers, youth leaders, volunteers, and caseworkers. The range of specialized coaching roles continues to grow across our society: personal trainers for physical development; spiritual directors for religious leaders; financial counselors; and specialized athletic coaches for particular skills like putting in golf or free-throw shooting in basketball.

Coaching and mentoring are high-value activities, albeit expensive at times. They require time, expertise, patience, influence, and concern. They play a pivotal role in our psychological, social, emotional, and economic development. Look back at your own life: Who made a difference in the defining, teachable moments you remember—a parent, a teacher, a coach, a friend, a mentor, a neighbor, a grandparent, a boss, or a colleague?

It is no accident that the decline in available coaching resources has occurred simultaneously with the decline in relationships. The adverse effect of the rise of single-parent families that have halved the on-site coaching capacity of traditional families, two-income families with less time to coach, downsized organizations that have removed layers of management, and discontinued formal training and mentoring programs, including apprenticeships, have taken their toll.

Coaching and mentoring are nitty-gritty practices of relational leaders at the most local of levels, which, with little fanfare, make extraordinary differences in our society. It is not just an extravagant resource for some; it is a necessity for all. The good news is that it is making a comeback.

RECLAIMING THE ROLE OF THE MENTOR/COACH

If we are worried about the poor, then we must find ways to address the relational poverty of children raised with limited parental and family relational leadership. If we are worried about our ability to remain competitive in a global economy, we need to be concerned about our families, schools, communities, and places of work and worship as environments that transform potential into competence and commitment.

Here's the deal: We are all coaches and mentors. At home with our children, grandchildren, nieces and nephews, neighbors and their kids, at school, at church, at work—we are surrounded by others who could benefit from our concern, attention, knowledge, and skills. Not everyone is looking for our advice or wisdom, but there are many opportunities to listen, care, and share experiences; to be present for those in need—which is all of us. Are we ready to take the mantle of relational leadership by seeking the coaching and mentoring opportunities that show up in our lives?

Although the road ahead is long, there is progress to report. The early social programs taught us a lot about what not to do. So much of public assistance, including government housing and welfare programs, provided no coaching and mentoring or incentives and accountability for becoming independent. In recent years, there have been attempts to move those receiving public assistance to greater self-sufficiency. While far from perfect, programs like Welfare to Work and the before-mentioned Nurse–Family Partnership have attempted to advance independence rather than incentivizing the status quo.[18] Unfortunately, these programs are costly and resources are limited.

The volunteer group that I am part of coaches and mentors two families one night every week. While the organization provides housing to meet their immediate needs, the focus is hands-on coaching to help mostly single mothers find jobs, make better spending decisions, and deal with other issues such as child support. As mentioned earlier, historically about 65 percent of the program's participants graduate to independent living within a few months. These results truly embody the well-known words of Lao Tzu: "Give a man a fish and you feed him for a day, teach him to fish and you feed him for a lifetime."[19] The business of coaching is really about relationships that change people's lives.

Coaching and mentoring are essential leadership components for rebuilding relationships that foster a successful society. They cannot be forced uninvited from above, but must be called forth locally from families, villages, providers, colleagues at work, and volunteer groups. A recent visit with J.T., the guy who runs cattle on our ranch, reminded me just how disarmingly simple all this is.

> Several of J.T.'s cows had calved during a recent severe winter storm where snowdrifts reached the tops of the corrals. He lamented that one of the calves froze before he could get to it, but in spite of the ice underneath the snow, he saved all of the other calves.
>
> One just-born calf got stuck in a deep snowdrift and was nearly frozen before J.T. found it, pulled it out, and took it home. His wife and three young daughters spent the rest of the night rubbing and drying it with towels, and stroking the calf while they fed it warm milk. J.T. said the main difference between the calves that survive out in the cold and those who don't is the behavior of their mothers. The best cows unrelentingly lick, nudge, stroke, and goad those little calves to get them up on their wobbly legs, to nurse, and to keep moving. It is what's required to get all the parts of a baby calf functioning, and it is crucial in the midst of subfreezing conditions.

In caring for that calf, J.T.'s wife and girls simply replicated what those attentive bovine mothers do. And there really is no simpler recipe for relational leadership: attentively and unrelentingly lick, nudge, stroke, and goad others up onto their wobbly legs to take nourishment in all its forms and to keep moving. It is what is required with our children, in helping the homeless, and in our organizations. It is what each of us requires in varying forms throughout our lives. We all have experienced times in our lives when we received something that saved us and kept us going and growing. And we have all served as leaders in providing that something to others.

For us and those around us to fulfill our purpose, we must receive as well as provide coaching and mentoring, both of which are most potent coming from strong, established relationships. It is circular, both requiring relationships and producing relationships.

It comes down to this. Our loss of relationships is destroying us because we have assigned so little value to them—the most valuable and value-creating things we have. We became distracted, inattentive, and even addicted to lesser, selfish things such as money, power, performance, and technology. Now the unintended consequences are hollowing us out. Turning it all around is not someone else's job; it is our job to make relationships a priority, to re-embrace local community, and to adopt relational leadership that restores us and ushers in this emerging age of hope—the Age of Relationship.

Epilogue

I opened this book with the story of my family ranch and how a relationship back in 1936 was pivotal to saving it. Let me conclude with the rest of the story and how a symphony of relational leaders came together to save and enrich us all.

My wife and I were ecstatic when our younger daughter told us she and her fiancé wanted to be married at our family ranch. She is a fourth-generation descendant of the ranch and it is, for her, holy ground. Since most of their friends lived in New York and had never set foot on a working ranch, we felt just a little pressure to get it right.

We selected a location on the south hillside within walking distance of the stone ranch house. Early on, our son-in-law-to-be had a vision of a stone altar with a gothic arch that would anchor the ceremony. The ranch house was constructed from large, hand-cut stone taken from the hillside just east of the ceremony site, carried up the hill by mule-driven wagons almost 100 years ago. We located some of that stone left over from a subsequent renovation to build an arch and altar that sat atop four steps.

He also wanted something of meaning from his family to be a part of the altar. At 11 years old, he lost his father after a three-year bout with cancer. In memory of him, he crafted a wooden cross from the first piece of furniture his dad had bought his mom—a dining table—and set it atop the arch.

The wedding was set for mid-June of 2011 and construction of the altar was well under way when in early April a fire swept across our ranch, transforming the ceremony site into a black, ashen heap. Fortunately, the house, barns, and partially constructed altar were unscathed, thanks to fast action from J.T. and his family, who lease the pasture. By the time I arrived that Saturday night it looked so bad that I could not muster the courage to even take a picture. I was just sick.

Meanwhile, the rock work for the altar was running several weeks behind schedule. Woodrow, my cousin, advised us to bring in sod to cover the distressed construction site, but there was no water line available. So my wife's brother Bill stepped in to lay a water line down to the ceremony site. My niece's husband, B.G., my brother-in-law, Ron, and my sisters, Joan and Karon, all showed up and in a myriad of ways helped us catch up and get ready.

Finally the day arrived. The grass was green and the remaining trees were lush, providing a beautiful backdrop.

As I escorted my daughter out of the house and we made the long procession down the sloping hillside toward the altar, I could hear the hauntingly beautiful violin playing. Time slowed and for those few moments we were totally present, mesmerized in the majesty of this sacred stroll.

In the first row was my beloved wife, Linda, and across the aisle was Liz, the groom's mother, accompanied by his sisters. As a widow and the very embodiment of a "steel magnolia," she had been left with almost a million dollars in medical bills and nothing else after her husband's death, and yet she managed to send all three kids to college on a teacher's salary. And in the next rows were people—precious relationships—that came to our aid: J.T. and his family, who fought the fire; Woodrow, who sweated the altar; Bill and his wife, Delores, who baked the great blackberry cobbler for the wedding feast; B.G., Joan, Karon, and Ron; and others like Larry who jumped in to help save the day.

And in my mind's eye, hovering just above was a large cloud of witnesses—my grandfather who died in the fall of 1936 in despair, thinking the ranch was lost; and my deceased parents, who gave everything they had to save it. And yes, from down the road was the late Buzz Newton, who cosigned that pivotal note that hangs on the ranch house wall.

Also, there was the groom's dad, who died knowing his wife was worse than broke and alone. Yet her friend Mary, sitting behind Liz along with people of his hometown of Madison, Mississippi, had jumped in with pie suppers and other fund-raising to help them get through it all. And Coach Smith, one of the groomsmen up at the altar, had served valiantly as a mentor to the young, fatherless teen.

As we came down the aisle entering this grand cocoon of family and friends, and feeling the presence of those absent, it all came home to me. The ranch, the hillside, the altar, the music—all were just symbols of something much greater. Sacred relationships, some going back almost 100 years through countless relational acts—large and small—now formed the communal path down which we trod. The physical elements of drought, fire, disease, separation, financial hardship, and even death, so central to the human experience, were trumped by the invisible force and reach of leaders in the cause of relationships. Nothing is more valuable, tangible, or hopeful than these—our courageous relationships.

Endnotes

Introduction

1. Edward Gibbon, *The Decline and Fall of the Roman Empire*, 1776.
2. D. T. Niles, *That They May Have Life* (New York: Harper, 1951).

Chapter 1

1. Lionel Tiger, anthropologist, Rutgers University, as quoted in "You've Got Male!" *Wall Street Journal*, December 17, 2005.
2. Charles Seifert, "An Elephant Crack-up," *New York Times*, October 6, 2006.
3. Clarence Page, "Obama's Culture War," *Chicago Tribune*, May 18, 2008.
4. Sabrina Tavernise, "Married Couples Are No Longer a Majority, Census Finds," *New York Times*, May 26, 2011; U.S. Census, Section 2 of 2003 Statistical Abstract of the U.S., page 4, Table 83; page 4 of pdf http://www.census.gov/prod/2004pubs/03statab/vitstat.pdf.
5. Barbara Dafoe Whitehead and David Popenoe, National Marriage Project, "The State of Our Unions: The Social Health of Marriage in America," Rutgers University, July 2005.
6. Whitehead and Popenoe.
7. Whitehead and Popenoe.
8. Whitehead and Popenoe.
9. D'Vera Cohn, Jeffrey Passel, Wendy Wang, and Gretchen Livingston, "Barely Half of U.S. Adults Are Married—A Record Low," Pew Research Center, December 14, 2011.

10. Japanese Teens, Married Couples Losing Sex Drive: Report, *Huffington Post*, January 16, 2011.

11. Whitehead and Popenoe.

12. "Births: Final Data for 2006," National Vital Statistics Reports, National Center for Health Statistics, U.S. Department of Health and Human Services, January 7, 2009.

13. Jason DeParle, Sabrina Tavernise, "For Women Under 30, Most Births Occur Outside Marriage," *New York Times*, February 17, 2012.

14. Whitehead and Popenoe.

15. "50 Million Children Lived With Married Parents in 2007," U.S. Census Bureau, press release, July 28, 2008.

16. Sharon Jayson, "Couples Study Debunks 'Trial Marriage' Notion of Cohabiting" *USA Today*, July 8, 2009.

17. Jason DeParle, Sabrina Tavernise, "For Women Under 30, Most Births Occur Outside Marriage," *New York Times*, February 17, 2012.

18. David Brooks, "Dollars and Sense," *New York Times*, January 26, 2006.

19. Jay Zagorsky, "The National Longitudinal Survey of Youth," Center for Human Resource Research, Ohio State University, based on interviews of participants beginning in 1979 through January 19, 2006.

20. Nancy Schimelpfening, "Men More Prone to Depression After Divorce Than Women," About.com Guide to Depression, May 29, 2007, citing research from Statistics Canada.

21. Neelima Mahajan, "As Material Wealth Has Risen, So Has Depression," *Times of India*, February 18, 2007.

22. Michael R. Haines, "Fertility and Mortality in the United States." EH. Net Encyclopedia, edited by Robert Whaples. March 19, 2008.

23. Hamilton, B.E., Martin, J.A., Ventura, S.J. "Births: Preliminary Data for 2007." National Vital Statistics Reports, Web release; vol. 57, no. 12. Hyattsville, MD: National Center for Health Statistics. Released March 18, 2009.

24. Rachel Zimmerman, "Researchers Target Toll Kids Take on Parents' Sex Lives," *Wall Street Journal*, April 24, 2007.

25. DeNavas-Walt, Carmen, Bernadette D. Proctor, and Jessica C. Smith, U.S. Census Bureau, Current Population Reports, P60–239, *Income, Poverty, and Health Insurance Coverage in the United States: 2010*, U.S. Government Printing Office, Washington, D.C., 2011. Table 4.

26. Robert Rector, "Married Fathers: America's Greatest Weapon Against Child Poverty," The Heritage Foundation, June 16, 2010. Web Memo heritage.org

27. Robert Rector and Kirk A. Johnson, "The Effects of Marriage and Maternal Education in Reducing Child Poverty," The Heritage Foundation, August 2, 2002. heritage.org

28. Joyce A. Martin and others, U.S. Department of Health and Human Services, Division of Vital Statistics, Births: Final Data 2006, Vol. 57, No. 7, published January 7, 2009, http://www.cdc.gov/nchs/data/nvsr/nvsr57/nvsr57_07.pdf.

29. Mark M. Kishiyama and others, "Socioeconomic Disparities Affect Prefrontal Function in Children," *Journal of Cognitive Neuroscience*, June 2009.

30. Chris Coughlin and Samuel Vuchinich, "Family Experience in Preadolescence and the Development of Male Delinquency," *Journal of Marriage and Family*, Vol. 58, No. 2 (1996), pp. 491–501.

31. Deborah A. Dawson, "Family Structure and Children's Health and Well-Being: Data from the 1988 National Health Interview Survey on Child Health," *Journal of Marriage and Family*, Vol. 53, No. 3 (August 1991), pp. 573–584.

32. Wendy D. Manning and Kathleen A. Lamb, "Adolescent Well-Being in Cohabiting, Married, and Single-Parent Families," *Journal of Marriage and Family*, Vol. 65, No. 4 (2003), pp. 876–893. Data came from the Add Health study. See also Deborah A. Dawson, "Family Structure and Children's Health and Well-Being: Data from the 1988 National Health Interview Survey on Child Health," *Journal of Marriage and Family*, Vol. 53, No. 3 (August 1991), pp. 573–584.

33. Timothy Biblarz and Greg Gottainer, "Family Structure and Children's Success: A Comparison of Widowed and Divorced Single-Mother Families," *Journal of Marriage and Family*, Vol. 62 (May 2000), pp. 533–548.

34. Lawrence K. Altman, "Sex Infections Found in Quarter of Teenage Girls, First National Study of Four Common Sexually Transmitted Diseases Among Girls/Young Women," *New York Times*, March 12, 2008.

35. Miller McPherson, Matthew E. Brashears, and Lynn Smith-Lovin, "Social Isolation in America: Changes in Core Discussion Networks over Two Decades," *American Sociological Review*, June 2006.

36. "Stay-at-Home Moms Are More Likely Younger, Hispanic and Foreign-Born Than Other Mothers," October 1, 2009, U.S. Census Bureau.

37. "Pets Are 'Members of the Family' and Two-Thirds of Pet Owners Buy Their Pets Holiday Presents," Harris Interactive, December 4, 2007.

38. McPherson, Brashears, and Smith-Lovin.

39. James Surowiecki, *The Wisdom of Crowds* (New York: Random House, 2004).

40. Henri Nouwen, "Moving from Solitude to Community to Ministry," *Leadership*, Spring 1995.

41. Elizabeth O'Connor, *Call to Commitment* (New York: Harper & Row, 1963).

42. Robert Putnam, *Bowling Alone* (New York: Simon & Schuster, 2000).

43. Caitlin Flanagan, "'Are You There God? It's Me, Monica' or How Nice Girls Got So Casual About Oral Sex," *The Atlantic*, November 2005.

44. Robert Putnam, "*E Pluribus Unum:* Diversity and Community in the Twenty-First Century—The 2006 Johan Skytte Prize Lecture," *Scandinavian Political Studies*, June 15, 2007.

45. Paul Galder, "Avid Boarders Bypass Branded Gear," *Wall Street Journal*, July 27, 2007, citing estimates by American Sports Data, a research firm located in Cortland Manor, New York.

46. SGMA Sports Participation Trends, Selected Years 1987–2003.

47. Sporting Goods Manufacturers Association (SGMA) annual participation study on team sports—*U. S. Trends in Team Sports* (2010 edition), September 22, 2010.

48. Peter Block, quoting Mike Butler, Police Chief, Longmont, Colorado, in *Community: The Structure of Belonging* (San Francisco: Berrett-Koehler Publishers, 2008), p. 132.

49. James Q. Wilson, "The Family Way: Treating Fathers as Optional Has Brought Big Social Costs," *Wall Street Journal*, January 7, 2003.

50. McPherson, Brashears, and Smith-Lovin.

51. Garance Franke-Ruta, "Remapping the Culture Debate," *American Prospect*, February 2006.

52. Ross Douthat and Reihan Salam, "The Party of Sam's Club," *Weekly Standard*, November 24, 2005.

53. Rich Morin and Rakesh Kochhar, "Lost Income, Lost Friends—and Loss of Self-Respect: The Impact of Long-Term Unemployment," Pew Research Center, July 22, 2010.

54. Lois A. Fingerhut and Joel C. Kleinman, "International and Interstate Comparisons of Homicide Among Young Males," *Journal of the American Medical Association*, June 27, 1990, Vol. 263, No. 24.

55. Gary Fields, citing research at Northeastern University, "Murders of Black Teens Are Up 39% Since 2000-01," *Wall Street Journal*, December 29, 2008.

56. Adam Liptak, "U.S. Imprisons One in 100 Adults, Report Finds," *New York Times*, February 29, 2008.

57. Liptak.

58. Erick Eckholm, citing an analysis of the U.S. census conducted by Steven Raphael of the University of California, Berkeley, "Plight Deepens for Black Men," *New York Times*, March 20, 2006.

59. Liptak.

60. Christopher B. Swanson, "Cities in Crisis: A Special Analytic Report on High School Graduation," America's Promise Alliance, April 1, 2008, partially funded by Bill and Melinda Gates Foundation.

61. Review & Outlook, "Obama's 'Race to the Top,'" *Wall Street Journal*, July 31, 2009.

62. "College Enrollment and Work Activity of 2009 High School Graduates," Economic News Release, Bureau of Labor Statistics, April 27, 2010.

63. Peg Tyre, "The Trouble With Boys," *Newsweek,* January 30, 2006.

64. Seifert.

Chapter 2

1. Phillip Kotler, *Kotler on Marketing* (New York: Free Press, 1999).

2. Sheila Bonini, David Court, and Alberto Marchi, "Rebuilding Corporate Reputations," *McKinsey Quarterly*, June 2009.

3. 2009 Edelman Trust Barometer, Edelman.com, a global study conducted annually about where the public places its trust.

4. California real estate agent in interview with Steve Croft, CBS's *60 Minutes*, May 25, 2008.

5. Marc Beaujean, Jonathan Davidson, and Stacey Madge, "The 'Moment of Truth' in Customer Service," *McKinsey Quarterly*, 2006, No. 1.

6. Don Peppers and Martha Rogers, "Customer Acquisition Makes a Comeback," 1 to 1 Magazine's Weekly Digest, November 17, 2005.

7. Andrew Greenyer, VP International Marketing, Pitney Bowes Group 1 Software, "Survey: Customer Churn Rates Rise by 15 Percent," *Customer Think*, February 4, 2008.

8. Elizabeth Schatz, "Cellphones: We Dial for Some Sweeter Deals," quoting Roger Etner, Yankee Group, *Wall Street Journal*, May 20, 2003.

9. Greenyer.

10. Bernard Simon, Shannon Bond , and Emma Saunders, "The Decline of U.S. Autos," *Financial Times*, May 29, 2009.

11. J.D. Power III, Founder and Chairman, J.D. Power, "Next Exit, the Auto Megastore," *Wall Street Journal*, October 28, 2003.

12. Don Peppers and Martha Rogers, "Customer Engagement Must Actually Involve Customers," citing Booz, Allen, Hamilton study, Inside 1to1 Media, March 27, 2006.

13. ARS Reports "Decline in Loyalty for Many Consumer Goods Brands During Recession," press release, comscore.com, May 4, 2010.

14. John Gaffney, "The Myth of Customer Loyalty," 1to1 Media, March 2006.

15. Robert E. Hall, *The Streetcorner Strategy for Winning Local Markets* (Austin, Texas: Bard Press, 1994).

16. Elizabeth Glagowski, "Where Has All the Trust Gone?" Inside 1to1, March 27, 2006, quoting from Datamonitor report, "Building and Profiting from Consumer Trust," by Data Monitor.

17. National Retail Federation news release, study by Adjoined Consulting, "Retail Demand Insights 2006: What Drives Consumers?" January 16, 2006.

18. Alex Berenson, "Big Drug Makers See Sales Decline With Their Image," *New York Times*, November 14, 2005.

19. Kaiser Family Foundation, *Health Poll Report Survey,* February 25, 2005.

20. Benedict Carey, "In the Hospital, a Degrading Shift from Person to Patient," *New York Times*, August 16, 2005.

21. Malcolm Gladwell, *Blink* (New York: Little, Brown and Company, 2005).

22. "Conference Board: 2009 Job Loss Could Hit 2 Million," *Wall Street Journal*, January 12, 2009.

23. Anne Fisher, "Playing for Keeps," *Fortune*, January 27, 2007.

24. Department of Labor, Bureau of Labor Statistics, "U.S. Annual Employee Total Separation Rates by Industry and by Geographic Region," Nobscot. com, through August 2006.

25. Cora Daniels, "By the Numbers," *Fortune*, December 27, 2004.

26. E. D. Cain, "High Teacher Turnover Rates are a Big Problem for America's Public Schools," *Forbes*, March 8, 2011.

27. "American's Job Satisfaction Falls to Record Low," Associated Press, January 5, 2010.

28. Michael Lowenstein, "The Trust Equation," CRMguru.com, February 14, 2006.

29. "Survival on the Front Lines: Best Practices for Building a Sales Culture," Bank Administration Institute, 2000. Research Report.

30. Greg Ip, "Wages Fail to Keep Pace with Productivity Increases, Aggravating Income Equality," *Wall Street Journal*, March 27, 2006.

31. David Wassel, "Is Inequality Over Wages Worsening?" *Wall Street Journal*, January 19, 2006, citing analysis of Bureau of Labor Statistics data by Harvard economist Lawrence Katz.

32. Erin White, "To Keep Employees, Domino's Decides It's Not All About Pay," *Wall Street Journal*, February 15, 2005.

33. Herbert Meyer, Former Vice Chairman of the CIA's National Intelligence Council and Associate Editor of *Fortune*, "What in the World Is Going On? A Global Intelligence Briefing for CEOs," February 20, 2007.

34. 100 Best Companies, citing research from the Food Marketing Institute, *Fortune*, January 24, 2005.

35. *National Leadership Index 2008*, JFK Center for Public Leadership, Harvard University.

36. Chuck Lucier, Rob Schuyt, and Junichi Handa, "CEO Succession 2003: The Perils of 'Good' Governance," Booz Allen Hamilton.

37. "CEOs Get the Boot," *Dallas Morning News* and Associated Press, April 18, 2008.

38. Carol Hymowitz, "Top Marketing Officers Finds Getting Together Helps Them Do Their Job," *Wall Street Journal*, January 11,2005, citing a survey conducted by the Spencer Stuart search firm, *Wall Street Journal*, January 11, 2005.

39. David McCann, according to Heidrick and Struggles, CFO.com, February 29, 2008.

40. Review and Outlook, "Off With Their Heads," *Wall Street Journal*, August 1, 2006.

41. "Chief Executive Succession: Bad Heir Days," *The Economist*, May 5, 2005.

42. John Birger, "Founders Keepers," *Fortune*, April 13, 2006.

43. Scott Thum, "Directors Now Prefer Insiders in Search for CEOs," *Wall Street Journal*, May 2, 2007.

44. Amy Zipkin, "The Wisdom of Thoughtfulness," *New York Times*, May 31, 2000.

45. Scott W. Spreier, Mary H. Fontaine, and Ruth L. Malloy, "Leadership Run Amok," *Harvard Business Review*, June 2006.

46. Ray Sasser, "And Then There Were Two: Angry Transient Buck Provides Hunter an Unusual Double," *Dallas Morning News*, January 9, 2005 (quoting whitetail deer expert James Kroll).

47. Justin Fox, "Why So Short Sighted?" *Fortune*, April 17, 2006.

48. Cheryl Hall quoting John Bogle, former founder and CEO, Vanguard Group Inc., in "Bogle: We're Lost in an Ethical Morass Here," *Dallas Morning News*, May 7, 2006.

49. John C. Bogle, "Restoring the Faith in the Financial Markets," *Wall Street Journal*, January 18, 2010.

50. Bogle.

51. Vikas Bajaj, "Household Wealth Falls by Trillions," *New York Times*, March 12, 2009.

52. Thomas K. Brown, CEO of Second Curve Capital, "The Evolution of Public Ownership," *Bank Director Magazine*, First Quarter, 2006.

53. Justin Fox, "Why Wall Street Had a Record Year and You Didn't," *Fortune*, February 6, 2006.

54. Aaron Lucchetti and Stephen Grocer, "Wall Street on Track to Award Record Pay," *Wall Street Journal*, October 14, 2009.

55. John C. Bogle, "The Battle for the Soul of Capitalism," speech delivered at the University of Virginia, February 8, 2006.

56. Benjamin E. Hermalin, "Trends in Corporate Governance," *Journal of Finance*, June 2004.

57. "Telecommunication Mergers & Acquisitions: How Do They Impact Customer Experience?" quoting a Marist survey, Reuters, March 4, 2008.

Chapter 3

1. Thomas Friedman, "Where Did 'We' Go?" *New York Times*, September 29, 2009.

2. Cate Malek, "Red/Blue Polarization" July, 2005, www.beyondintractability. org/casestudy/malek-red.

3. Malcolm Gladwell, *Blink* (New York: Little, Brown and Company, 2005), citing John Gottman, University of Washington.

4. Andrew Sullivan, "Goodbye to All That," TheAtlantic.com of the Atlantic Monthly Group, November 6, 2007.

5. James Davison Hunter, *Culture Wars* (New York: Basic Books, 1991).

6. E. J. Dionne Jr., "Why the Culture War Is the Wrong War," *The Atlantic Monthly*, January/February 2006.

7. Morris Fiorina, Samuel J. Abrams, and Jeremy C. Pope, *Culture War: The Myth of a Polarized America*, 3rd ed. (New York: Longman, 2010).

8. John Chambers, head of the Sovereign Ratings, S & P, Wolf Blitzer interview, CNN, August 6, 2011.

9. Dennis Cauchon, "Lead in U.S. Debt Hits Taxpayers with 12% More Red Ink," *USA Today*, May 5, 2009.

10. Thomas Friedman, "Dumb as We Wanna Be," *New York Times*, April 30, 2008.

11. Pew Survey Center, "Distrust, Discontent, Anger and Partisan Rancor, The People and Their Government," April 18, 2010.

12. John Harwood, "America's Economic Mood: Gloomy," *Wall Street Journal*, August 2, 2007.

13. National Leadership Index 2006, Harvard University, Center for Public Leadership, John F. Kennedy School of Government.

14. Doris Kearns Goodwin, *Team of Rivals: The Political Genius of Abraham Lincoln* (New York: Simon & Schuster, 2005).

15. Larry Diamond and Marc F. Plattner, eds., *The Global Divergence of Democracies* (Baltimore: Johns Hopkins University Press, 2001).

16. World War I and World War II Casualties, Wikipedia.

17. Dana Priest and Mary Jordon, "Top U.S. Generals Fear Civil War," *Washington Post*, August 4, 2006.

18. "Inconclusive Election Leaves Israel in Limbo," MSNBC, Associated Press, February 11, 2009.

19. Stephen Castle, Steven Erlanger, "Dutch Voters Split, and Right Surges," *New York Times*, June 10, 2010.

20. Bill Bishop, *The Big Sort: Why the Clustering of Like-Minded America is Tearing Us Apart* (New York: Houghton Mifflin, 2008), p. 246.

21. Nolan McCarty, "Polarization," NolanMcCarty.com, December 24, 2008.

22. James McGregor, "No More Chinese Whispers," *Wall Street Journal*, September 12, 2006.

23. Matthew Dowd, "The Politics of Polarization," *Washington Post*, December 16, 2002.

24. Michael Barone, "It's the Partisan Economy, Stupid," *The American*, January 23, 2008, based on research from the Pew Research Center.

25. Jeffrey M. Jones, "Obama Approval Continues to Show Party, Age, Race Gaps," Gallup.com, May 11, 2010.

26. Pew Survey Center, "Distrust, Discontent, Anger and Partisan Rancor, The People and Their Government," April 18, 2010.

27. James Wolcott, "When Democrats Go Post-al," *Vanity Fair*, June 2008.

28. Cate Malek, "Red/Blue Polarization," BeyondIntractability.org case study, July 2005.

29. "Reelection Rates Over the Years," Opensecrets.org, The Center for Responsive Politics.

30. Alan I. Abramowitz, Brad Alexander, and Matthew Gunning, "Incumbency, Redistricting, and the Decline of Competition in U.S. House Elections," Annual Meeting of the Southern Political Science Association, January 6–8, 2006.

31. Doug Mataconis, "Incumbent Reelection Rates in the 2010 Mid-Terms," Outside the Beltway, November 9, 2010, http://www.outsidethebeltway.com/incumbent-re-election-rates-in-the-2010-mid-terms.

32. Opensecrets.com, based on Federal Election Commission data January 6, 2010.

33. Florida PIRG, *Money & Politics News*, March 28, 2007.

34. Lobbying Database, OpenSecrets.org, Center for Responsive Politics, updated July 26, 2010.

35. R. J. Dionne Jr., "Why the Culture War Is the Wrong War," quoting political scientist Morris Fiorina, *The Atlantic Monthly*, January/February 2006.

36. Salena Zito, quoting Lana Brown, professor of political science, Villanova University, "Political Class Ignoring at Their Peril," *Pittsburgh Tribune-Review*, September 20, 2009.

37. "Independents Take Center Stage in Obama Era," Pew Research, May 21, 2009.

38. James Davison Hunter, description of his book, *Culture Wars: The Struggle to Define America*, Department of Sociology website, University of Virginia, http://www.virginia.edu/sociology/publications/hunterculturewarsthestruggletodefineamerica.htm.

39. Andrew Sullivan, "Goodbye to All That," TheAtlantic.com of the Atlantic Monthly Group, November 6, 2007.

40. Morris P. Fiorina and Samuel J. Abrams, *Disconnect: The Breakdown of Representation in American Politics*, (Norman, Oklahoma: University of Oklahoma Press, 2009).

41. Alan I. Abramowitz, *The Disappearing Center: Engaged Citizens, Polarization, and American Democracy*, (New Haven, Connecticut: Yale University Press, 2010).

42. James Davison Hunter, description from his website.

43. Pew Research Center, "Distrust, Discontent, Anger and Partisan Rancor," April 18, 2010.

44. Fox News Poll: 57% Think Next Generation Will Be Worse Off, Foxnews. com, April 9, 2010.

45. Center for Public Leadership, John F. Kennedy School of Government, National Leadership Index, Harvard University, 2009.

46. David Brooks, "The Power Elite," *New York Times*, February 18, 2010.

47. J. A. F. Stoner, "A Comparison of Individual and Group Decisions Involving Risks," unpublished master's thesis, School of Industrial Management, MIT, 1961.

48. James Surowiecki, *The Wisdom of Crowds* (New York: Anchor Books, 2004), p. 10.

49. Bill Bishop, *The Big Sort: Why the Clustering of Like-Minded America is Tearing Us Apart* (New York: Houghton Mifflin, 2008), pp. 6, 9, 73.

50. Malek.

51. Adam Wolfson, "Red and Blue Nation? Causes, Consequences, and Correction of America's Politicized Politics," The Brookings Institute, Issues in Governance Studies, May 2006.

52. Center for Public Leadership, John F. Kennedy School of Government, National Leadership Index, Harvard University, 2009.

53. Bishop, p. 286.

54. "Survey: U.S. Falls to 5th in Global Competitiveness," World Economic Forum, Geneva, Switzerland, Associated Press, September 7, 2011.

Chapter 4

1. Sam Dagher, "An Arab Winter Chills Christians," *Wall Street Journal*, December 5, 2011.

2. "American Attitudes Toward Religion in the Public Square," a national poll of 800 American adults, Anti-Defamation League, Marttila Communications Group, October 2005.

3. "Trends in Attitudes Toward Religion and Social Issues: 1987–2007," Pew Research Center, March 22, 2007.

4. Robert Putnam, *Bowling Alone*. (New York: Simon & Schuster, 2000).

5. Robert D. Putnam and David E. Campbell, *American Grace* (New York: Simon & Schuster, 2010).

6. Bill Bishop, *The Big Sort*, quoting Martin Marty.

7. Francis S. Collins, *The Language of God* (New York: Free Press, 2006) pp. 210–211.

8. American Attitudes Toward Religion in the Public Square," a national poll of 800 American adults, Anti-Defamation League, Marttila Communications Group, October 2005.

9. Arthur C. Brooks, "The Ennui of Saint Teresa," *Wall Street Journal,* September 24, 2007.

10. Alan Finder, "Matters of Faith Find a New Prominence on Campus," *New York Times,* May 2, 2007.

11. "A New Generation Expresses Its Skepticism and Frustration with Christianity," The Barna Group Ltd., September 24, 2007.

12. Bruce Feiler, *Abraham: A Journey to the Heart of Three Faiths* (New York: HarperCollins, 2002).

13. "Prospects for Inter-Religious Understanding: Will Views Towards Muslims & Islam Follow Traditional Trends?" International Conference on Faith & Service, The Pew Forum on Religion & Public Life, March 22, 2006.

14. "The Great Divide: How Westerners and Muslims View Each Other," Pew Global Attitudes Project, Pew Research Center, June 22, 2006.

15. "The Great Divide."

16. "Prospects for Inter-Religious Understanding."

17. "Prospects for Inter-Religious Understanding."

18. "Prospects for Inter-Religious Understanding."

19. "Prospects for Inter-Religious Understanding."

20. "Prospects for Inter-Religious Understanding."

21. Drew DeSilver, "'After the Prophet': Sunni and Shia Explained," *Seattle Times,* September 18, 2009.

22. Iraq Body Count Project, September 3, 2009, http://www.iraqbodycount.org/databa se.

23. Zaffar Abbas, "Pakistan's Schisms Break Into Present," BBC News, October 7, 2004.

24. Thomas L. Friedman, "The Central Truth," *New York Times,* September 8, 2006.

25. John Tierney, "One Nation Divisible," *New York Times,* October 24, 2006.

26. David B. Barrett and others, *World Christian Encyclopedia : A Comparative Survey of Churches and Religions in the Modern World* (New York: Oxford University Press, 2001).

27. Laurie Goodstein and David D. Kirkpatrick, "Conservative Group Amplifies Voice of Protestant Orthodoxy," *New York Times,* March 22, 2004.

28. Suzanne Sataline, "Strategy for Church Growth Splits Congregants," *Wall Street Journal*, September 5, 2006.

29. Judie Jacobson, "Sociologist Barry Kosmin Offers His Take on American Jewish Trends," *Jewish Ledger*, October 20, 2005.

30. Egon Mayer, Barry Kosmin, and Ariela Keysar, American Jewish Identity Survey, 2001.

31. Rabbi Stuart Federow, "What Jews Believe," www.whatjewsbelieve.org/explanation.

32. *Jewish News*, July 22, 2010.

33. Matthew Kalman, "The Jewish Religious Conflict Tearing at Israel," *Time*, June 17, 2010.

34. Ethan Bronner and Isabel Kershner, "Israelis Facing a Seismic Rift Over the Role of Women," *New York Times*, January 15, 2012.

35. Putnam and Campbell.

36. Sam Harris, *The End of Faith* (New York: W. W. Norton & Company, 2005).

37. "The Great Divide" Pew Research Center.

38. "Pakistani Schools Teach Intolerance of Hinduism: U.S. Report," Associated Press, November 9, 2011.

39. "A New Generation Expresses Its Skepticism and Frustration With Christianity," The Barna Update, September 24, 2007, excerpts from *unChristian: What a New Generation Really Thinks About Christianity and Why It Matters,* David Kinnaman and Gabe Lyons (Grand Rapids, MI: Baker Books, 2007).

40. Harris, p. 39.

41. Nicholas Kristof, "Looking for Islam's Luthers," *New York Times*, October 15, 2006.

42. Sam Huntington, "Clash of Civilizations?" *Foreign Affairs*, Summer 1993.

43. Larry M Bartels, "Who's Bitter Now?" *New York Times*, April 17, 2008.

44. Harris, p. 27

45. "Modest Rise in Concern About Islamic Extremists," Pew Forum on Religion & Public Life, November 18, 2009.

46. Dan Harris, "America Is Becoming Less Christian, Less Religious," American Religious Identification Survey, ABC News.com, March 9, 2009.

47. Barna Research Group, citing Religious Tolerance.org, "Trends Among Christians in the U.S.," October 18, 2006.

48. Barry A. Kosmin and Ariela Keysar, American Religious Identification Survey, Trinity College, March 2009.

49. "Faith in Flux: Changes in Religious Affiliation in the U.S.," Poll, Pew Forum on Religion & Public Life, April 27, 2009.

50. Jeffrey MacDonald, "Congregations Gone Wild," *New York Times*, August 7, 2010.

51. Jerry Adler, "In Search of the Spiritual," *Newsweek*, August 21, 2005.

52. Barna Research Group, citing Religious Tolerance.org, "Trends Among Christians in the U.S.," October 18, 2006.

53. Cathy Lynn Grossman and Anthony DeBarros, "Church Struggles with Change," *USA Today*, November 7, 2004.

54. "Faith in Flux."

55. "Trends Among Christians in the U.S.," Religious Tolerance.org, October 18, 2006.

56. *National Leadership Index*, Harvard University, Center for Public Leadership, John F. Kennedy School of Government, 2009.

57. Francis X. Rocca, "Pope Faces Growth of Pentecostals, Unbelief in Trip to Brazil," Pew Forum on Religion & Pubic Life, May 2, 2007.

58. Reinhold Niebuhr, American theologian.

59. Peter Gomes, *The Good Life* (San Francisco: Harper, 1998).

Chapter 5

1. Rob Stein, "Study Says Happiness Makes the Rounds in World," *Washington Post*, December 4, 2008, quoting James Fowler, political scientist and study coauthor.

2. Dr. Richard Klausner, former executive director of global health, Bill and Melinda Gates Foundation, as quoted by Thomas Friedman, *The World is Flat* (New York: Farrar, Straus, and Giroux, 2005).

3. John Gottman, "The Mathematics of Love," Edge, The Third Culture, publication of the Edge Foundation, April 4, 2004. http://www.edge.org/3rd_culture/gottman05/gottman05_index.html.

4. Richard Rohr, *Everything Belongs* (New York: Crossroad, 1999), p. 119, quoting Diamuid O'Murchu, *Quantam Theology* (New York: Crossroad, 1997).

5. J. Holt-Lunstad, T. B. Smith, and J. B. Layton, "Social Relationships and Mortality Risk: A Meta-analytic Review," *PLoS Medicine*, July 2010, 7(7): e1000316. doi:10.1371/ journal.pmed.1000316.

6. John Ortberg, *Everybody's Normal Till You Get to Know Them* (Grand Rapids, Mich.: Zondervan, 2003), p. 33. quoting from Robert Putnam's *Bowling Alone*.

7. David Brooks, "The Relationship Blend," *New York Times*, July 27, 2006.

8. Bradford C. Johnson, James M. Manyika, and Lareina A. Yee, "The Next Revolution in Interactions," *McKinsey Quarterly*, 2005, No. 4.

9. Robert Putnam, *Bowling Alone* (New York: Simon & Schuster, 2000).

10. Frederick F. Reichheld, "The One Number You Need to Grow," *Harvard Business Review*, December 2003.

11. J. S. House, K. R. Landis, and D. Umberson, "Social Relationships and Health," July, 1988, *Science* 241, pp. 540–545.

12. Sam Harris, *The End of Faith* (New York: W.W. Norton, 2004), pp. 226–227.

13. Sharon Begley, "Beyond Stones and Bones," *Newsweek*, March 15, 2007; see also Donna Hart and Robert W. Sussman, *Man the Hunted: Primates, Predators and Human Evolution* (New York: Basic Books, 2005).

14. Craig Lambert, "The Science of Happiness: Psychology Explores Humans at Their Best," *Harvard Magazine*, January–February 2007, quoting George Valliant, M.D., professor of psychiatry, Harvard Medical School.

15. Michael Tomasello, "For Human Eyes Only," *New York Times*, January 13, 2007.

16. Holt-Lunstad, Smith, and Layton.

17. J. M. Tither and B. J. Ellis, "Impact of Fathers on Daughters' Age at Menarche: A Genetically and Environmentally Controlled Sibling Study," *Developmental Psychology* 44, 2008, pp. 1409–1420.

18. Bettina Arndt, "Without a Dad, Little Girls Grow Up Too Fast," *Sydney Morning Herald*, March 9, 2002.

19. Katherine Harmon, "As Increasingly Early Puberty Ups Breast Cancer Risks, Researchers Search Environment for Clues," *Scientific American*, November 30, 2009.

20. Bruce Ellis and others, "Does Father Absence Place Daughters at Special Risk for Early Sexual Activity and Teenage Pregnancy?" *Child Development*, May–June 2003, www.ncbi.nlm.nih.gov/pmc/articles/PMC2764264.

21. Lee T. Gettlera, Thomas W. McDadea, Alan B. Feranilc, and Christopher W. Kuzawa, "Longitudinal Evidence That Fatherhood Decreases Testosterone in Human Males," *Proceedings of the National Academy of Sciences*, September 13, 2011.

22. Gina Kolata, "Find Yourself Packing It On? Blame Friends," *New York Times*, July 26, 2007.

23. Lambert.

24. Karen Kaplan, "Happiness Is Contagious, Research Finds," *Los Angeles Times*, December 5, 2008.

25. Daniel Gilbert, "Compassionate Commercialism," *New York Times*, March 25, 2007.

26. George Will, "The Coming Backlash Against the Clintons," *Washington Post*, March 5, 2007.

27. Dr. Henry S. Lodge, "You Can Stop 'Normal' Aging," *Parade*, March 18, 2007.

28. A. Nyberg and others, "Managerial Leadership and Ischaemic Heart Disease Among Employees: The Swedish WOLF Study," *Journal of Occupational and Environmental Medicine*, November 2008.

29. Henrik Ibsen, 19th-century Norwegian playwright.

30. John Gottman, "Making Relationships Work," *Harvard Business Review*, December 2007.

31. Thomas Keating, *Awakenings* (New York: Crossroad, 1990).

32. Putnam, *Bowling Alone.*

33. Kenneth Arrow, *The Limits of Organization* (New York: Norton, 1974), p. 23.

34. Doris Kearns Goodwin, *Team of Rivals* (New York: Simon & Schuster, 2005), p. 713.

35. Benedict Carey, "Study on I.Q. Prompts Debate on Family Dynamics," *New York Times*, June 25, 2007.

36. Robert Putnam, *Bowling Alone.*

37. Pope John Paul II on his visit to the United States in 1995.

38. Ortberg, p. 90.

39. Bruce Perry, "The First Core Strength," Early Childhood Today, Scholastic. com.

40. Jennifer Szetho, Australian Vietnamese International, www.icasn.org/jenniferstory.html.

41. Daniel Goleman, Richard Boyatzis, and Annie McKee, *Primal Leadership* (Boston: Harvard Business School Publishing, 2002).

Chapter 6

1. Stephen M.R. Covey, *The Speed of Trust* (New York: Free Press, A Division of Simon & Schuster, 2006), p. 255, citing 2005 study by Russell Investment Group.

2. Sven Rusticus, "Creating Brand Advocates," a chapter in the book *Connected Marketing* (London: Butterworth-Heinemann, 2006), citing research by McKinsey.

3. Bill Bishop, *The Big Sort* (New York: Houghton Mifflin, 2008), pp. 259, 264, citing research by Gerber and Green at Yale University.

4. David J. Lynch, "Global Trade Requires Foreign Language Skills," *USA Today*, February 8, 2006, quoting Angel Cabrera, president, Thunderbird School of Global Management.

5. Don Peppers and Martha Rogers, "New Research Links Customer Loyalty to Retailer Performance, Study: Carlson Relationship Builder 2007" 1to1 Weekly, June 18, 2007.

6. John H. Fleming, Curt Coffman, and James K. Harter, "Manage Your Human Sigma," *Harvard Business Review*, July–August 2005, citing research conducted by the Gallup Organization.

7. Robert E. Hall, *The Streetcorner Strategy for Winning Local Markets* (Austin, TX: Performance Press, 1994).

8. Jim Cole, "Marketing Study Touts Cross-Sell over Cold Calling," *American Banker*, February 22, 2006, citing a Greenwich study on cross-selling.

9. Paul McAdam and Joseph B. Pine III, "Customer Experiences Rule," *Banking Strategies*, March/April 2006.

10. "BB&T Ranks No. 1 Among Financial Services Firms in National Survey of 'Customer Advocacy,'" *American Banker*, August 19, 2003.

11. Marc Beaujean, Jonathan Davidson, and Stacey Madge, "The 'Moment of Truth' in Customer Service," *McKinsey Quarterly*, 2006, No. 1.

12. McAdam and Pine.

13. Pete Blackshaw, "Emotionomics, Anyone?" The ClickZ Network, Nielsen Online, September 4, 2007, review of Dan Hill's book, *Emotionomics*.

14. Robert Levering, "100 Best Companies to Work For," *Fortune*, January 24, 2005.

15. Beth Kowitt, "Inside Trader Joe's," *Fortune*, September 6, 2010.

16. Howard Behar, *It's Not About the Coffee*, quoting Starbucks CEO Howard Schultz (Portfolio Hardcover, 2007).

17. Jeff Taylor and Gina Pingitore, J.D. Power and Associates, "Why Can't Some People Commit?" *Banking Strategies*, March/April 2006.

18. Carolyn Beeler, "Outsourced Call Centers Return, to U.S. Homes," NPR, August 25, 2010, citing Joshua Brockman and CFI Group's 2010 Contact Center Satisfaction Index.

19. Christopher Lawton, "Consumer Demand and Growth in Laptops Leave Dell Behind," *Wall Street Journal*, July 21, 2006.

20. Nate Boaz, John Murnane, and Kevin Nuffer, "The Basics of Business-to-Business Sales Success," *McKinsey Quarterly*, May 2010.

21. Elizabeth Glagowski, Inside 1to1: Privacy, quoting from the study "Customers Say What Companies Don't Want to Hear," by Dick Lee and David Mangen, June 12, 2006.

22. "The Global CEO Study," IBM Global Business Services, 2006.

23. Kenneth Kline, "Reinventing Management by Empowering Employees," BAI, *Banking Strategies*, November 2006, interview of Gary Hamel, author of *Leading the Revolution*.

24. "Organizing for Success in the 21st Century," Booz Allen Hamilton–Kellogg School of Management joint research study, January 30, 2002.

25. Sigal Barsade and Lakshmi Ramarajan, Wharton School, University of Pennsylvania, "What Makes the Job Tough? The Influence of Organizational Respect on Burnout in Human Services," Knowledge@Wharton, November, 2006.

26. Daniel Goleman, Richard Boyatzis, and Annie McKee, *Primal Leadership* (Boston: Harvard Business Review Press, 2002), pp. 18, 19.

27. Jonathan Sacks, "Reversing the Decay of London Undone," citing research in *American Grace* by Robert Putnam, *Wall Steet Journal*, August 20, 2011.

28. "Independents Take Center Stage in Obama Era," Pew Research Center, May 21, 2009.

29. David Brooks, "The Limits of Policy," *New York Times*, May 5, 2010, quoting Susan Mayer's book, *What Money Can't Buy*.

30. Keith J. Winstein, "Ability to Quit Smoking Affected by Friendship," *Wall Street Journal*, May 22, 2008.

31. "Families Drawn Together by Communication Revolution," Pew Research Center, February 21, 2006.

32. Jay Zagorsky, "The National Longitudinal Survey of Youth," Center for Human Resource Research, Ohio State University, based on interviews of participants beginning in 1979 through January 19, 2006.

33. David Olson and Matthew Turvey, "Marriage & Family Wellness: Corporate America's Business," A Marriage Commission Research Report, Minneapolis, MN, 2006.

34. Bureau of Labor Statistics, Labor Force Statistics including the National Unemployment Review, Characteristics of the Unemployed, Chart 24.

35. Robert Rector, "Married Fathers: America's Greatest Weapon Against Child Poverty," WebMemo, Heritage Foundation, June 16, 2010.

36. Barbara Dafoe Whitehead and David Popenoe, The National Marriage Project, "The State of Our Unions: The Social Health of Marriage in America," Rutgers University, July 2005.

37. Linda J. Waite and Maggie Gallagher, The Case for Marriage (New York: Doubleday, 2000).

38. Rachael Emma, "Silverman Working on Your Marriage—at Work," Wall Street Journal, May 31, 2007.

49. Olson and Turvey.

40. Katherine Boo, "Children of the Bayou," The New Yorker, February 2006.

41. Christine Ademec and William Pierce, The Encyclopedia of Adoption (New York: Facts on File, 2000).

42. Rachel Tolbert Kimbro, "Together Forever? Relationship Dynamics and Maternal Investments in Children's Health," Center for Research on Child Wellbeing, Working Paper 2006-32-FF, University of Wisconsin, Madison, November 2006.

43. Kay S. Hymowitz, Marriage and Caste in America: Separate and Unequal Families in a Post Marital Age (Chicago: Ivan R. Dee, 2006).

44. Bruce D. Perry, "Maltreatment and the Developing Child: How Early Childhood Experience Shapes Child and Culture," Inaugural Lecture: Margaret McCain Lecture Series, September 24, 2004.

45. Tara Parker-Pope, "Hint of Hope as Child Obesity Rates Hit Plateau," New York Times, May 28, 2008.

46. Kevin Helliker, "Alcoholic Anonymous: It Works Even If Science Is Missing," Wall Street Journal, October 18, 2006.

47. John McKnight, The Careless Society (New York: Basic Books, 1995).

48. Goleman, Boyatzis, and McKee, Primal Leadership, citing research from the Annals of Internal Medicine, 1992, p. 6.

49. Geeta Anand, "Rationing Becomes a Reality as Costs Skyrocket," Wall Street Journal, September 12, 2003.

Chapter 7

1. David B. Myers, The American Paradox: Spiritual Hunger in an Age of Plenty (New Haven: Yale University Press, 2000).

2. Michael J. Silverstein and Neil Fiske, Trading Up: The New American Luxury (New York: Portfolio, 2003).

3. "Rate of Growth in Consumer Debt Slowed in December," Associated Press, as quoted in *New York Times*, February 8, 2008.

4. Federalbudget.com, January 31, 2011.

5. U.S. Department of Labor, Bureau of Labor Statistics (December 2010), "Labor Force Statistics from the Current Population Survey: Current News Releases: Employment Situation," Bureau of Labor Statistics (website). Retrieved January 23, 2011.

6. Bill Bishop, *The Big Sort* (New York: Houghton Mifflin, 2008).

7. Jean Twenge, San Diego State University, citing the largest study ever conducted on generational changes in narcissism, news press release, February 27, 2007.

8. L. Heise, M. Ellsberg, and M. Gottemoeller, "Ending Violence Against Women," *Population Reports*, Series L, No. 11, December, 1999.

9. Noemic Emery, "The Natural and His Wife," *Weekly Standard*, January 14, 2008.

10. Rick Warren, *The Purpose Driven Life* (Grand Rapids, MI: Zondervan, 2002).

11. Daniel Henninger, "Western Civ 101: Benedict's Seminar on Fundamentals," *Wall Street Journal*, December 1, 2006.

12. Andrew Kohut and Carroll Doherty, "What Was—and Wasn't—On the Public's Mind in 2007," Pew Research Center for the People and the Press, December 19, 2007.

13. Dalton Conley, *Elsewhere, U.S.A.* (New York: Pantheon, 2009).

14. Clarence Page, "Oprah's Truth Does Not Hurt," *Chicago Tribune*, January 8, 2006.

15. Ward Justice, in his review of *The Price of Privilege* by Madeline Levine, *The Week*, September 15, 2006.

16. Robert Frank, "Marrying for Love . . . of Money," *Wall Street Journal*, December 14, 2007.

17. Rod Dreher, "Not Even Our Parks Are Safe," *Dallas Morning News*, September 23, 2007, quoting Alan Ehrenhalt, author of *The Lost City*.

18. Douglas B. Sosnik, Matthew J. Dowd, and Ron Fornier, *Applebee's America* (New York: Simon & Schuster, 2006), p. 199.

19. David Brooks, "A Nation of Villages," *New York Times*, January 19, 2006.

20. Barbara Dafoe Whitehead and David Popenoe, The National Marriage Project, "The State of Our Unions: The Social Health of Marriage in America," Rutgers University, July 2005.

21. Donna Freitas, "Sex Education," *Wall Street Journal*, April 4, 2008.

22. Mary Eberstadt, Hoover Institute, "Eminen Is Right," Hoover Institute, January 1, 2006.

Chapter 8

1. James P. Owen, *Cowboy Ethics: What Wall Street Can Learn from the Code of the West* (Ketchum, ID: Stoecklein, 2005).

2. Steven Landsburg, "A Brief History of Economic Time," *Wall Street Journal*, June 9, 2007.

3. Michael S. Malone, review of Jacob Needleman's *Money and the Meaning of Life*, in *Fast Company*, June 30, 1997.

4. Jane Spencer and Juliet Ye, "Toxic Factories Take Toll on China's Labor Force" *Wall Street Journal*, January 15, 2008.

5. David Wessel, "A Source of Our Bubble Trouble," *Wall Street Journal*, January 17, 2008.

6. Simon Johnson, "The Quiet Coup," *The Atlantic*, May 2009.

7. Peter Brimelow, "Kevin Phillips Is Still a Populist," *Market Watch*, May 26, 2008, commenting on *Bad Money: Reckless Finance, Failed Politics, and the Global Crisis of American Capitalism*.

8. Steve Kaplan and Joshua Rauh, "Wall Street and Main Street: What Contributes to the Rise in the Highest Incomes?" NBER, Working Paper 13270, July 2007, online at http://www.nber.org/papers/w13270.pdf.

9. "Right Direction or Wrong Track," Rasmussen Reports, January 11, 2012.

10. Douglas Sosnik, Matthew Dowd, and Ron Fournier, *Applebee's America* (New York: Simon & Schuster, 2006), pp. 180–181.

11. Theresa Y. Sun, James R. Blaylock, and Jane E. Allshouse, "Dramatiac Growth in Mass Media Food Advertising in the 1980s," *Food Review*, September–December 1993.

12. Malcolm Gladwell, *The Tipping Point* (Boston: Little, Brown, 2000), p. 98.

13. Eric Lichtblau, "Lobbyist Says It's Not About Influence" *New York Times*, July 1, 2010, citing information from the Center for Responsive Politics.

14. "Junk TV: Study Says Kids Get a Heavy Diet of Food Ads," wire reports—Kaiser Family Foundation, *Dallas Morning News*, March 27, 2007.

15. Dalton Conley, *Elsewhere, U.S.A.* (New York: Pantheon, 2009), p. 34, quoting Jeffrey J. Saliaz, *The Labor of Luck: Work and Politics in the Global Gambling Industry* (Berkeley: University of California Press, 2009).

16. American Society of Aesthetic Plastic Surgery, www.surgery.org

17. Tara Parker-Pope, "Role Models: How Images of Smoking May Affect Kids," *Wall Street Journal*, May 15, 2007.

18. Andrea Coombs, "Mail Glut," *Market Watch*, April 2006.

19. Deborah Charles, "Big Money in Politics—Sign of Excess," Reuters, March 26, 2008.

20. Karl Rove, "The New Role of Politics," *Wall Street Journal*, January 31, 2008.

21. Nielsen Online, "Buzz Metrics," September–December 2008.

22. Edward Boches, "The Consumer Will See You Now," *Creativity_Unbound*, May 18, 2010.

23. Jim Edwards, "Broken Promises," *Brandweek*, May 22, 2006.

24. Don Peppers, Inside 1to1, "The Shift Is On for Marketing Dollars," August 28, 2006.

25. David Enrich, "Bruised Banks Salve Their Pain with More Fees for Consumers; Overdraft, ATM Charges Climb as Lenders Scrape for Revenue," *Wall Street Journal*, January 26, 2008.

26. John Fabian Witt, "First, Rename All of the Lawyers," *New York Times*, October 24, 2006.

27. Lee Gomes, "Vendors Still Paying for IT Research That Flatters Them," *Wall Street Journal*, January 30, 2008.

28. Anna Wilde Mathews, "At Medical Journals, Paid Writers Play Big Role," *Wall Street Journal*, December 13, 2005.

29. Alex Berenson, "Big Drug Makers See Sales Erode with Image," *New York Times*, February 19, 2005, quoting Marcia Angell, a former editor in chief of the *New England Journal of Medicine*.

30. Daniel Golden, "How Lowering the Bar Helps Colleges Prosper," *Wall Street Journal*, September 9, 2006.

31. Golden.

32. Mark Earls, *Herd: How to Change Mass Behaviour by Harnessing Our True Nature* (Wiley, 2007)

33. Earls.

34. Business Insider, "U.S. Advertising Revenue, by Medium," quoting Barclays Capital, October 27, 2009.

35. Earls, pp. 177–178.

Chapter 9

1. Nicolas Carr, "The Terrifying Future of Computing," *Wired* Magazine, December 20, 2007, quoted in interview with Spencer Reiss.

2. Carr.

3. Stefanie Kranjac, quoting John O'Neill, director of addictions services, Menninger Clinic, Houston, Texas, "Technology Overload Can Ruin Relationships," Reuters Life! January 23, 2008. Jeremy Laurence, "Addicted! Scientists Show How Internet Dependency Alters the Human Brain," *Independent*, January 12, 2012.

4. Jeremy Laurence, "Addicted! Scientists Show How Internet Dependency Alters the Human Brain," *Independent*, January 12, 2012.

5. Kim Painter, "Teens Do Better With Parents Who Set Limits," *USA Today*, February 7, 2010.

6. Kimberlee Salmond, Girl Scout Research Institute, and Kristen Purcell, Pew Research Center's Internet and American Life Project, "Trends in Teen Communication and Social Media Use: What's Really Going On Here?" Webinar, Wednesday, February 9, 2011.

7. Roman Friedrich, Michael Peterson, Alex Koster, and Sebastian Blum, "The Rise of Generation C," *Strategy + Business*, a management magazine published by Booz & Co., Spring 2011.

8. Salmond and Purcell.

9. Friedrich, Peterson, Koster, and Blum.

10. Amanda Lenhart, Rich Ling, Scott Campbell, and Kristen Purcell, "Teens and Mobile Phones," Pew Internet, April 20, 2010.

11. Lee Rainie and others, "The Strength of Internet Ties," Pew Internet and American Life Project, January 25, 2006.

12. Robert Kraut and others, "Internet Paradox Revisited," Carnegie Mellon University, May 4, 2001.

13. Gwenn Schurgin O'Keeffe, Kathleen Clarke-Pearson, and Council on Communications and Media, "Clinical Report: The Impact of Social Media on Children, Adolescents, and Families," *Pediatrics*, published online Mar 28, 2011.

14. Nassim Nicholas Taleb, *The Black Swan* (New York: Random House, 2007), p. 144.

15. Ibid.

16. Lenny T. Mendonca and Matt Miller, "Crafting a Message that Sticks: An Interview with Chip Heat," *McKinsey Quarterly*, December 20, 2007.

17. "Online and Isolated," On the Media, NPR, November 20, 2010, interviewing Lee Rainie, director of Pew Internet and American Life Project.

18. George Bullard, *Pursuing the Full Kingdom Potential of Your Congregation* (St. Louis, MO: Lake Hickory Resources, 2005) pp. 157–158.

19. Kenneth M. Dixon, "Researchers Link Use of Internet, Social Isolation," based on the study: "What Do Americans Do on the Internet," Stanford Report, February 23, 2005.

20. Barbara Rose, "iPod Isolation," *Chicago Tribune*, April 2, 2006.

21. Jamie Ginsbery, "Facebook Statistics Are Thru the Roof," Best Practices, Facebook, January 21, 2010, http://www.sonicallstar.com/2010/01/facebook-statistics-are-thru-the-roof.

22. Dixon.

23. Kranjac.

24. Anuradha Raghunathan, "Banks Are Battling for Branch Space," *Dallas Morning News*, September 26, 2003, quoting research from Synergistics Research Corporation

25. Candice Choi, "Banks Smarten Up Branches to Woo Customers," Associated Press, December 16, 2010.

26. David Enrich, "Bruised Banks Salve Their Pain with More Fees for Consumers; Overdraft, ATM Charges Climb as Lenders Scrape for Revenue," *Wall Street Journal*, January 26, 2008.

27. Alana Semuels, "Employers Embracing Automation to Cut Costs, Red Tape," *Los Angeles Times*, October 14, 2010.

28. Ellen Gamerman, "Schools Discover Automated Calling and Go Wild," *Wall Street Journal*, March 16, 2007.

29. About.com, quoting research from Radicati Group in April 2010.

30. Ieva M. Augstums and Maria Halkias, "E-mail: You're Fired" *Dallas Morning News*, August 30, 2006.

31. Jared Sandberg,"Employees Forsake Dreaded Email for the Beloved Phone," *Wall Street Journal*, September 26, 2006.

32. Thomas Friedman,"The Taxi Driver," *New York Times*, November 1, 2006.

33. Brad Stone, "Facebook Expands into MySpace's Territory," *New York Times*, May 25, 2007.

Chapter 10

1. John Harwood, "America's Economic Mood: Gloomy," *Wall Street Journal*, August 2, 2007, quoting pollster Peter Hart, Wall Street Journal/NBC Poll.

2. Henri Nouwen, *The Road to Daybreak: A Spiritual Journey* (New York: Doubleday, 1988).

3. Peggy Noonan, "Look Ahead with Stoicism—and Optimism," *Wall Street Journal*, December 31, 2009.

4. Sir Antony Jay, "Confessions of a BBC Liberal," *Sunday Times*, August 12, 2007.

5. General Social Survey, Cumulative Data File 1972–2008, http://sda.berkeley.edu/archive.htm.

6. Louis V. Gerstner Jr., former CEO of IBM and author of *Who Says You Can't Teach Elephants to Dance*.

7. Geoffrey West,"Connecting Maverick Minds," *Harvard Business Review*, March 2006.

8. Donald L. Laurie, Yves L. Doz, and Claude P. Sheer, "Creating the New Growth Platform," *Harvard Business Review*, May 2006.

9. "Smaller, Better High Schools," editorial, *New York Times*, July 6, 2007.

10. Barry A. Kosmin and Ariela Keysar, American Religious Identification Survey, Trinity College, March 2009, Table 3.

11. Rod Dreher, "Wendell Berry's Time Is Now," *Dallas Morning News*, October 26, 2008.

12. Ginny Parker Woods, "In Aging Japan, Young Slackers Stir Up Concern," *Wall Street Journal*, December 29, 2005.

13. Robert E. Litan,"Innovators Matter Most," *Wall Street Journal*, February 27, 2007.

14. Paul McAdam and Joseph B. Pine III, "Customer Experiences Rule," *Banking Strategies*, March/April 2006.

15. Steven Bills, "A Big Name Could Be a Recipe for Distrust," American Banker, August 19, 2003.

16. Leonard Sweet, *Out of the Question . . . Into the Mystery* (Colorado Springs: Waterbook Press, 2004), cited in *Interactives*.

17. Guatam Naik, "Faltering Family M.D.s Get Technology Lifeline," *Wall Street Journal*, February 23, 2007.

18. Mike Malone, "The Next American Frontier," *Wall Street Journal*, May 19, 2008.

Chapter 11

1. Thomas L. Friedman, "The Class Too Dumb to Quit," *New York Times*, July 21, 2009.

2. University of Michigan American Customer Satisfaction Survey, Annual Survey, 2010.

3. Miguel Helft and Ashlee Vance, "Apple Passes Microsoft as No. 1 in Tech," *New York Times*, May 26, 2010.

4. Eric Ogg, "Secrets of Apple's Customer Success," C-Net News, September 20, 2010.

5. Gardiner Morse, "Retail Isn't Broken, Stores Are," *Harvard Business Review*, December 2011, interview with Ron Johnson, former senior VP of retail at Apple and builder of the Apple Store, now CEO of JCPenney.

6. George Strait, "Let's Fall to Pieces Together."

7. David Brooks, "The Conservative Revival," *New York Times*, May 9, 2008.

8. Sherry Jacobson, "Families Will Get More Space, More Comforts in the New Parkland Hospital," *Dallas Morning News*, April 7, 2011.

9. Betsy McKay, "Out Front in the Fight on Fat," *Wall Street Journal*, April 26, 2011.

10. Dr. Bernard Lown, *The Lost Art of Healing* (New York: Ballantine, 1999) (http://www.bernardlown.org).

11. Scott Burns, "Being Rich Isn't Just About Cash," *Dallas Morning News*, June 1, 2006.

12. William R. Easterly, "Why Bill Gates Hates My Book," *Wall Street Journal*, February 7, 2008.

13. David Brooks, "For Love or Money," *New York Times*, May 25, 2006.

14. "The Global CEO Study," IBM Global Business Services, 2006.

15. Stephen Grocer, "Banks Set for Record Pay," *Wall Street Journal*, January 15, 2010.

16. Walter Isaacson, *Steve Jobs* (New York: Simon & Schuster, 2011).

17. Arthur C. Brooks, "Money Buys Happiness," *Wall Street Journal*, December 8, 2005.

18. Arie de Geus, author of *The Living Company*, as quoted on TomPeters.com.

19. Peter Lattman, "You Say You Want a Big-Law Revolution," April 3, 2007, *Wall Street Journal* online.

20. Gary Loveman, "Diamonds in the Data Mine," *Harvard Business Review*, May 2003.

21. Donna St. George, "Despite Mommy Guilt, Time with Kids Increasing," *Washington Post*, March 20, 2007.

22. "U.S. Divorce Rate Falls to Lowest Level Since 1970," Associated Press, MSNBC , May 10, 2007.

23. "Births, Marriages, Divorces and Deaths: Provisional Data for 2009," National Vital Statistics Report, August 27, 2010, Vol. 58, No. 25.

24. David Von Drehle, "The Myth about Boys," *Time*, July 26, 2007.

25. "Catalysts for Change: The Implications of Gen Y Consumers for Banks," Deloitte Center for Banking, 2008.

26. Maria Halkias,"The Container Store Up for Sale," *Dallas Morning News*, February 18, 2007.

27. Anne Fisher, "Playing for Keeps," *Fortune*, January 27, 2007.

28. Lisa Takeuchi Cullen, "Defending Jerks at Work," *Time*, March 22, 2007.

29. Gerald F. Seib and John Harwood, "America's Race to the Middle," *Wall Street Journal*, May 10, 2008.

Chapter 12

1. Jeff Milchen, "The Power of Local," *Yes!* February 18, 2010.

2. John Schuhmann, "Homecourt Is an Advantage . . . Especially in the Playoffs," NBA.com, April 17, 2009.

3. Peter Block, *Community: The Structure of Belonging* (San Francisco: Berrett-Koehler, 2008), p. 95.

4. Louis Uchitelle, "The Richest of the Rich, Proud of a New Gilded Age," *New York Times*, July 15, 2007, quoting David Nasaw, author of *Andrew Carnegie* (London: Penguin Press, 206).

5. Rory Stewart, "What We Can Do," *New York Times*, March 27, 2007.

6. Paige Brady, "#18 on the 100 Best Companies to Work For List, Whole Story," Whole Foods market blog, January 21, 2010, citing "100 Best Companies to Work For," *Fortune*, February 8, 2010.

7. Kim Severson, "When Local Makes It Big," *New York Times*, May 12, 2009.

8. Sue Shellenbarger, "Tractor, Laptop: Family Farm Tools," *Wall Street Journal*, July 16, 2011.

9. Susan Saulny, "Cutting Out the Middlemen, Shoppers Buy Slices of Farms," *New York Times*, July 10, 2008.

10. Kim Pierce, "The ABCs of CSAs," *Dallas Morning News*, April 6, 2011.

11. Amy Truab, Research Director, Drum Major Institute for Public Policy, January 21, 2010, *Huffington Post*.

12. Suzanne Vranica, "A Small Agency's Battle to Shed Boutique Stigma," *Wall Street Journal*, April 8, 2007.

13. Advertisement for The Luxury of Leather, *Dallas Morning News*, p. 23A, December 4, 2011.

14. Julia Werdigier, "McDonald's, but With Flair," *New York Times*, August 25, 2007.

15. "In Search of More Growth, Wal-Mart Follows Best Buy in Move to Tailor Stores to Individual Markets," *Supply Chain Digest*, September 21, 2006.

16. Sarah Yall, "Britain Plans to Decentralize Health Care," *New York Times*, July 25, 2010.

17. Jeff Taylor and Gina Pingitore, J.D. Power and Associates, "Why Can't Some People Commit?" *Banking Strategies*, March/April 2006.

18. John J. Fiakla, "Wildcat Producer Sparks Oil Boom on Montana Plains," *Wall Street Journal*, April 5, 2006.

19. "Small Schools," editorial, *New York Times*, June 30, 2010, citing research from MRDC, "Transforming the High School Experience," by S. Bloom, Saskia Levy Thompson, and Rebecca Unterman, with Corinne Herlihy and Collin F. Payne, June 2010, www.mdrc.org/about.htm.

20. "Think Tank Pushes for Smaller Schools," Associated Press, October 5, 2008.

21. Associated Press, based on an analysis by Johns Hopkins University of Department of Education data 2004–2006, http://hosted.ap.org/specials/interactives/wdc/dropout/index.html.

22. Katherine Boo, "Children of the Bayou," *The New Yorker*, March 2, 2007.

23. Peter Block, *Community*.

24. Keith Epstein, "Crisis Mentality," *Stanford Social Innovation Review*, Spring 2006.

25. Cathy Lynn Grossman, "Christians Celebrate 'Simple' Easter," quoting a January 2011 Barna survey, *USA Today*/Religion, April 22, 2011.

26. Sue Shellenbarger, "The Power of Myth: The Benefits of Sharing Family Stories of Hard Times," *Wall Street Journal*, December 22, 2005.

27. Peter Block, *Community*.

28. U.S. Department of Education, National Center for Education Statistics, "1.5 Million Homeschooled Students in the United States in 2007," December 2008, http://nces.ed.gov/pubs2009/2009030.pdf.

29. Brian D. Ray, "Research Facts on Homeschooling," National Home Education Research Institute, July 2, 2008, at www.nheri.org/Research-Facts-on-Homeschooling.html (January 6, 2009).

30. Dan Garfield, "The Power of Local Mobile Search," Orange Soda, July 6, 2010, www.orangesoda.com.

31. Nassim Nicholas Taleb, *The Black Swan* (New York: Random House, 2007), p. 94.

32. Ann Lee, "The Banking System Is Still Broken," *Wall Street Journal*, October 15, 2009.

33. Wendy Pollack, "Despite Growth, Starbucks Can't Dislodge Local Rivals," *Wall Street Journal*, December 28, 2007.

34. Michael H. Seid, *Franchise Update Magazine*, WhichFranchise.org.

Chapter 13

1. Michael Cooley, *Rock Bottom: From the Streets to Success* (Mustang, Okla.: Tate Publishing, 2011).

2. Louis V. Gerstner Jr., *Who Says Elephants Can't Dance?* (New York: Harper, 2002).

3. Brink Lindsey, "The Culture Gap," *Wall Street Journal*, July 9, 2007.

4. Louis V. Gerstner Jr., *Who Says Elephants Can't Dance?*

5. Wendy Kopp, SMU Women Lecture Series, October 4, 2007.

6. Teach for America, "5,200 New Teach for America Teachers Join Efforts to Expand Educational Opportunity Nationwide," press release, June 7, 2011.

7. Daniel Goleman, Richard Boyatzis, and Annie McKee, *Primal Leadership* (Boston: HBS Press, 2002).

8. Daniel Goleman, *Emotional Intelligence*, (New York: Bantam Books, 1995).

9. Louis V. Gerstner Jr., *Who Says Elephants Can't Dance?*

10. John Birger, "Founders Keepers," *Fortune*, April 17, 2006.

11. National Leadership Index 2010, Center for Public Leadership, Harvard Kennedy School.

12. John Mackey, "Why Sky-High CEO Pay Is Bad Business," *Harvard Business Review*, June 17, 2009.

13. Teach for America, "5,200 New Teach for America Teachers Join Efforts to Expand Educational Opportunity Nationwide," press release, June 7, 2011.

14. Geoff Colvin, "The 100 Best Companies to Work For 2006," *Fortune*, January 23, 2006.

15. www.Consciouscapitalism.org.

16. Stratford Sherman and Alyssa Freas, "The Wild West of Executive Coaching," *Harvard Business Review*, November 2004.

17. "The Market for Self-Improvement Products and Services, Marketdata Report, October 2008.

18. Katherine Boo, "Children of the Bayou," *The New Yorker*, February 2006.

19. Lao Tzu, the Father of Taoism, www.chebucto.ns.ca/Philosophy/Taichi/lao.html.

Acknowledgments

This book about relationships is really a product *of* a series of relationships. First, I go back to more than two hundred colleagues and one hundred clients at my company ActionSystems, where together we studied, developed, taught, implemented, and measured—lived and breathed—relationships for well over twenty years. So much of what I learned about the challenges and incredible value of customer, employee, management, and shareholder relationships, as well as organizational relationships, I initially learned there.

Second, for the past decade in my work with the homeless, I have learned about and seen firsthand the unraveling of family, friend, and community relationships that so often accompanies homelessness. Likewise, I have learned about the power of relationships to heal, restore, and get families back on the road to recovery. As mentor and coach to scores of these families, I have learned from and been inspired by them.

Along with my gritty personal and organizational hands-on experience, I have been profoundly influenced by a legion of researchers and writers who have put relationships—at home, at work, in politics, and in faith—under the microscope to examine their decay as well as their accompanying costs, causes, and potential cures. There are way too many to identify here, but three of them warrant special acknowledgment. First is Robert Putnam, because of his seminal research and writing on the collapse of community and civic engagement since the 1950s, which culminated in his best-selling book *Bowling Alone*. Second is the team of David Popenoe and Barbara Defoe Whitehead, who from 1997 through 2009 at Rutgers University directed The National Marriage Project and published the annual report titled "The State of Our Unions: The Social Health of Marriage in America." Their comprehensive research provided great insight into the decline of marital relationships and rise of single-parent families. Third is David Brooks, a cultural and political commentator for the *New York Times* and author of, among other popular books, *The Social Animal*. His deep insight in connecting political issues to the causes and consequences of cultural trends has informed the content of this book greatly.

The editing help on this book was crucial both because of the breadth of the topic and my own need for Lap-band as a card-carrying member of the verbally obese. Ann Cain was my first go-to person to help me conceptually organize and then pare the length. Ann read my first draft and has been such a valuable sounding board and encourager throughout. Suzy Spencer helped with the first draft of chapter one, which aided in setting the standard for the remainder of the book. Cynthia Zigmund did the most significant editing in helping me reorganize and trim in some major ways; her extensive publishing background has been invaluable. Linda O'Doughda made organizational changes that really added to the book's value, and Karen Cakebread along with Jeanne Pinault brought it all home to final form.

I would especially like to recognize a group of friends and colleagues who read an early draft. Their feedback really shaped the content and style of the final product: Tom and Ellen Boehmer, Ann Cain, Mike Cooley, Lucille DiDomenico, Karen and Chris Ebling, Herb Reed, Larry Spencer, Craig Spencer, Matt Starcevich, Marlene Stjernholm, and Arnold Sykes.

A special thanks to Ray Bard at Bard Press who helped me with great advice and timely encouragement throughout as I worked on this project. Ray published my first book, and as this was not a business book, he introduced me to the talented people at Greenleaf Book Group. I had already heard great things about them, and they have indeed been a wonderful partner in publishing *This Land of Strangers* quickly and expertly. Their guidance with marketing, platform building, and the like are rare value-addeds in today's "skinnied-down" publishing world. In addition to Linda's, Karen's, and Jeanne's editorial expertise, Justin Branch, Abby Kitten, Neil Gonzalez, Bryan Carroll, and Kris Pauls have been so very helpful. I would also like to thank Rob Nissen, my publicist, who has been such a strong advocate for a complex and daunting message.

Thanks to my two wonderful sisters, Joan Faubion and Karon Young, who were great encouragers and the source of specific ideas and stories in the book. Their feedback on early drafts really added to the soul of the book. Also, thanks to my beloved daughters Sarah and Lauren. They have taught me much about the real meaning and value of relationships; several of the stories herein are theirs—not to mention their valued help with naming and some of the book positioning.

Finally, I would like to thank Linda, my wife, soul mate, and closest relationship over the past forty-plus years. Linda has discussed "relationships" ad nauseam; I am grateful to her not only for putting up with me but also for listening, encouraging, reading, and providing feedback from beginning to end. Also, in her role as CEO at Interfaith Housing Coalition (she retired last year), Linda has provided such a rich source for my work with homeless families. (As a serial social worker, she has flunked retirement, of course, as evidenced by her latest venture, The Wisdom Project, for families homeless due to the daunting medical costs of special needs children.) Nothing substantiates my view that relationships are our most valuable possession more than my relationship with her.

This book is dedicated to my beloved family, this generation and all the ones that have gone before.

To access a Discussion Guide, The State of Your Relationships Question-naire, and additional content for *This Land of Strangers*, or to learn more about Robert, visit www.RobertEHall.com

Index

A

abandonment, 175–77
Aberdeen Group, 195
Abraham, 92
Abramoff, Jack, 195
accountability, 133–34
advertising. *See* commercialism
Afghanistan, 61, 79, 105, 239, 266
African American population, 13, 18, 29, 30
Age of Relationship, 237, 258–59. *See also*
    leadership roles; revaluing relationships;
    small and local restoration
Air Canada, 180
Alcoholics Anonymous, 155
Altman, Drew, 41
Altria, 195
Amazon, 233
American Airlines, 180
American Association for Justice, 195

Apple, Inc., 233, 239–41, 275, 288
Arab Spring, 86, 206
Arthur Young & Company, 255
Association of Trial Lawyers of America, 195
atheists, 91, 108, 121
attachment components
    give and take, 127–28
    grace and accountability, 133–34
    ongoing and obligated, 127
    serving and being served, 129–32, 285–87
author's personal story, 1–3, 295–97
Axelrod, David, 184

B

Bakker, Jim, 107
banking industry
    business relationships and, 33–34, 44, 56
    commercialism in, 179–80, 193
    harvesting in, 249

business relationships and (continued)
  institutionalization of, 227, 230
  monetary view, 138, 143
  small and local restoration, 267, 268
  technology in, 214
Bank of America, 33–34, 59
Bank One, 180
Beck, Glenn, 83
Beckwith, Bob, 80
Beltzer, Ben, 131
big, concept of, 223–24, 231–32
Big Brothers Big Sisters, 291
Big Rocks exercise, 260
bin Laden, Osama, 104
Blair, Tony, 71, 228
Bloomberg, Michael, 259
Bogle, John, 54, 56, 157
Bono, 149
bootlegger's still story, 263–64
branding, 180, 185, 231
Brown, Gordon, 70
Buffett, Warren, 58, 149
Bush, George H. W., 72
Bush, George W. (and administration), 63,
  65–66, 72, 73, 79, 80, 184, 259
business relationships. See also commercialism; institutionalization of relationships;
  leadership roles; management relationships
boards of directors, 57–58
  customers and, 37–42
  employees and, 42–47, 58, 145–48, 174
  financial vs. manufacturing sector profits,
    183
  goals and metrics, 255–58
  harvest mode, 249–51, 254
  individualism effects on, 172
  monetary view, 140–41
  overview, 33–36, 58–59
  profitability and, 53
  relational capacity, 245–48
  revival of, 241–42, 258–59
  shareholders and, 54–58

small and local organizations, 275–78
C
capital, concept of, 118
caring, economics of, 155–57, 270
Carter, Jimmy, 66, 72
celebrity culture, 169–72, 188, 197
Chick-fil-A, 268
children, 18–21, 153–55, 169, 170, 175–
  76, 188, 272
Christianity, 89, 92, 94, 96–98, 102–3,
  106–8, 121
Churchill, Winston, 182, 253
Citibank, 180, 233
Civil War, 61–62, 129
Clinton, Bill (and administration), 66, 72,
  80, 167
Clinton, Hillary, 74
coaching and mentoring, 290–94
cohabitation, 15–16, 173–74
commercialism
  branding and, 180, 185, 231
  bribery and, 195–96
  broken relationships, 194–97
  commercial forces influences, 186–88
  deceptive fees, 193
  distrust from, 191–93, 197–98
  growth of, 182
  marketing roles, 184–86, 189–91
  media and, 185–88
  naming rights, 179–80
  overview, 179–84, 198–99
  reputations, 180, 195
  viral marketing, 288–89
  word of mouth, 139, 197–98
community relationships, 24–27, 274–75.
  See also small and local restoration
Congressional dysfunction, 66, 67, 71–72,
  75–77, 80
Conscious Capitalism, 287–88
consumerism
  abandonment and, 175–77
  loneliness, 167–69
  materialism, 169–75

narcissism, 165–67
overview, 161–65, 177
The Container Store, 259, 287
contempt, concept of, 63–64
Costco, 258
Coulter, Ann, 64, 90
Countrywide, 34
cultivating growth and development, 248–54
culture, concept of, 281–82
customer relationship management (CRM), 37
customers
definition, 37
distrust by, 192–93
economic relationships with, 141–44
economics of emotion, 142–44
institutionalization of relationships, 226
loyalty of, 37–42, 119, 143–44, 230

D
Darwin, Charles, 121
Dawkins, Richard, 90
deer management, 52
Dell, 145
Deloitte & Touche, 259
Delta Airlines, 180
depression, 17, 170
Diana, Princess of Wales, 149
Disturbed (band), 176
diversity, 23–26, 81–82
divorce
business analogy, 38–39, 50
consumerism and, 171
economics of, 151–53
family relationship and, 14–19
hierarchy effects and, 232
physiological and evolutionary views, 122–23
Domino's Pizza, 46
doubt, engagement of, 289
Duke University, 197

E

Ebbers, Bernie, 48
economics, concept of, 140
economics of relationships. *See also* social economics of relationships
business views, 140–41
customer emotions, 142–44
customers, 141–42
employees, 145–48
human capital and, 244–45
overview, 137–40, 157–58
economies of scale, 141, 152, 222–25, 228, 229–30, 246. *See also* small and local restoration
education, 30–31, 43, 104, 170, 242, 269, 274, 281
Eisenhower, Dwight, 72
elephant culture, 11–12, 32
emotional impact of relationships, 123–26, 142–44
employee relationships, 42–47, 51–54, 58, 145–48, 174, 226
employers. *See* business relationships
entrepreneurs, 230, 250
escalation, 74, 81, 83, 103
ESPN, 277
evolution, 121–23, 124–25
Exxon Mobil, 233

F
Facebook, 127, 165, 167, 209, 219, 233
failure, 134, 288
family relationships. *See also* children; divorce; marriage
abandonment, 175–77
costs of decline in, 17–18
decline in, 13–17
economics of, 150
economy of scale in, 152, 229–30
history relevance, 1–3, 295–97
home, concept of, 13, 261, 264, 271–74
parenting roles, 16
relational capacity, 245–48
relational goals, 255–56
revival of, 241

family relationships (continued)
  small and local restoration, 271–74
  surrogate members, 22–23
  technology effects on, 211–13
Feiler, Bruce, 92
First RepublicBank Corp., 33–34
Fleet Bank, 180
Fleming, Jim, 85
food localization, 266–67
Ford, Gerald, 72
Forman, Milos, 253
franchise organizations, 277
Friedman, Thomas, 66, 95, 215, 239, 255
friend, concept of, 202, 219
friendships, 21–24

G
Gandhi, Mohandas, 103
Gates, Bill and Melinda, 149
General Electric, 233
General Motors, 39, 73, 233
generational gap, 206–9
goals and metrics for relational growth, 255–57
Gogh, Vincent van, 86
Google, 233, 259
Gottman, John, 63–64, 116, 132
grace, 133–34
growth consequences. See institutionalization of relationships
growth of relationships. See revaluing relationships
Gumbel, Nicky, 260

H
Habitat for Humanity, 149, 275
Hacohen, Aviad, 99
Hall, Bob, 1–2
Hannity, Sean, 65, 83
Harper, Stephen, 71
Harrah's, 257
Harris, Sam, 90, 100, 103, 104, 121
harvest mode, 249–51, 254

health care. See medical profession
Hillstone, 268
Hispanic population, 13, 18, 19, 29, 30, 169
Hitchens, Christopher, 90
home, concept of, 13, 261, 264, 271–74
HP, 265
human capital, 244–45
humiliation and humility concepts, 166
Hussein, Saddam, 95

I
IBM, 225, 233, 281
indifference, 274–75
individualism, 168
innovation, 230, 275, 288–89
institutionalization of relationships
  big, concept of, 223–24, 231–32
  caring and, 225–26
  confidence and, 224–25
  consequences of, 233–34
  dysfunction and distrust, 228–29
  growth effects, 227, 229–32
  overview, 221–23, 234–35
integrity, concept of, 131
Interfaith Housing Coalition, 131
Iraq, 61, 70, 79, 86–87, 95–96, 105, 239, 255, 266
Islam, 86, 89, 92–96, 101, 104, 105, 107, 108
Israel, 85, 93, 98
Italy, 273–74

J
Jackson, Phil, 289
Japan, 14–15, 228
Jesus Christ, 121
Johnson, Lyndon, 72
Jolie, Angelina, 149
Judaism, 92, 93, 98–100, 106, 108

K
Kelly, Cynthia, 113–15, 119, 137–38
Kemp, Buddy, 34

Kennedy, John, 72
Klausner, Richard, 115, 116
Korn (band), 176
Koslowski, Dennis, 48

L
Lamott, Anne, 90
Lao Tzu, 293
Lauren, Ralph, 197
lawsuits, 41
Lay, Ken, 48
leadership roles. *See also* management relationships
    coaching and mentoring, 290–94
    components, 283–88
    engagement, 287–90
    in military, 80
    overview, 237, 279–82
    philanthropy, 149–50
    relationship building, 282–83
Leno, Jay, 187
Letterman, David, 187
Lewis, Ken, 33, 34, 48
Limbaugh, Rush, 82, 188
Lincoln, Abraham, 129
Linkin Park (band), 176
Local Harvest, 267
local relationships. *See* small and local restoration
loneliness, 148, 167–69
love, 109, 121, 127, 132
loyalty, 37–42, 119, 143–44, 230
lust, 174–75

M
Maayan, Channa, 99
Mackey, John, 286, 287
Madoff, Bernie, 195
Maher, Bill, 82–83
management relationships. *See also* business relationships; leadership roles
    compensation excesses, 53–54, 56, 249, 285–86
    distrust, 48–51

employee performance and, 51–54, 58
    financial statements and, 57–58
    outside hires, 50–51
    turnover, 43, 49–51
marketing. *See* commercialism
marriage
    abandonment, 175–77
    consumerism and, 171
    economics of, 17–18, 151–55
    family relationship declines, 14–17
    hierarchy in, 232
    physiological and evolutionary views, 122–23
    serving and being served, 132
materialism, 169–75
Matthews, Chris, 83
McCain, John, 74, 79
McColl, Hugh, 33–34
McDonald's, 268
media, 82–83, 126–27, 165, 185–88, 206–7, 209, 250–51
medical profession, 41, 196, 232, 269–70
mentoring and coaching, 290–94
mergers and acquisitions, 58, 226–28
Merkel, Angela, 70, 71
Merrill Lynch, 34
Microsoft, 222, 240
military-industrial complex, 76
Moore, Michael, 64–65
Moynihan, Brian, 59
Muhammad, Prophet, 95, 101
multitasking, 215–16
Muslims. *See* Islam

N
narcissism, 78, 165–67, 231
Nardelli, Robert, 48
NCNB, 33–34
Neiman Marcus, 113–15, 119, 137–38
Netanyahu, Benjamin, 70, 99
Netflix, 265
Newton, Buzz, 2–3, 137–38, 297
Nixon, Richard, 72
Nouwen, Henri, 221–22

Nurse-Family Partnership, 269–70, 292

O
Obama, Barack (and administration), 66, 70, 73, 75–76, 79, 80, 184, 259
obesity, 123, 154–55, 242
Occupy Wall Street, 184, 265
Olbermann, Keith, 64, 83
O'Reilly, Bill, 64, 83
organizations, 275–78

P
Pace, Peter, 70
Pacific Bell, 180
Palin, Sarah, 74
patience, concept of, 127, 204
peer relationships, 45, 289
personal relationships. *See also* consumerism; family relationships
    author's personal story, 1–3, 295–97
    community and, 24–27, 274–75
    cost of loss of, 27–29
    friends, 21–24, 202, 219
    overview, 11–13, 31–32
    violence trends, 29–31
    volunteerism and, 88, 217
Petraeus, David, 266
pets as family members, 23
pharmaceutical industry, 196
philanthropy, 149–50
Philip Morris, 195
physiological impact of relationships, 121–23
Pickens, T. Boone, 149
political dysfunction
    beneficiaries of, 76–77
    bias and polarization, 81–83
    causes of, 78–81
    Congress, 66, 67, 71–72, 75–77, 80
    contempt and, 63–64
    domestic trends, 71–73
    incumbency, 74–78
    individualism effects on, 172

international views, 68–70, 72
inter-party discord, 74
marketing and, 184, 190, 192
money and spending, 75–77
overview, 61–65, 83–84
partisanship, 65–68
presidential campaigns, 63, 71, 73–78, 79, 190
religion and, 87–88, 108
poverty, 18, 19–21, 27–29, 164, 170, 183, 244–45

Q
Qwest Communications, 180

R
RadioShack Corporation, 214
Rall, Ted, 63
Rauch, Doug, 287
Reagan, Ronald, 72
reciprocity, 131, 132
relating, concept of, 127
relational capacity, 245–48. *See also* revaluing relationships
relational disregard, 211–15
relational leadership, 282–83. *See also* leadership roles
relationship capital, 6, 116–17, 118–20, 139–40
relationship decline, 3–5, 9. *See also* business relationships; personal relationships; political dysfunction; religion
relationship decline causes, 159. *See also* commercialism; consumerism; institutionalization of relationships; technology
relationship revaluation. *See* revaluing relationships
relationships. *See also* Age of Relationship; economics of relationships; social economics of relationships; value of relationships
    concept of, 5, 126
    diversity effects on, 23–26, 81–82

importance of, 1–3
societal well-being and, 6–7, 9
religion
  believers *vs.* nonbelievers, 89–91
  commercialism and, 192
  divide among different faiths, 92–94
  divide consequences, 100–105
  divide within faiths, 94–100
  house church movement, 270–71
  individualism effects on, 172
  intolerance, 95, 100–103, 105
  moderation, 103–4
  overview, 85–87, 109–10
  politics and, 87–88, 108
  relationship decline, 87–88
  trends, 105–9
revaluing relationships. *See also* value of relationships
  broadening networks, 242–43
  goals and metrics, 255–57
  growth and development model, 248–54
  human capital, 244–45
  overview, 237, 239–41, 260
  relational capacity, 245–48
  renewed relationship focus, 243–44, 258–59
  social revival, 241–42
Roman Empire, 4–5
Romney, Mitt, 190
Roosevelt, Franklin, 222
Rove, Karl, 184, 190
Royal Bank of Canada, 40

S
Sarkozy, Nicolas, 70
Schwarzenegger, Arnold, 259
segmentation and separation, 216–19
September 11, 2001 terrorist attacks, 69, 80, 86, 265–66
serving, concept of, 129–32, 285–87
shareholder relationships, 54–58
Skilling, Jeffrey, 48
small and local restoration

community learning and innovation, 274–75
family and home, 261, 264, 271–74
organizational rebuilding, 275–78
overview, 237, 261–62, 278
resurgence of, 262–65, 268–71
rise of small scale, 265–68
small businesses, 230, 275–78
social capital, 24, 118–19, 131
social economics of relationships
  care, 155–57
  family relationships, 150
  marriage, 151–55
  overview, 148–49
  philanthropy, 149–50
social media, 126–27, 165, 185, 206–7, 209
societal relationships, 6–7, 9, 104. *See also* business relationships; personal relationships; political dysfunction; religion
Southwest Airlines, 193
Sports Illustrated, 189
stakeholder relationships, 35, 51, 53–54, 226, 232, 246–48, 281, 288–90
Starbucks, 144, 173, 193, 258, 276
status quo, 229–32
Stewart, Jon, 83, 187
stockholder relationships, 54–57
strangers, 25–26, 50–51, 185–86, 188, 190, 223, 275–76
suffering, 127
surrogate family members, 23
Susan G. Komen for the Cure, 149
Swaggart, Jimmy, 107

T
Taxi, 267
Teach for America, 282, 286
Tea Party, 73, 265
technology
  addiction to, 203, 213–14
  blogs, number of, 185
  generational differences, 165, 206–9
  information overload, 210–11

technology (continued)
  overview, 201–5, 219–20
  partial tasking and interruption, 215–16
  promise of, 205–6
  relational disregard and, 211–15
  segmentation and separation, 216–19
  social media, 126–27, 165, 185, 206–7,
    209
Teresa, Mother, 148
terrorism, 68–70, 86, 265–66
Thomas, Cal, 63
Tiller, George, 87
Tindell, Kip, 287
Trader Joe's, 144, 287
trust, 128
trust deficiency, 40, 48–51, 191–93, 197–
    98, 228–29
Turner, Ted, 149
Tutu, Desmond, 119

V
value of relationships. *See also* economics of
    relationships; revaluing relationships
  attachment components, 126–34
  emotional impacts, 123–26, 142–44
  overview, 111, 113–15, 134–35
  physiological impacts, 121–23
  relationship capital, 118–20
  value creation, 115–18
Victoria's Secret, 189

violence, 29–31, 62–63, 74, 87, 95, 105,
    177
volunteerism, 88, 149–50, 217, 251–54

W
Wagoner, Rick, 48
Wallis, Jim, 90
Walmart, 222, 268
Warren, Rick, 97–98, 167
wealth, 104, 164, 170–71, 183, 244–45,
    265
Wegmans Food Markets, 47
Welfare to Work, 226, 292
Whole Foods, 266, 286, 287
Winfrey, Oprah, 149, 170, 188

Z
Zapatero, José Luis Rodríguez, 71